Levia DiNardo Hayes • Bradley Waltman

Words on Paper
Essays on American Culture for College Writers

A Third Custom Edition

Taken from.

Words on Paper: Essays on American Culture for College Writers
by Levia DiNardo Hayes and Bradley Waltman

Cover Art: Courtesy of Comstock.

Taken from:

Words on Paper: Essays on American Culture for College Writers
by Levia DiNardo Hayes and Bradley Waltman
Copyright © 2009 by Pearson Education, Inc.
New York, New York 10013

Pearson Learning Solutions, 330 Hudson Street, New York, New York 10013
A Pearson Education Company
www.pearsoned.com

Printed in the United States of America

11   17

000200010272013883

EEB/KS

ISBN 10: 1-323-25848-5
ISBN 13: 978-1-323-25848-4

CONTENTS

Rhetorical Contents vii

To the Student ix

INTRODUCTION 1

Chapter 1: THE PROCESS
OF GOOD WRITING 3
Invention 4
Writing 9
Revision 13
Other Elements of Good Writing 14
Putting It All Together 16
Avoiding Plagiarism 20

Chapter 2: READING TO WRITE 21
Be an Active Reader 22
Read to Understand 23
Expand Your Vocabulary through Reading 23
College Reading Strategies 24
Mechanics and Grammar: Correction Symbols 30

Chapter 3:   INTROSPECTION   34

Ewa Zadrynska, "A Bracelet, an Odd Earring,
    Cracked Teacups"   35

Langston Hughes, "Salvation"   39

Caroline Hwang, "The Good Daughter"   42

Deborah Work, "What's in a Name?"   46

Jennifer Crispin, "No Place Like Home"   51

Writing Suggestions   54
In-Sight   55
Peer Critique   56
Mechanics and Grammar: The Parts of Speech   57

Chapter 4:   FAMILY   67

Leslie Kaufman, "Just a Normal Girl"   68

Amy Tan, "Two Kinds"   75

Jamaica Kincaid, "Girl"   86

Craig Swanson, "The Turning Point"   89

Michael Dorris, "Father's Day"   92

Bonnie Smith-Yackel, "My Mother
    Never Worked"   94

Writing Suggestions   98
In-Sight   99
Peer Critique   100
Mechanics and Grammar: Verbs   101

Chapter 5:   LIFE EXPERIENCES   112

Irma Sonnenberg Menkel, "I Saw Anne Frank Die"   113

Shirley Geok-lin Lim, "Pomegranates
    and English Education"   117

Richard Wright, "Black Boy"   126

Serena Nanda, "Arranging a Marriage in India"   132

Denise Gonsales, "I'm Afraid to Look,
    Afraid to Turn Away"   142

Writing Suggestions   145
In-Sight   145

Peer Critique   146
Mechanics and Grammar: Commonly Confused Words   148
Mechanics and Grammar: Subject–Verb Agreement   156

Chapter 6:   POPULAR CULTURE   158

Josh Tyrangiel, "Andy Was Right"   160

Andrew Sullivan, "The 'M Word': Why It
Matters to Me"   163

Lola Ogunnaike, "'Yours Truly, the E-Variations"   166

Deborah Netburn, "Young, Carefree
and Hooked on Sunlamps"   170

Marie Winn Miller, "Family Life"   176

Katha Pollitt, "Why Boys Don't Play
with Dolls"   186

Stephanie Ericsson, "The Ways We Lie"   190

Karen Goldberg Goff, "Social Networking Benefits
Validated"   200

Writing Suggestions   199
In-Sight   204
Peer Critique   205
Mechanics and Grammar: Spelling   207

Chapter 7:   THE CALL OF THE WILD   209

William Blake, "The Tyger"   210

Rafe Martin, "The Brave Little Parrot"   213

Jerry Adler, "Vanity, Thy Name Is . . ."   216

Robert Frost, "The Road Not Taken"   219

Jeanie French, "To Everything There Is a Season"   221

Ian Frazier, "Trust Me. In These Parts,
Hot Dogs Actually Repel Bears"   226

Writing Suggestions   231
In-Sight   232
Peer Critique   233
*Mechanics and Grammar: The Mysterious
Comma and Semicolon   234*

Chapter 8: ISSUES AND
CONTROVERSIES   237

Marc Santora, "Burgers for the Health
Professional"   238

Barbara Mujica, "No Comprendo"   242

Thomas Jefferson, "The Declaration
of Independence"   245

Patricia Dalton, "Have Today's Schools
Failed Male Students?"   250

Margaret Atwood, "The Female Body"   254

Linda M. Hasselstrom, "Why One Peaceful Woman
Carries a Pistol"   258

Facts on File, "Reality Television: Issues and
Controversies"   266

Writing Suggestions   265
In-Sight   269
Peer Critique   270
Mechanics and Style: Using and Acknowledging Sources   272

Kerri Mertz, "Wayward Cells"   274

Chapter 9: DOCUMENTATION
IN THE HUMANITIES:
MLA STYLE   278

Appendix: A Guide to Avoiding Plagiarism   288
Index   308

RHETORICAL CONTENTS

Narration

Ewa Zadrynska, "A Bracelet, an Odd Earring,
    Cracked Teacups" 35
Langston Hughes, "Salvation" 39
Caroline Hwang, "The Good Daughter" 42
Deborah Work, "What's in a Name?" 46
Jennifer Crispin, "No Place Like Home" 51
Richard Wright, "Black Boy" 126

Description

Langston Hughes, "Salvation" 39
Jamaica Kincaid, "Girl" 86
Michael Dorris, "Father's Day" 92
William Blake, "The Tyger" 210
Rafe Martin, "The Brave Little Parrot" 213
Margaret Atwood, "The Female Body" 254

Example

Ian Frazier, "Trust Me. In These Parts, Hot Dogs Actually Repel
    Bears" 226

Process
Craig Swanson, "The Turning Point"   89
Rafe Martin, "The Brave Little Parrot"   213

Cause and Effect
Leslie Kaufman, "Just a Normal Girl"   68
Serena Nanda, "Arranging a Marriage in India"   132
Denise Gonsales "I'm Afraid to Look, Afraid to Turn Away"   142
Lola Ogunnaike, "'Yours Truly,' the E-Variations"   166
Deborah Netburn, "Young, Carefree and Hooked
    on Sunlamps"   170
Jeanie French, "To Everything There Is a Season"   221

Compare and Contrast
Amy Tan, "Two Kinds"   75
Shirley Geok-lin Lim, "Pomegranates and English Education"   117
Robert Frost, "The Road Not Taken"   219

Classification and Division
Stephanie Ericsson, "The Ways We Lie"   190

Definition
Bonnie Smith-Yackel, "My Mother Never Worked"   94

Argumentation
Bonnie Smith-Yackel, "My Mother Never Worked"   94
Josh Tyrangiel, "Andy Was Right"   160
Andrew Sullivan, "The 'M Word': Why It Matters to Me"   163
Marie Winn Miller, "Family Life"   176
Katha Pollitt, "Why Boys Don't Play with Dolls"   186
Karen Goldberg Goff, "Social Networking"   200
Marc Santora, "Burgers for the Health Professional"   238
Barbara Mujica, "No Comprendo"   242
Thomas Jefferson, "The Declaration of Independence"   245
Patricia Dalton, "Have Today's Schools Failed Male Students?"   250
Linda M. Hasselstrom, "Why One Peaceful
    Woman Carries a Pistol"   258
Facts on File, "Reality Television: Issues and Controversies"   266

TO THE STUDENT

One of the goals of this book is to teach you that reading and writing are linked. Improvement in one cannot occur without improvement in the other. Reading generates writing, and practice in writing must be supplemented by reading texts by good and interesting writers. Reading other students' work also provides models and ideas for your own writing. Relying on your own writing alone to achieve proficiency only continues your faults. Other writers teach the meaning of "style," afford examples of precision in the use of words, and enlarge your vocabulary.

It is not the goal of this book to provide you with some secret formula for the composition of perfect writing. Instead our intent is to instill in you a respect for language, to demonstrate the difference between good writing and bad writing, and to suggest a means of improving writing.

The most important objectives in writing are having something to say and creating some interest and purpose in expressing those ideas. It is also important for writers to pay attention to details that will ensure the correct, clear, and effective communication of their ideas to readers. The whole process of writing consists of (1) finding out what we think and feel about people, places and happenings, and (2) communicating those thoughts and feelings in words on paper. The first step is thinking and the second is writing: the two are inseparably linked. The first step is often referred to as "invention." Good invention strategies will be explored in Chapter 1.

The only way to learn to write is to write. As students of writing, you have the luxury of having an expert instructor who will criticize and guide your writing in an attempt to improve your writing. Frequent writing gives practice that will help you express your ideas effectively.

Planning is an important element in writing, because without planning, you run the risk of getting into the middle of a project, finding that what you are doing has no direction, and having to begin again. This is as true of writing a composition as of planting a garden, preparing a meal, or running a business. A well-planned approach to a problem helps to most effectively solve it.

As you read Chapter 1 and begin writing essays, keep the following in mind:

1. Why write? Are you writing to tell a story, show your reader something, define a term, describe how to do something, persuade your reader, or argue your opinion? Perhaps your work has some other **purpose**. Knowing your purpose will help you formulate whatever you are writing.

2. Who is the reader? Is it your professor, your professor and your fellow students, an examining board, your parents, your boss? It is critical that you know your **audience**. Audience helps determine the word choices we make and the level of formality in our writing. For example, if you are working in the legal field and are writing for a group of lawyers, you can use the terms "motion" and "plaintiff" without defining them. However, if you are writing the same information for a general audience, you need to define these terms in your writing.

3. What evidence and details should be provided? If the purpose is to persuade your reader, the **evidence** provided must build a strong case and perhaps include expert testimony or statistics. However, if your purpose is to tell a story, then the evidence provided would be drawn largely from personal examples and experience.

4. How should the essay be constructed? Is there a sequencing of events in the essay? Then perhaps you should tell it in that order, or chronologically. Are you describing something? Then perhaps you should describe from the outside to the inside or from the top to the bottom or spatially. Are there points to be made? The essay could move from most important to least important point, or vice versa. Your essay needs some system of **organization**.

Does the essay have a beginning, a middle, and an ending? In other words, do you have an introduction, body, and conclusion in your essay?

5. Can everyone understand the essay? Everyone comes to college with a different way of speaking. In college, you learn that most people use Standard English to communicate their thoughts. Readers will better understand writers who use Standard English. The attainment of this type of writing involves adapting to specific mechanical and stylistic ways of written and oral communication. This involves improving your **grammar and mechanics**.

6. How will the writing be assessed? Has the instructor provided guidelines for assessment? If not, it is a good idea to inquire how a writing assignment will be assessed and graded.

To summarize, you must know your purpose for writing, your audience, your evidence, your organization, and your grammar and mechanics. You must also be aware of how your writing will be assessed. ***Words on Paper* will teach you all of these key elements in the writing process.**

DEVELOPMENTAL WRITING SUPPLEMENTS

Student Supplements

The Pearson Student Essays Booklet (0-205-60544-3) This brief booklet of student models includes two essays from each of the nine modes. It also includes an essay that showcases the writing process from beginning to end, crystallizing the importance of revision for all writers.

The Pearson Visual Writing Guide for Developing Writers by Ileen L. Linden (0-205-61984-3) This thematic supplement is designed to stimulate reading comprehension through an authentic perspective of visual imagery. Each assignment challenges the learner to think beyond the text to the image, expanding their worldview as they navigate through complex or unfamiliar issues. This approach teaches deconstruction, a problem-based strategy that reveals important social and cultural interrelationships across the curriculum. Instructors will find this a practical guide for assignments directed toward journaling, reflection, argumentative essay writing, and more.

100 Things to Write About by Ron Koertge (0-673-98239-4) This brief book contains over 100 individual writing assignments, on a variety of topics and in a wide range of formats, from expressive to analytical writing.

The Pearson Student Planner (0-205-66301-X) This unique supplement provides students with a space to plan, think about, and present their work. In addition to the yearly planner, this portfolio includes an assessing/organizing area; daily planner for students including daily, weekly, and monthly calendars; and a useful links page.

The Pearson Writer's Journal by Mimi Markus (0-321-08639-2) Provides students with their own personal space for writing and contains helpful journal writing strategies, sample journal entries by other students, and many writing prompts and topics to get students writing.

Applying English to Your Career by Deborah Davis (0-131-92115-0) This supplement includes a brief page of instruction on 25 key writing skills, followed by practice exercises in these skills that focus on seven specific career fields.

The New American Webster Handy College Dictionary, Third Edition (0-451-18166-2) This is a paperback reference text with more than 100,000 entries.

The Oxford American Desk Dictionary and Thesaurus (0-425-18068-9) From the Oxford University Press and Berkley Publishing Group comes this one-of-a-kind reference book that combines both of the essential language tools—dictionary and thesaurus—in a single, integrated A-to-Z volume. The

1,024-page book offers more than 150,000 entries, definitions, and synonyms so you can find the right word every time, as well as appendices of valuable quick-reference information including signs and symbols, weights and measures, presidents of the United States, U.S. states and capitals, and more.

The Oxford Essential Thesaurus, Second Edition (0-425-16421-7) From Oxford University Press, renowned for quality educational and reference works, comes this concise, easy-to-use thesaurus—the essential tool for finding just the right word for every occasion. The 528-page book includes 175,000 synonyms in a simple A-to-Z format, more than 10,000 entries, extensive word choices, example sentences and phrases, and guidance on usage and punctuation.

The Pearson ESL Workbook, Second Edition, by Susan Peterson Miller and Karen Standridge (0-131-94759-1) This workbook is divided into seven major units, each of which provides thorough explanations and exercises in the most challenging grammar topics for non-native speakers of English. Topics include nouns, articles, verbs, modifiers, pronouns, prepositions, and sentence structure.

Eighty Practices by Maxine Hairston Emerita (0-673-53422-7) A collection of ten-item exercises that provide additional practice for specific grammatical usage problems, such as comma splices, capitalization, and pronouns.

The Pearson Grammar Workbook, Second Edition, by Jeanette Adkins (0-131-94771-0) This workbook is a comprehensive source of instruction for students who need additional grammar, punctuation, and mechanics assistance. Covering such topics as subject-verb agreement, conjunctions, modifiers, capital letters, and vocabulary, each chapter provides helpful explanations, examples, and exercises.

Learning Together: An Introduction to Collaborative Learning by Tori Haring-Smith (0-673-46848-8) This brief guide to the fundamentals of collaborative learning teaches students how to work effectively in groups.

Pearson Editing Exercises (0-205-66618-3) and Instructor Answer Key (0-205-66617-5) by Anna Ingalls and Don Moody The Editing Exercises booklet contains 50 one-page editing paragraphs that provide students with opportunities to learn how to recognize and correct the most common types of sentence, grammar, and mechanical errors in context. Embedding the errors within the context of informative paragraphs rather than using discrete sentence exercises simulates a more natural writing situation, allowing students to draw upon their intuitive knowledge of structure and syntax, as well as specific information from class instruction. The booklet makes an ideal supplement to any grammar, sentence, or writing text. Various editing topics can be assigned to coordinate with class lessons, or they may be assigned individually based on problems observed in students' writing. Students may also complete selected exercises as an enrichment activity, either on their own or in collaboration with other students. Additionally, the variety of topics in the paragraphs themselves can also be used as springboards for discussion or journaling, or as models for writing assignments if desired.

Penguin Discount Novel Program

In cooperation with Penguin Putnam, Inc., Pearson is proud to offer a variety of Penguin paperbacks at a significant discount when packaged with any Pearson title. Excellent additions to any English course, Penguin titles give students the opportunity to explore contemporary and classical fiction and drama. The available titles include works by authors as diverse as Toni Morrison, Julia Alvarez, Mary Shelley, and Shakespeare. To review the complete list of titles available, visit the Pearson-Penguin-Putnam website: http://www.pearsonhighered.com/penguin.

What Every Student Should Know About (WESSKA) Series

The **What Every Student Should Know About . . .** series is a collection of guide books designed to help students with specific topics that are important in a number of different college courses. Instructors can package any one of these booklets with their Pearson textbook for no additional charge, or the booklets can be purchased separately.

What Every Student Should Know About Preparing Effective Oral Presentations by Martin C. Cox (0-205-50545-7)

What Every Student Should Know About Researching Online by David Munger and Shireen Campbell (Student / 0-321-44531-7)

What Every Student Should Know About Citing Sources with APA Documentation by Chalon E. Anderson, Amy T. Carrell, and Jimmy L. Widdlefield, Jr. (0-205-49923-6)

What Every Student Should Know About Citing Sources with MLA Documentation by Michael Greer (Student / 0-321-44737-9)

What Every Student Should Know About Avoiding Plagiarism by Linda Stern (0-321-44689-5)

Multimedia Offerings

MyWritingLab (www.mywritinglab.com) MyWritingLab is a complete online learning system with better practice exercises to make students better writers. The exercises in MyWritingLab are progressive, which means within each skill module students move from literal comprehension to critical application to demonstrating their skills in their own writing. The 9,000+ exercises in the system do rehearse grammar, but they also extend into the writing process, paragraph development, essay development, and research. A thorough diagnostic test outlines where student have not yet mastered the skill, and an easy-to-use tracking system enables students and instructors to monitor all work in MyWritingLab.

State Specific Supplements

For Florida Adopters

Thinking Through the Test: A Study Guide for the Florida College Basic Skills Exit Test, by D. J. Henry and Mimi Markus FOR FLORIDA ADOPTIONS ONLY. This workbook helps students strengthen their reading skills in preparation for the Florida College Basic Skills Exit Test. It features both diagnostic tests to help assess areas that may need improvement and exit tests to help test skill mastery. Detailed explanatory answers have been provided for almost all of the questions.

Package item only—not available for sale.

Available Versions:

Thinking Through the Test: A Study Guide for the Florida   0-321-38740-6
College Basic Skills Exit Tests: Reading and Writing,
without Answers, Third Edition

Thinking Through the Test: A Study Guide for the Florida   0-321-38739-2
College Basic Skills Exit Tests: Reading and Writing,
with Answers, Third Edition

Thinking Through the Test: A Study Guide for the Florida   0-321-38741-4
College Basic Skills Exit Tests: Writing,
with Answers, Third Edition

Thinking Through the Test: A Study Guide for the Florida   0-321-38934-4
College Basic Skills Exit Tests: Writing,
without Answers, Third Edition

Preparing for the CLAST, Seventh Edition, by H. Ramsey Fowler (0-321-01950-4) These two, 40-item objective tests evaluate students' readiness for the Florida CLAST exams. Strategies for teaching CLAST preparedness are included.

For Texas Adopters

The Pearson THEA Study Guide, by Jeannette Harris (0-321-27240-4) Created specifically for students in Texas, this study guide includes straightforward explanations and numerous practice exercises to help students prepare for the reading and writing sections of THEA Test.

Package item only—not available for sale.

For New York/CUNY Adopters

Preparing for the CUNY-ACT Reading and Writing Test, edited by Patricia Licklider (0-321-19608-2) This booklet, prepared by reading and writing faculty from across the CUNY system, is designed to help students prepare for the CUNY-ACT exit test. It includes test-taking tips, reading passages, typical exam questions, and sample writing prompts to help students become familiar with each portion of the test.

Instructor Supplements

Pearson is pleased to offer a variety of support materials to help make teaching developmental English easier on teachers and to help students excel in their coursework. Many of our student supplements are available free or at a greatly reduced price when packaged with a Pearson writing textbook. Contact your local Pearson sales representative for more information on pricing and how to create a package.

Instructor's Manual for Words on Paper: Essays on American Culture for College Writers by Maria Shockey (0-205-57323-1)

Printed Test Bank for Developmental Writing (0-321-08486-1) Features more than 5,000 questions in all areas of writing, from grammar to paragraphing through essay writing, research, and documentation.

Electronic Test Bank for Developmental Writing by Checkett (CD 0-321-08117-X) Features more than 5,000 questions in all areas of writing, from grammar to paragraphing through essay writing, research, and documentation. Instructors simply choose questions from the electronic test bank, then print out the completed test for distribution OR offer the test online.

Diagnostic and Editing Tests and Exercises, Ninth Edition (0-321-41524-8)
This collection of diagnostic tests helps instructors assess students' competence in standard written English to determine placement or to gauge progress.

The Pearson Guide to Community Service-Learning in the English Classroom and Beyond (0-321-12749-8) Written by Elizabeth Rodriguez Kessler of University of Houston, this monograph provides a definition and history of service-learning, as well as an overview of how service-learning can be integrated effectively into the college classroom.

INTRODUCTION

We developed *Words on Paper: Essays on American Culture for College Writers* largely out of frustration. With over twenty years of teaching English between us, we recognized the vital connection between reading and writing, but we could not find a writing text that treated the two as inseparable. Taking our combined experiences in the classroom, along with lively and thought-provoking essays, and an abundance of exercises, we have developed just that text.

The essays in this text were selected to excite and motivate readers into sharing their experiences and opinions in writing. The text also reflects a diversity of backgrounds, not only among its American writers but also with selections from British, Canadian, Jamaican, and Asian writers, to name a few. This rich presentation of readings empowers students to interact proactively and constructively with all types of essays.

We also chose these selections because they serve as superior models of writing and invite discussion that will facilitate writing. The process begins when we read a resonating text, such as an interesting essay. Some part of the essay— a described incident, a character, a place, an outcome—can excite us to tell our own stories.

To further build writing/reading connections, we include two chapters on reading and writing, and we equip each essay with pre-reading and post-reading questions and exercises. Each thematic chapter concludes with skill-building exercises that further reinforce reading and writing abilities.

In addition to the essays and exercises, students are further supported in the honing of their writing skills with "Mechanics and Grammar" or "Mechanics and Style" sections that conclude Chapters 2 and 9.

We have tried to make this text both teacher and student friendly. Chapters 3 through 9 each focus on a topic important to students: self-examination, family, people and places, heroes, popular culture, the great outdoors, and issues and controversies. We believe that writers learn from the familiar then move to the abstract. We have selected essays we hope will facilitate students' ease in writing.

We sincerely invite suggestions and opinions from fellow instructors and their students on the content and organization of our text. We would also like to thank those instructors who provided commentary on early drafts of the book:

Cheryl Cardoza, *Truckee Meadows Community College*

Lynn Clark-Lambert, *James Madison University*

Tyson L. Dutton, *Chemeketa Community College*

Edward Glenn, *Miami Dade College*

Alexander Howe, *University of the District of Columbia*

Robert A. Mayer, *College of Southern Idaho*

Sarah O'Connor, *James Madison University*

Judy Welch, *Miami Dade College*

Courtesy of Peter Dennis/DK Images.

1

THE PROCESS OF GOOD WRITING

The writing process has three core elements: invention, writing, and revision. Before you write, *invention* strategies help you formulate ideas. *Writing* involves your first attempt at creating a rough draft of your essay. Many students write their first draft straight through, without stopping to make changes as they go along. As a result, some passages are likely to need rewriting or polishing. The process of rewriting and polishing is called *revision*, which involves filling in needed elements missing from your first draft as well as making certain that grammar, spelling, and mechanics are correct.

INVENTION

As noted, the first element of the writing process is invention. Selecting the best invention strategies for writing will help you come up with important writing ideas. Before we look at each of the invention strategies more closely, let's first discuss the writing process by discussing how to get started.

How Do You Start?

You will most likely start the writing process with an assignment from your instructor. However, before you can begin writing, you need to understand the **purpose** of the writing assignment you are about to embark on and the **audience** who will be reading your work.

In a nutshell, purpose is your reason for writing. Your purpose might be explaining a topic so that readers have a better understanding of it, telling an interesting story about something so that readers are entertained and motivated, comparing and contrasting two topics in order to make a point, or persuading your readers about something. If you are unsure what your purpose is in a particular writing assignment, be sure to ask your instructor for clarification.

Your audience is those people who will read your writing. Are you writing a particular piece for your instructor? Your instructor and your classmates? A friend? Your boss? Are you writing for a general audience (such as readers of your school's newspaper) or a specialized audience (such as members of a chess club)?

Knowing your audience is key to your writing. Imagine you are working as a nurse in a busy hospital and need to write a report on "code blue" procedures. If you were writing for an audience of nurses, you could use many terms familiar to nurses without fully explaining those terms. However, if you were writing to a more general audience (such as hospital patients), you would need to use many more definitions and clarify steps in the process. Thus, audience and purpose are critical for you to understand before you even begin the writing process.

Once you understand your purpose and audience, you are ready to begin the writing process. There are several invention strategies that can help you—brainstorming, freewriting, stream of consciousness, looping, outlining, clustering, and journalistic questions.

Brainstorming

The first invention strategy we will discuss here, **brainstorming,** may prove to be the most useful to you in your writing because it is so easy. Brainstorming involves taking a blank sheet of paper, putting your writing assignment topic at the top, and then writing down all of the ideas that randomly pop into your head about the topic. Don't worry about keeping your ideas in order or presenting them logically. You are simply attempting to get as many ideas out as quickly as possible.

Here is a sample brainstorm on the subject of wearing uniforms in public schools.

School Uniforms in Public Schools

No individualism	Hyde Park School
Cheaper	No expression
Anti-American	Militaristic
Easy to dress in morning	Identity theft
Less fighting	Uncomplicated
Equality?	Too many rules
Costs less for parents	Brings respect

As you can see, the student who brainstormed here had no trouble coming up with ideas and details about school uniforms in public schools. This student can now extend the brainstorming to further elaborate on some of these ideas.

The next step in brainstorming would be to see whether any of the writing ideas and details you came up with are relevant (or irrelevant) to the writing topic.

Example:

No individualism	Hyde Park School
Cheaper	No expression
~~Anti-American~~	Militaristic
Easy to dress in morning	~~Identity theft~~
Less fighting	Uncomplicated
~~Equality?~~	Too many rules
Costs less for parents	Brings respect

After you have decided on the ideas and details you will cover in your writing assignment based on your brainstorming session, you may either begin the rough draft of your first few paragraphs or, if you still don't feel that you are ready to begin writing, you can extend your brainstorming list with freewriting.

Freewriting

The second strategy to explore in the invention process is **freewriting**. This technique helps students who have problems putting pen to paper. For a freewriting exercise, you are given a topic to write on. You first write the topic at the top of a clean sheet of paper. Then you are given an amount of time (usually five or ten minutes) in which you *must* write. You cannot stop writing until the time has expired. The goal of freewriting is to write as much as possible during the five or ten minutes. You are not concerned with grammar, punctuation, spelling, or even making a lot of sense when you freewrite. You should try to stay on the topic, but, if you cannot, you must continue to write anyway, even if you only produce filler such as "I can't think of anything to write." The theory is that once you have put pen to paper, ideas will begin to flow. It usually works, but sometimes it doesn't. Give it a chance to succeed!

Once you have finished freewriting, you may want to write one sentence that states the most important thing you said. Once you have written your most important sentence, you can freewrite on that sentence until you have exhausted the topic.

Set a timer for five minutes and give it a try. Remember, do not lift the pen from the paper. Just keep writing whatever pops into your head. Try freewriting for five minutes on the topic School Uniforms in Public Schools.

Stream of Consciousness

Stream of consciousness is a form of freewriting. It is often used as a technique in creative writing but can prove effective in academic writing as well. If you are really having trouble writing about a topic, select one word dealing with the topic (of major or minor importance) and begin writing about that word. Be as creative as you dare. Let your thoughts grow until your mind and your writing are moving from one thought to another with no connection necessary between them.

For example, if your writing assignment is about an environmental issue such as recycling, you could begin your stream of consciousness writing with the word "waste." First you might describe your local park and its garbage cans overflowing with trash. Then you might remember the expensive green jacket that you wore only once, to a wedding, and that stayed in the back of your closet for years, but also how much fun you had dancing the polka at the wedding, and so on. Who knows? You may find a potential topic. This technique tends to lower anxiety involved with writing assignments.

Looping

Many students enjoy the creativity involved with the stream of consciousness strategy for invention. Others may prefer a more structured technique known as **looping.**

In looping, as in stream of consciousness, you begin with simply one word— often a keyword in your topic. You write about this word for approximately ten minutes. Then, go back over your writing and reflect on your brainstorm. Select the best sentence that you have written on the topic. Place that sentence at the top of a new sheet of paper. Beginning with that sentence, write for another ten-minute loop. Then, repeat this process. Repeat the process until you have at least three loops.

The benefits of looping are that you are concentrating on a topic that is relevant to your final writing project. You are also able to focus more directly with the looping method than with the previous brainstorming activities.

Go ahead and try this technique. Choose from the following topics and perform three ten-minute loops:

- Discrimination
- Military obligation for eighteen-year-olds
- Greed
- Stereotypes
- College education

Outlining

Outlining can be an invention strategy of its own or perhaps a continuation of brainstorming and freewriting.

A complete outline consists of three parts: the title, the purpose statement, and the body of the outline. The main divisions or units of the body are represented by roman numerals; their divisions, in turn, are marked by capital letters. Arabic numerals and lowercase letters indicate successive subdivisions. These units follow a progressive system of indention so that the relation and relative importance of topics may be seen at a glance.

Here is an example:

School Uniforms in Public Schools

Topic sentence: There are both drawbacks and benefits when schools mandate that public school students wear uniforms.

I. Uniforms are easier for both students and parents.
   A. Uncomplicated
   B. Cheaper
   C. Easy to dress in the morning
II. Many schools have reported positive outcomes from uniform policies.
   A. Equality
   B. Less fighting
   C. Brings respect

III. Many students do not like the idea of school uniforms.
  A. No individualism
  B. Militaristic
  C. Too many rules

Outlining is useful when you are clear about what you want to cover in your essay. It allows you to break your essay into topics or paragraphs to be written. In writing an outline, you can often tell if you have enough evidence to support your topic or whether more evidence will be needed.

Clustering

Clustering is another extension of brainstorming. It involves taking the major ideas that you have about your writing topic and extending details from them that you will explore further.

To cluster, you begin by writing a topic in the middle of a sheet of paper. Then you let your mind move out from the central topic in different directions. You quickly write down any word or idea that comes to you, sometimes connecting it to the previous word with a line.

When a different idea comes to your mind, one unrelated to the previous word, you begin a new branch off the main topic. When you're finished, your page will have a map or design of all your ideas.

Clustering allows the mind to bring forth ideas and thought patterns you might not see if you were simply writing. Because you jot down thoughts immediately, without judging their appropriateness or logic, you can often come up with new and creative ideas and relationships. Try using the clustering technique on the topic of School Uniforms in Public Schools.

Journalistic Questioning

Another invention strategy involves responding to six basic **journalistic questions** on your topic: Who? What? Where? When? Why? How? Journalists often use these questions to assure themselves that they have explored every angle of their story. You can start with these questions to see whether you have considered all aspects of your topic.

Try answering the following questions on the topic of School Uniforms in Public Schools:

Who?

What?

Where?

When?

Why?

How?

Once you have answered all of these questions on your topic, you can proceed with any new questions that you may have. This will lead you toward a stronger essay.

We have given you several invention techniques and strategies. We cannot guarantee that they will all work for you. We are all individual writers and we arrive at our final drafts through different avenues. Try all of the previous techniques and find one or two that work best for you. Perhaps you'll even come up with a technique of your own.

WRITING

Now that you are familiar with invention strategies, let's turn our attention to the second element of the writing process: writing.

The First Draft

Now that you have the ideas you want to explore in your writing, you can put those ideas down in essay format.

Start your writing assignment with the basic five-paragraph essay. Some instructors refer to this as the traditional academic essay. The five-paragraph essay is merely a starting point for beginning college writers. You will quickly discover that a good essay could easily have four paragraphs or ten paragraphs or more. There is no magic formula for good writing, but the five-paragraph essay is a good place to start.

In essay writing, you must consider your purpose, audience, and the evidence available to support your contentions. If your essay is to be based largely on your own experiences, then it will be largely narrative (story-telling) and you will rely on your own knowledge to write the essay. If it is for any other purpose, you will probably need evidence from sources such as books, newspapers, databases, journals, magazines, interviews, or other materials. If you use other sources in your writing, be sure to credit those sources or you will be guilty of plagiarism.

Plagiarism is academic theft. It means that you have quoted or paraphrased (used someone else's thoughts in your own words) without giving the writer credit. For more about this issue, see the section on avoiding plagiarism at the end of this chapter. Correct procedures for crediting other sources will be covered in Chapter 9.

No matter what your purpose is, your essay will need a beginning, middle, and ending. In writing, we refer to these parts of the essay as the introduction, body, and conclusion. The basic format for a five-paragraph essay is discussed next.

The Five-Paragraph Essay

The Title

Often an overlooked element of the essay, the title is important in both interesting readers and informing them of your topic. Who has not been led to read a certain book, magazine article, or story because of its attractive title? Give your essay a great title and you will have taken an important step in making your whole essay effective. A well-chosen title will also help you stick to your topic throughout your writing.

Paragraph 1: The Introduction

Following the title is your **introductory paragraph.** This paragraph includes a **thesis statement,** or a statement of your position on the topic. For example, if you were to write a thesis statement for an essay on school uniforms in public schools, it might read: **School uniforms should be implemented in Nevada to instill pride in Nevada students.** Through this statement, it is clear that the writer supports the wearing of uniforms in public schools and will use the essay to attempt to persuade readers to also support this point of view.

Sometimes a thesis statement is a statement of purpose rather than persuasion. Consider this thesis statement: **Secrets repeat themselves and create family history.** With this kind of thesis, you must show the reader what you mean by the statement. Here is an entire introductory paragraph developed from this sentence:

Secrets and the Family

Secrets repeat themselves and create family history. Skeletons that are left in the closet may be hereditary. For instance, when I was growing up, I repeatedly heard family gossip about one of my aunts; this gossip shaped how I thought of her. The story goes that my Aunt Freda loved to gamble. In fact, she gambled so much, that in her ninth month of pregnancy, she left California and traveled several hours to Las Vegas to play the slot machines. In the middle of this gambling spree, my aunt went into labor. During labor, with her contractions six minutes apart, she refused to stop gambling. While she was heavily involved in a poker game, the labor pains progressed to two to four minutes apart and she still continued to play. As she was enjoying a winning streak, she intended to see it out.

This introductory paragraph propels the reader to read further.

A good introduction gains the reader's attention and entices him or her to continue reading. Perhaps the most commonly used opening is either a combination of narrative and descriptive details or a summary of ideas to follow.

Ideas for introductions include

- a short personal story or anecdote
- a startling statistic
- a quotation
- a question
- a direct personal appeal
- the report of a conversation

Student Writing Sample: Title and Introductory Paragraph

Burning in Salem

During the Salem Witch Trials, religion was the answer to what people didn't understand. As a result, ministers and priests were extremely powerful because they were the only people that were "qualified" to interpret the rules of the religion. They were considered to be the voice of God. Back in Salem, how could anything have been more powerful than that? Nobody could question the priests because they would then be questioning God, which of course was completely taboo. Thus, a person in such a position of power could say nearly anything they wanted, such as deciding that "cleansing" was needed in Salem. As a result, people would listen and it would be done but not necessarily deemed right by all the parishioners. This same pattern has repeated itself throughout history and continues today.

This introduction is interesting, states its thesis, and provides questions the writer will tackle in the essay.

Paragraphs 2 through 4: The Body

The body of the essay should further explain the topic. It should provide key examples and details about the topic.

Evidence supporting the thesis statement usually comes in the body paragraphs.

Evidence can come from your own experiences, the experiences of those close to you, and citations from secondary sources (such as books, journals, and magazines).

A sample body paragraph written by a student is provided below. It is a continuation of the student essay begun previously concerning religion and Salem.

> In the 1950s the idea of an imbalance of power was still an issue. After just starting to recover from the Holocaust (fueled by the very same need of "cleansing" as in Salem but on a larger scale), Americans were bewildered as to how easily people could be manipulated by those in a position of great power. Hitler had just basically accused millions of being "witches." Americans could see how weak they were. They did not question the government, the military, or the church. This led to the red scare led by Senator Joe McCarthy. Those refusing to name names, just like the citizens of Salem hundreds of years before, were persecuted.

This body paragraph is interesting, insightful, and provides an excellent example for the student's thesis.

Paragraph 5: The Conclusion

The writer can end with a summary of the major details covered in the overall essay. For a more active conclusion, the writer can make a recommendation or call to action for the reader of the essay. You want readers to continue thinking about your topic even after they have finished reading your essay.

The following is an example of a student's conclusion to the essay on Salem and religious freedom.

> As history has shown us, the injustices that occurred during the Salem Witch Trials continue to go on even today. People who define the ideologies and beliefs by which we live will always exist. Sadly, the accusations made by one group of select individuals toward groups of others in order to support their cause will continue as well. As a global society, we must strive for more freedom and tolerance of all individuals, beliefs, and religions.

This conclusion serves as both a summary and a call to action.

An important thing to remember in concluding the essay is this: When you have said what you intended to say, stop. Do not write a conclusion simply for the sake of having a conclusion. A rambling and wordy ending will destroy the effect of what has been said. Also, except in argumentative (persuasive) writing, there is little use for the words "In conclusion" or "Let me restate."

REVISION

The third and final element of the writing process is revision. The first step in revision is *reading* your essay again. First read your essay to see whether your purpose has been fulfilled. Have you supported the thesis statement in the introductory paragraph? When you first read your essay, don't concern yourself with making any corrections to grammar or style. You just want to make sure that the substance of the essay is presented clearly.

When you read your essay for a second time, identify weaknesses in your writing. What details need to be filled in? What grammar needs checking or correcting?

You will then need to read your essay a third time to see whether your purpose is becoming more solid.

No one gets it perfect the first time—no one. Not your instructor, not your instructor's instructors, not even an accomplished writer who has been on the *New York Times* best-seller list gets it perfect the first time, or even almost perfect. When students do not read and revise their own texts, they are holding themselves back from learning and improving as college writers.

Allow as much time as possible to elapse between writing the essay and revis-iting it. If there is sufficient time between the two steps, you will see errors that were not apparent to you when you just completed writing it.

Often you cannot see all of the errors that you made because you are too close to your writing. It is a good idea to have a peer read your writing and offer suggestions before making your final revision. A peer comment and evaluation sheet is provided at the end of each chapter for your use. The best students are those who can take active and constructive criticism on their writing. It is also a good idea to form reading circles with fellow classmates to gain many differ-ent perspectives on your writing.

Your instructor will read your work and give you feedback for improvement, but he or she will not be able to accurately gauge your abilities and improve-ments if you do not reread your essay, revise weak areas, and look for your own mistakes and correct them before handing in your paper.

OTHER ELEMENTS OF GOOD WRITING

Other key elements of good writing besides invention, writing, and revision are unity, coherence, and clarity, which will be discussed next.

Unity

Unity in an essay gives readers a clear road map to your ideas and overall pur-pose for writing. An essay has unity when it relates all of its parts (introductory paragraph, body, and conclusion) to the thesis statement.

An essay should clearly and fully develop the topic discussed, but it should avoid being overly wordy. Omit irrelevant material or "padding." Stick to the topic and your controlling purpose. There is nothing more confusing or irritat-ing to a reader than the insertion of irrelevant detail when the connection with the main topic is not obvious.

An irrelevant introduction or conclusion violates the principle of unity. A story that has nothing to do with the subject but is told merely for its own sake violates unity. After you have determined your purpose, be careful to attempt nothing except reaching your predetermined goal.

Coherence

Coherence, or the logical flow of ideas within an essay, is essential to good writ-ing. Without coherence, there can be no clear communication or thought from writer to reader. An essay is coherent when its parts have been carefully woven together and the reader is never confused about relationships of ideas.

An outline (as illustrated earlier in the section on invention strategies) is helpful in achieving coherence because it helps you arrange ideas in proper order. An outline alone will not ensure coherence, however. You must also be sure that you have left no gaps in thought (so that readers can follow the thought process of the essay) and that you carefully *review* the order of ideas presented to ensure that logical connections are made.

If the parts of an essay are properly arranged and no gaps in thought occur, coherence is usually achieved. Sometimes, however, the progress of thought should be marked, so that the reader knows when one point has finished and another is about to begin. **Transitional words** signal readers of a change in direction of the writer's thought. Here are some examples of transitional words and phrases:

Addition or repetition: again, also, finally, in addition, furthermore, moreover

Time: first, second, finally, last, afterward, meanwhile, simultaneously, later

Comparison: similarly, likewise, in the same manner, also

Contrast: however, but, even so, nevertheless, whereas, on the contrary, in contrast

Cause and effect: thus, consequently, therefore, as a result, furthermore

Summary or conclusion: finally, in summary, all things considered, in short, in conclusion

Transitional words such as those presented here not only signal readers of a change in direction within an essay but also help organize an essay.

There are several ways to organize your essays effectively. The most common is a time organization. **Time** organization is usually referred to as "chronological organization." That is, the writer moves from the past to the present to the future. The writer could also go from the past to the present and end there. Also, a writer could write far back in time and move to a nearer time in the past to finish his or her essay. Time organization is often used in process essays, or "how to" essays. For example, if you were writing an essay about how to apply for financial aid, you would begin with Step 1 then move to Step 2, and so on. If you were telling a story or giving directions on how to reach a certain destination or how to bake a cake, the natural order would be a time order.

Another method of organizing is **space** organization. A space order is useful when the writer wishes to report what he or she sees. The movement of the paragraph and essay thus follows the movement of the eyes. That movement must have some continuity a reader can recognize and follow. It need not start at the far left and move steadily to the far right, or vice versa, since an observer's gaze is likely to be drawn quickly to the most conspicuous detail. But there should be some natural or logical progression from one descriptive detail to the next. It may be very confusing to move haphazardly from left to right, to center, then to left again.

In a coherent essay, each paragraph must seem to grow out of the preceding one. Finally, the reader must be able to see clearly that the whole essay has made orderly progress from beginning to end, without gaps in thought, obscurity, or fruitless backward movement.

Clarity

Clarity, along with correctness and effectiveness, is essential to good writing. An idea may be incorrectly and ineffectively expressed, yet if it is understood by others, you have achieved communication, the purpose of all writing. But it is certainly possible for the essay to be substantially correct in the details of writing and not be clear to the reader. It is impossible for writing to be effective without being clear.

How does a writer achieve clarity? One way is to define all terms that are not completely clear. All thinking begins with terms (concepts, ideas, names), and the reader cannot understand your thought process unless he or she understands the terms used. Another way to achieve clarity is to make every statement reasonable. Reasoning is based on facts and inferences. That is, conclusions are drawn from facts. Avoid making questionable statements unless you are prepared to defend them. Make meaning clear to the reader by offering evidence based on facts. Sound thinking is essential to clarity.

PUTTING IT ALL TOGETHER

Now that you have learned all of the essential elements of good writing, it is time to pull all of them together in a final draft.

The Final Draft

Although you may have finished your paper and feel satisfied that you have addressed all of the key elements of good writing, you will need to do one additional critical reading of it before you turn it in to your instructor. When reviewing your final draft, check for page design, proper documentation, and overall appearance. You might have heard the saying that neat IRS forms are rarely pulled for audits, but sloppy forms often lead to further scrutiny. Whether this is absolute truth or not may be questionable. You know, however, that in job applications, appearance can get you the job or lose you the job. The same is true with the submission of projects to your instructors.

Ask yourself these questions before submitting your writing assignment:

1. Have I adhered to the instructor's guidelines on spacing, margins, font size, and page numbering?
2. Are the page header and page numbers correct?
3. Are my headings (if any) short and to the point?
4. Have I correctly followed MLA documentation guidelines?
5. Have I used quality paper and ink?
6. Have I spelled my instructor's name correctly?

Now that you have read about the writing process as well as the attributes of good writing, the next page shows an example of a completed academic essay. Different instructors have different writing guidelines, so it is always important to ask your instructor about his or her expectations for your project.

The following essay is an example of a traditional essay. The essay was written by a beginning college student. This is a good student essay but can use a little improvement. As you read the student essay, point out its strengths and weaknesses.

This essay was written in response to a popular play entitled *The Crucible* by Arthur Miller. It was written in the 1950s and was based in part on the Salem witch trials. Miller and many other writers, actors, and directors were labelled as communists during the McCarthy congressional hearings in the 1950s and experienced their own version of a witch hunt. Miller tried to show that, historically, "witch hunts" have always existed and will probably continue.

```
                                            Smith 1


    Jonathon Smith

    Professor Walburg

    English 100

    12 October 2004
                    Burning in Salem
        During the Salem Witch Trials, religion was

    the answer to what people didn't understand. As

    a result, ministers and priests were extremely

    powerful because they were the only people that

    were "qualified" to interpret the rules of the

    religion. They were considered to be the voice
```

of God. Back in Salem, how could anything have been more powerful than that? Nobody could question the priests because they would then be questioning God, which of course was completely taboo. Thus, a person in such a position of power could say nearly anything they wanted, such as deciding that "cleansing" was needed in Salem. As a result, people would listen and it would be done, but not necessarily deemed right by all the parishioners. This same pattern has repeated itself throughout history and continues today.

In the 1950s the idea of an imbalance of power was still an issue. After just starting to recover from the Holocaust (fueled by the very same need of "cleansing" as in Salem but on a larger scale), Americans were bewildered as to how easily people could be manipulated by those in a position of great power. Hitler had just basically accused millions of being "witches." Americans could see how weak they were. They did not question the government, the military, or the church. This led to the red scare led by Senator Joe McCarthy. Those refusing to name names, just like the citizens of Salem hundreds of years before, were persecuted.

At the time when The Crucible was first performed, something was taking place that was very like the Salem Witch Trials. In Washington, Senator McCarthy had played on the communist fears of Americans by exploiting his position

Smith 3

for the gain of fame. He forced Hollywood
actors and writers (easy scapegoats)
to name names of those who had communist
leanings. This led to the persecution of many
innocent individuals. Actors, writers, and
directors were interrogated and blacklisted for
not "naming names." As a result, these
individuals lost livelihoods and lifelong
friendships in the process.

Another example of witch hunting is
happening today after the events of 9/11. Muslim
Americans often find themselves under suspicion,
much the same as Japanese Americans did during
World War II.

The Patriot Act enacted by Congress
following the tragedy of the Twin Towers has
diminished the rights of individuals guaranteed
by our U.S. Constitution. Again, we see the
"naming of names" and ugly suspicion rear its
ugly head.

As history has shown us, the injustices that
occurred during the Salem Witch Trials continue
to go on even today. People who define the
ideologies and beliefs by which we live will
always exist. Sadly, the accusations made by one
group of select individuals toward groups of
others in order to support their cause will
continue as well. As a global society, we must
strive for more freedom and tolerance of all
individuals, beliefs, and religions.

COMPREHENSION QUESTIONS ON THE PAPER

1. The student essay above is organized, interesting, and complete. What is the writer's thesis? You can find it at the end of his first paragraph.
2. What does the writer use to support this statement? List his examples.
3. Who is the writer's audience?
4. What technique does the writer use to conclude his essay?
5. Although this student wrote a very good essay, all writing can be revised. If you were advising the writer on revisions, what would you suggest?

AVOIDING PLAGIARISM

One final caution: **plagiarism** is academic theft. It occurs when you use someone else's words or ideas and represent them as your own. There is nothing wrong with using someone else's ideas and expert testimony to support the ideas in your writing, as long as you give credit where credit is due. This credit is done through the use of in-text and post-text citation. Citation is fully explained in Chapters 9 and 10. Citation involves identifying your sources (author, title, publisher, and page numbers) to ensure that the reader can find the original text. This way, the reader can read the complete work. It also gives the author credit for writing on the topic.

Often, the act of plagiarism can result in an "F" on a paper or failing a course. In more extreme cases, it can result in the termination of an academic career or even a lawsuit. Plagiarism must be avoided at all times. See the Plagiarism Appendix at the end of this book for more information on avoiding plagiarism.

2

READING TO WRITE

The two skills that all college students are called on to use and improve throughout their college career are reading and writing. English courses are required for all students because without strong reading and writing skills it will be next to impossible to graduate from college. You will be held responsible for information that you gather through reading assignments, and you will often be asked to use the knowledge you obtained from the assigned reading in some way, such as in a classroom discussion, activity, written assignment, or exam. For this reason, it is important to build reading skills while working on becoming a college-level writer. Working with this book, you will find that as your writing improves, so will your reading, and, as your reading improves, you will learn more about what good writing is, and how to write essays that others will be interested in reading.

Like writing, reading is an interactive process between the reader and the writer of the text. Reading is a communicative process that asks you to take in information and then relate the unknown to the known. In other words, who you are and the life you have lived will have a direct effect on how you and the text you are reading will interact. The minute you pick up a text and begin to read it, the text changes. The interaction changes with each text and each reader.

The texts gathered in this book should challenge you in ways that will improve your reading skills without causing frustration. The following suggestions will help you become a more confident reader of college-level texts.

BE AN ACTIVE READER

Being an active reader involves looking at text in a variety of ways in order to give yourself a better understanding of the material before, during, and after reading. Before you read a text, for example, your instructor might ask you to think about or look for certain ideas or themes in the text. You might preview the material by looking at the title of the reading, subheadings, and other visual aids in order to gain some preliminary information on what you are about to read.

Here are some useful questions to ask yourself when previewing material:

- What is the subject of the reading?
- What do I already know about this subject?
- What are my opinions on this subject, and will my opinions affect my reading?

During reading, you might review the material as a possible model for your own writing and assess any insights or philosophies that the writer shares to see if you agree or disagree with the writer's findings. You might also note questions that you have about the material you are reading that the writer has not answered to your satisfaction.

Here are some questions to ask yourself during reading:

- Do I understand this material? (If not, reread a sentence or paragraph, look up confusing words in the dictionary, or ask your instructor for further clarification.)
- What is it about this reading that I find interesting or motivating?

- Do I agree or disagree with the writer's assertions?
- Does this reading material serve as a good model for my own writing? Why?

After reading, you might think again about the reading. Recall key facts or opinions from the text, and think about what you have learned from the reading.

Here are some questions to ask yourself after reading:

- How did I feel about what the author wrote?
- Did the author effectively back up his or her thesis?
- What were the author's strong points?

As you can see, active readers do not simply read the words on the page. They review, analyze, and evaluate texts. Now that you are familiar with the process of active reading, let's review the next strategy for becoming a confident reader: reading to understand.

READ TO UNDERSTAND

How can you be sure that you fully understand what a writer is trying to say? Is reading material once enough? Sometimes one read is sufficient to fully understand a text, but some reading material, especially college textbook material, often requires two or more readings to understand the author's main points. A second reading will usually bring out more clearly the author's main points and supporting ideas.

One method of assuring your understanding of a text is to take a few moments to write a short summary of the information in your own words. In writing the summary, you will notice that either it comes easily to you, or that you need to refer back to the text once more to feel confident that you understood the information. If even after several readings you still feel that you do not fully understand a text, write a summary on the parts that you did understand, and be prepared to ask questions in class about the parts that were confusing. Chances are you were not the only student who was confused.

The next reading strategy asks you to expand your vocabulary through the reading process.

EXPAND YOUR VOCABULARY THROUGH READING

It is not unusual for readers to encounter words they are not familiar with. This is a common occurrence and happens to all readers of all skill levels from time to time. Often readers can figure out the meanings of unfamiliar words through

context clues—other words in the sentence or related sentences may give clues to the meaning of the word. If you look again at the previous sentence, you'll notice that a context clue was used to help you figure out what the term "context clue" means. In this case, the context clue was: "other words in the sentence or related sentences may give clues to the meaning of the word."

Unfortunately, there are not always context clues in texts, or they are not always obvious, so it is important to write down or underline unfamiliar words and look them up in a dictionary. If you take the time to write the definitions of the unfamiliar words, you will find that you will remember what those unfamiliar words mean the next time you see them. Keep a dictionary on hand when reading, or take advantage of the free, online dictionaries found on the Web.

It is also a good idea to have a notebook with you when you read. Failure to master words because of your assumption that you "know the meanings well enough" will continue to prove the greatest single hindrance to your vocabulary development. And remember, after you have thoroughly studied a new word, use it in speech and writing until it is yours. Adding words to one's stock can be fascinating, but there must be a constant and systemic use of your will to study and employ these acquisitions.

COLLEGE READING STRATEGIES

Very few people walk into a college classroom for the first time and breeze through the required reading materials. It takes time and practice to achieve the skills necessary to be a college-level reader, but it is not an insurmountable task. It is our hope that your experiences reading the texts in *Words on Paper* will help you on your journey toward becoming a better reader while improving your writing skills. The reading strategies discussed below will help you become a more proficient reader.

Underline or Highlight Text

Many students underline or highlight key passages or memorable points in their texts in order to be able to find them again during class discussions, when writing a paper, or studying for a test. To make the most of this first reading strategy, be sure not to underline so much of the text that key information is not easily found; it is important to limit your underlining to only the most noteworthy information. If you prefer to highlight texts, it might be helpful to use different colored highlighters to note primary (the most important) information and secondary (less important, but still necessary for your overall understanding) information.

Annotate Text

As you read a text for a college course, you will often find yourself writing comments in the margins of what you are reading. This system of marking a text for increased knowledge is called **annotation.** Annotation creates a record of the reading experience. Your annotations might include very short comments on how the writer has structured the writing, your reactions to the writing, or questions you are left with. Annotating is most useful with difficult texts that require close reading in order to gain full understanding.

Summarize What You Have Read

Summarizing is somewhat time consuming, so few students take the time to do it; however, it is very useful for negotiating difficult texts or preparing information to be used in research. A **summary** is simply a restatement of what the author has said in your own words. Summarizing builds on underlining and annotating by creating an accurate account of what was read.

When you are summarizing, read with the writer's purpose in mind. Read the text very carefully, making no notes or marks and looking only for what the writer is saying. After reading, write down in one sentence the point that is made about the subject. Then look for the writer's purpose or thesis and underline it.

When you underline, underline with summarizing in mind. Once you clearly understand the writer's major point (or purpose) for writing, read the text again. This time underline the major points supporting the thesis; these should be words or phrases here and there, rather than complete sentences. In addition, underline key transitional elements (see Chapter 1 for more information on transitions), which show how parts are connected. Omit specific details, examples, description, and unnecessary explanations. **Note:** You may need to go through the essay twice in order to pick up everything you need.

You must then write, revise, and edit to ensure the accuracy and correctness of your summary. When writing a summary of an essay, for example, start with a sentence naming the writer and title of the essay and stating the essay's main idea. Then write your summary, making sure to include all of the main points. Conclude with a final statement reflecting the significance of the essay—not from your own point of view but from the writer's. Throughout the summary, do *not* insert your own opinions or thoughts; instead summarize what the writer has to say about the subject.

After you've completed a draft, read your summary and check for accuracy. Does your summary make the same point as the article? Have you omitted anything important? Does your summary read smoothly, with all parts clearly related? Keep in mind that a summary should generally be no more than one-fourth the length of the original. If your summary is too long, cut out words rather than ideas. Then look for non-essential information and delete it. Write another draft—still a draft for revision—and ask someone to read it critically. Can that person understand the sense of the article by reading your summary? Ask for criticism; then weigh these criticisms and make valid changes.

Finally, when editing your summary, correct grammar, spelling, and punctuation errors, looking particularly for those common in your writing. Then, write a clean draft and proofread for copying errors.

Use Exploratory Writing for Comprehension

Exploratory writing offers a way to think—on paper—about what you have read. It allows you to go beyond summary, annotation, and underlining and actually begin to make decisions about what you have read, what else it connects to, how it relates to other issues, or how it seems to confuse an issue. One way to think about exploratory writing is that it offers a way to test your own responses to public issues. With exploratory writing, it is possible to experiment with ways of explaining and justifying your reactions so that others will take them seriously, even if they do not completely agree.

After underlining, annotating, and summarizing a text, your exploratory writing would be a fuller expression of what has already been done. Exploratory writing will bring your reading into focus. Exploratory writing can sound quite personal in tone, but it isn't exactly private either. This type of writing is somewhere between annotated reactions and the public voice of formal essay writing.

Applying the Strategies to a Text

Now that the basic reading strategies have been covered, let's apply them to actual reading material. Read the following essay using the reading strategies presented.

```
        Masculinity in the Twenty-first Century
     Feminism has affected masculinity in ways that
have allowed men to be more open and given them
opportunities concerning family involvement and career
choices that their fathers and grandfathers might not
have had, in effect, giving men more freedom than ever
```

before. What does masculinity look like in the twenty-first century?

In some ways masculinity might seem like it has not changed much in the past fifty years. Most rap stars put on a persona of thugs, misogynists, and violent criminals, and sell millions of records. Athletes, who are revered for their abilities on the court or the playing field, are routinely front page news when they are arrested for "bad boy" antics like having weapons or getting into fights. It seems like young males today are confused as to where to look for role models. To define masculinity in today's society, it might be a good idea to examine masculinity in the context of violence, sports, and the changing roles of men and women.

Since 1996, school shootings have become increasingly commonplace, with the shootings at Columbine High School in 1999,the most famous. Boys have perpetrated almost all of the school shootings. Most of the young boys involved in school shootings were white, from middle-class families, and felt marginalized in some way. These young men saw violence as a means to create a sense of power, authority, and strength. In a society that encourages boys to keep their emotions in check, these boys saw violence as an acceptable "manly" alternative. Most of the boys had been bullied and teased by their peers for not living up to a standard of manhood that included being strong and sports-oriented.

Some consider sports, especially contact sports, the last place for "real men" to learn masculinity through participation. Playing sports often includes injuries, yet there is a lot of pressure on young men to show toughness, deny pain, and play despite being hurt, which could lead to some males actually distancing themselves from their own bodies.

Sports such as football are extremely popular, with high rates of participation among young boys. Football is a sport that involves team members participating in a sort of highly ritualized combat. Many young men see football as a site of masculine companionship, a source of identity, an area of prestige, a possible source for scholarship opportunities, and for a select few, a career. Although I enjoy watching football myself, I also see it as a form of revered and ritualized violence that often features players getting injured and playing injured for the concerned yet excited crowd.

Outside of hard-hitting contact sports, there are few professions in the twenty-first century that require substantial body size, such as some types of construction work that involves heavy equipment to be operated by hand, like a jackhammer, furniture movers, and intimidating professional positions such as bodyguards. In today's modern technological world, there are machines that can do almost all of the work that was once done using brute strength. Considering the fact that most young adults today come from families where both parents worked or where they were raised by one parent, most often their mother, recent generations have grown up with the idea that it is normal for women to pursue careers.

Men and the definition of masculinity have undergone some very positive changes in response to the working partnerships men now share with women. Men now often take a much more active role in child rearing, with some men actually opting to be stay-at-home dads and taking on the job of primary caregiver.

Jobs once thought of as primarily women's jobs, such as nursing, have suddenly become popular occupations for men as well. And taboos on men having feelings and being allowed to express them are slowly being lifted.

So what is the definition of masculinity in the twenty-first century? Unfortunately, too often, masculinity translates into violence. For some, that violence may be somewhat controlled through sports, for others it may translate into crime against other men and women, while for many men, violence is not part of their masculinity at all. Hopefully, masculinity in the twenty-first century will continue to grow and change to the point where it is much more normal for men to be caring and sensitive than violently aggressive. For this to happen, more positive role models need to emerge, and young boys need to understand that the thugs and law-breakers they see in the media are not real men but caricatures of men.

Summarizing Activity
What would a summary of the above essay look like? Take a few minutes to try to write a very brief summary of the above essay. It should only be about a paragraph or two long.

Exploratory Writing
Here is a real challenge. Try doing some exploratory writing on the above essay. What did you like about the essay? What didn't you like? What would you say to the author if you could discuss the essay with him or her? In what ways would your definition of masculinity be similar or different?

Hopefully, these reading suggestions and strategies will help you as you journey through this textbook and your college career. Remember, reading will continue to be a fundamental part of your education, but it does not have to be a source of frustration and struggle.

MECHANICS AND GRAMMAR
Correction Symbols

Below are some basic correction symbols that your instructor may use to indicate grammatical and mechanical errors on essays.

Frag   Fragment—the sentence is incomplete. Sentence is missing a subject or verb.

R-O   Run-on sentence. The sentence has too much information, making it confusing to the reader.

S-S   Sentence structure. The sentence does not follow the pattern of standard written American English.

S-V agr   Subject-verb agreement. The subject does not agree with the verb in number.

T   Tense. The sentence has an error in verb tense (time).

VF   Verb form. Part of a verb is incorrect in spelling or form.

Cap   Capitalization. The word is improperly capitalized or not capitalized.

Ap   Apostrophe. An error in apostrophe usage.

WW   Wrong word.

WF   Word form. The form of the word is used improperly. Usually in part of speech usage.

Hom   Homonym. An error in the use of a homonym.

WO   Word order. An error in the order of words.

Pl   Plural. The error in the plural form of a word is present.

Prep   Preposition. Preposition used is incorrect.

Art   Article. An error in article usage (a/an/the).

^   Insertion. A missing word.

Sp   Spelling. A spelling error.

Exercise 1

Correct each of the sentences below. Indicate the error in the sentence and give the proper form. The corresponding correction symbol for each error is located in the column next to the sentence.

1. Frag		Last Friday I went to a conference. In Chicago. When I arrived at the airport. My friend was waiting for me. She was dressed in a pink dress; just beautiful.
2. R-O		The conference took place on Friday I stayed in Chicago until Sunday. My plane left at 5:00p.m., I got to the airport at 4:45.
3. S-S		What I did before leaving for Chicago I packed two bags.
4. S-V agr		My friend live on the north side of Chicago. She teach at Malcolm X college.
5. T		Last Friday she drive to the airport to pick me up. When we arrive at the hotel, we have dinner.
6. VF		I have visit Chicago before, but it looked very different to me this time. Many new buildings had been build since I was there in 1980.
7. Cap		I stayed at the Knickerbocker hotel, which is just off of Michigan avenue. My Room was beautiful and i loved the view of the Lake from the window.
8. Ap		I couldn't believe the beautiful decorations. The hotels decorator certainly has taste.
9. WW		The best think about the hotel though was the food. It couldn't have been best.
10. WF		The beef was the most tenderest I have ever tasted. The chef certainly cooks good.
11. Hom		I ate to much. In fact, I ate sew much that I felt ill. Their was nothing to do but quit. I all most had to leave the table.
12. WO		Chicago is a exciting city very. There is something always to do.
13. Pl		The hotel, restaurant and theatre are my favorite place to visit.

14. Prep   When I arrived to the hotel, I found a lot of people waiting on
              the lobby.

15. Art   We went into the dining room and found a empty table. We
              ordered an bottle of wine.

16. ^   Visiting Chicago was fun, but I was happy to return to New
              York City. It's the greatest city in United States.

17. Sp   I'll take Manatten any day. And Brooklyn isn't too bad either.

Exercise 2

Which correction symbol would be appropriate for each of the errors below?
Correct the error in each sentence, then write the appropriate correction symbol corresponding to the error.

_____   This is the most biggest animal I have ever seen.

_____   Where is it located on the mapp?

_____   She has never insist that I correct her grammar.

_____   We cant forgive their problems.

_____   We only have a hour to finish the assignment.

_____   We live on the bering sea, which is close to russia.

_____   She is in the hospital at the emergency room.

_____   The people in the conference room believes we should finish the
          meeting.

_____   Many people have been said that Nevada is the best place to live.

_____   Yesterday I finish my homework and go to class.

_____   They finished there homework early.

_____   The pants was dirty.

_____   It was a lovely day and a sun was high in the sky.

_____   She always opens a door for me, I am an engineer in her company.

_____   He is an interesting person very.

_____   Who's coat is this?

_____   The University of Nevada has several openings for English Instructers.

_____   Where was you on July 4, 2002?

_____   How much are the dog?

Courtesy of /DK Images.

3

INTROSPECTION

In this chapter you will be looking at yourself as a catalyst for writing. It has often been said that good writers write what they know, and whom do you know better than yourself? If you don't think you know yourself very well, perhaps this first series of essays and this first writing assignment will help you to know and understand yourself a little better.

Writing about yourself will most likely require a degree of story-telling or narration. As you will see, narration tells a story in a logical order. Usually that order is chronological (time), but it does not have to be. A good writer draws readers in and let's them "see" what the writer is trying to show them with words.

As you read the essays "A Bracelet, an Odd Earring, Cracked Teacups" by Zadrynska, "Salvation" by Hughes, "The Good Daughter" by Hwang, "What's in a Name?" by Work, and "No Place like Home" by Crispin, pay attention to the ways in which the authors bring their stories to life through words. Make sure that when it is your turn to write, you do your best to show, not tell. Use as much descriptive language as you can while describing the events of your story.

PRE-READING QUESTIONS

1. What is your first memory of moving out of a house?
2. How did you adjust to your new surroundings?
3. What did you do to ease the transition?
4. What material objects do you remember bringing with you that held sentimental value?

A Bracelet, an Odd Earring, Cracked Teacups

Ewa Zadrynska

Born in Poland, Ewa Zadrynska left her homeland in 1983 after martial law was declared. She now lives in the East Village section of New York City. Her essay "A Bracelet, an Odd Earring, Cracked Teacups" appeared in the New York Times *on June 8, 1988. This essay tells about Zadrynska's discovery of a discarded trunk filled with another family's memories. It is about memory and about what is important to us all as humans, no matter what country or city we are from.*

1 I came to live in the United States believing I was profoundly prepared. I studied the works of Flannery O'Conner in Polish and had learned

Ewa Zadrynska, "A Bracelet, an Odd Earring, Cracked Teacups," *New York Times*, June 8, 1988.

English by reading J.D. Salinger's short stories. I had seen all of Woody Allen's movies, and could sing Duke Ellington's "Take the A Train."

2   But I found myself living in Washington Heights, at the end of Manhattan. . . . My only connection with the rest of the world was the famous A Train. But this train didn't lightly swing like Ellington's. It rocked and rolled like Motley Crue's heavy metal: slow, noisy, and crowded.

3   Then one day, in 1984, at the corner of Hillside Avenue and Broadway, I saw an old wooden trunk that looked very familiar. Only its location, next to some garbage cans, indicated that it was meant to be trash. Even the strange tag—"Destination America; Address Unknown"—didn't change my impression that I had seen this trunk before.

4   And I had.

5   In Poland, my sister stored her blankets and pillows in exactly the same kind of trunk. She had bought her vintage trunk in a small village in the vicinity of Wroclaw, within the so-called "post-German" regions.

6   When I forced the lid of this trunk open, I was not surprised to find yellowing postcards from Breslau—the German name for Wroclaw.

7   It was an "all-my-life-in-one-package" trunk. It contained a broken silver bracelet, an odd earring with the Star of David carved on it, two teacups, silk dresses for a very slim young woman and dresses for a more mature, older woman. There were bundles of letters, papers and photographs.

8   Once, the trunk had belonged to the Mueller family. The trunk and the Muellers came to the States in 1936. (The tag on the lid was dated August 1936.) They had probably lived in Wroclaw. At least in Germany they had been well off. One of the photographs was taken in an expensively furnished living room. They were in their 20's. Full of good expectations and confidence, they looked straight into the camera.

9   They were Jewish. (A later photograph, probably taken in the United States, showed the family celebrating Hanukkah.) They spent at least 50 years together. There was a letter written by Mr. Mueller to Mrs. Mueller in 1976. Hesitantly, I looked at it. As far as my German and shame let me understand it, Mr. Mueller was in Los Angeles visiting relatives. He was missing his wife and looking forward to seeing her.

10   Mr. Mueller probably died not long after. If he were alive, he wouldn't have dumped their personal letters. If he had died recently, there would have been men's clothing in the trunk.

11   She, or rather they, liked to drink tea. There were two old Meissen teacups with a pink and blue rose pattern. Mrs. Mueller must have been

fond of them. The cups had broken twice. The first accident was mended with an old-fashioned glue that left brown lines in the cracks; the second accident occurred much later, when better glues were available.

12   Only a person who cared about memories would have bothered to apply the glue. Mrs. Mueller cared, but whoever threw away the teacups judged them in cold blood.

13   How did she lose only one earring? And why did she keep the odd one? Maybe she believed, as do some Europeans, that things have souls and suffer when they are thrown away. There was also a bracelet that seemed to have been broken on purpose, deliberately twisted and bent in a few places. When I looked at the pieces, I could picture the infuriated Mrs. Mueller destroying the bracelet with the hope of punishing her husband. Later when the fury was gone, Mr. Mueller was forgiven and the bracelet, too. It was put back in its Tiffany cotton envelope and stored away. I think Mrs. Mueller meant to fix it someday.

14   The trunk contained not only Mr. and Mrs. Mueller's past but also some of mine. Two years after getting married, I tore apart a silver necklace I had received from my husband as a wedding gift. I keep a few silver pieces in a little box, and someday I am going to link them together. In Warsaw, I had a similar set of Meissen china cups. I would never throw out an odd earring. I store my correspondence—bound with a blue ribbon—the way Mrs. Mueller did. I even know the Wroclaw street pictured on one of her postcards.

15   I took home the broken bracelet, the earring and two photographs of the Mueller family. The trunk was too heavy to carry. But when I came back with my husband, Janusz, it had been taken away. Only the two china cups still leaned against the trash can, awaiting the sanitation truck. I thought about the Muellers drinking their afternoon tea for 50 years. Over my husband's protests, I took the cups home.

16   Two years later, when we were moving 180 blocks downtown, the cups broke again. I didn't glue them. I had just begun to work full time and to adjust to the American pace. I didn't have time to bother about two old cups. The cups, after all, were someone else's memory. By then I had my own New York past.

17   But I still have the broken bracelet and the nicely framed photo of Mr. and Mrs. Mueller in 1929. Too many times my friends asked, "Are they your grandparents?" so I slipped a picture of my daughter wearing her P.S. 41 sweatshirt into the frame. Zuzana doesn't know that behind her back there is a young couple, full of confidence, staring straight ahead.

WRITING TECHNIQUE

Telling a story is a powerful way for communicating our thoughts and actions in both oral and written form. Some cultures have strong story-telling legacies while others have stronger written legacies. The essay we just finished reading told a story and taught us a lesson in its telling. What lesson did you learn from this essay? We call the technique of telling a story **narration.**

When we tell a story, it is important that we organize and sequence the events logically for our readers. This will usually mean organizing the story chronologically from past to present to future. Other times, however, we may begin our stories in the present and move to the future by using flashbacks of past events to fill in detail for our readers.

Good narration needs to be planned. We simply cannot choose odd details and let our readers fill in the blanks. We need to select concrete, specific details that reveal the most for our readers and allow them to paint a vivid picture in their minds of the events we describe. Details must not be jumbled in our narration but must be selected with care.

To summarize, good narration has enough detail so that readers can visualize sharply what happened. Narration, to be effective, must also follow some order, usually the natural chronological order.

COMPREHENSION QUESTIONS

1. What do you think the author means by "all-my-life-in-one-package" trunk? What do we learn about the Muellers in the essay?
2. Explain the significance of the teacups. Why do they help to unify the story?
3. Reread the concluding paragraph. What does it show about the author's life today? What do you believe the concluding paragraph says about American culture?
4. What tense is used throughout the essay? When does that change? Why is this significant?
5. If the essay had been written by a man, how might the narrative have been different? Why?

QUESTIONS ON WRITING TECHNIQUE

1. Why did Ewa Zadrynska write this essay?
2. What is the significance of the title?
3. How does the title help tie everything together?
4. What precedes the essay?
5. How does the author introduce the essay in the first paragraph?

PRE-READING QUESTIONS

1. Did your parents ever have expectations of you that you could not fulfill? How did you handle that?
2. Did you ever tell a lie that you do not regret telling?
3. What are some of your most vivid memories of childhood?

Salvation

Langston Hughes

Langston Hughes is considered one of the most influential poets of the twentieth century. He also wrote essays and short stories. He was born in Joplin, Missouri, and started writing poetry in elementary school. He lived most of his life in Harlem, a part of New York City. He was strongly influenced by jazz, the blues, and spirituals. He wrote, as he put it, "to explain and illuminate the Negro condition in America."

1   I was saved from sin when I was going on thirteen. But not really saved. It happened like this. There was a big revival at my Auntie Reed's church. Every night for weeks there had been much preaching, singing, praying, and shouting, and some very hardened sinners had been brought to Christ, and the membership of the church had grown by leaps and bounds. Then just before the revival ended, they held a special meeting for children, "to bring the

---

"Salvation" from *The Big Sea* by Langston Hughes. Copyright © 1940 by Langston Hughes. Copyright renewed 1968 by Arna Bontemps and George Houston Bass. Reprinted by permission of Hill and Wang, a division of Farrar, Straus and Giroux, LLC.

young lambs to the fold." My aunt spoke of it for days ahead. That night I was escorted to the front row and placed on the mourners' bench with all the other young sinners, who had not yet been brought to Jesus.

2   My aunt told me that when you were saved you saw a light, and something happened to you inside! And Jesus came into your life! And God was with you from then on! She said you could see and hear and feel Jesus in your soul. I believed her. I had heard a great many old people say the same thing and it seemed to me they ought to know. So I sat there calmly in the hot, crowded church, waiting for Jesus to come to me.

3   The preacher preached a wonderful rhythmical sermon, all moans and shouts and lonely cries and dire pictures of hell, and then he sang a song about the ninety and nine safe in the fold, but one little lamb was left out in the cold. Then he said: "Won't you come? Won't you come to Jesus? Young lambs, won't you come?" And he held out his arms to all us young sinners there on the mourners' bench. And the little girls cried. And some of them jumped up and went to Jesus right away. But most of us just sat there.

4   A great many old people came and knelt around us and prayed, old women with jet-black faces and braided hair, old men with work-gnarled hands. And the church sang a song about the lower lights are burning, some poor sinners to be saved. And the whole building rocked with prayer and song.

5   Still I kept waiting to *see* Jesus.

6   Finally all the young people had gone to the altar and were saved, but one boy and me. He was a rounder's son named Westley. Westley and I were surrounded by sisters and deacons praying. It was very hot in the church, and getting late now. Finally Westley said to me in a whisper: "God damn! I'm tired o' sitting here. Let's get up and be saved." So he got up and was saved.

7   Then I was left all alone on the mourners' bench. My aunt came and knelt at my knees and cried, while prayers and song swirled all around me in the little church. The whole congregation prayed for me alone, in a mighty wail of moans and voices. And I kept waiting serenely for Jesus, waiting, waiting—but he didn't come. I wanted to see him, but nothing happened to me. Nothing! I wanted something to happen to me, but nothing happened.

8   I heard the songs and the minister saying: "Why don't you come? My dear child, why don't you come to Jesus? Jesus is waiting for you. He wants you. Why don't you come? Sister Reed, what is this child's name?"

9   "Langston," my aunt sobbed.

10   "Langston, why don't you come? Why don't you come and be saved? Oh, Lamb of God! Why don't you come?"

11   Now it was really getting late. I began to be ashamed of myself, holding everything up so long. I began to wonder what God thought about Westley, who certainly hadn't seen Jesus either, but who was now sitting proudly on the platform, swinging his knickerbockered legs and grinning down at me, surrounded by deacons and old women on their knees praying. God had not struck Westley dead for taking his name in vain or for lying in the temple. So I decided that maybe to save further trouble, I'd better lie, too, and say that Jesus had come, and get up and be saved.

12   So I got up.

13   Suddenly the whole room broke into a sea of shouting, as they saw me rise. Waves of rejoicing swept the place. Women leaped in the air. My aunt threw her arms around me. The minister took me by the hand and led me to the platform.

14   When things quieted down, in a hushed silence, punctuated by a few ecstatic "Amens," all the new young lambs were blessed in the name of God. Then joyous singing filled the room.

15   That night, for the first time in my life but one—for I was a big boy twelve years old—I cried. I cried, in bed alone, and couldn't stop. I buried my head under the quilts, but my aunt heard me. She woke up and told my uncle I was crying because the Holy Ghost had come into my life, and because I had seen Jesus. But I was really crying because I couldn't bear to tell her that I had lied, that I had deceived everybody in the church, that I hadn't seen Jesus, and that now I didn't believe there was a Jesus anymore, since he didn't come to help me.

COMPREHENSION QUESTIONS

1. What does it mean to be "saved" in most faiths? What was Hughes's interpretation of "being saved"? Why does young Langston Hughes expect to be saved at this meeting? Why does it take him so long to walk to the altar to be "saved"?

2. Why do you think the audience reacted the way they did when Hughes finally approached the altar? What did they believe happened?

3. Do you think it was right for the aunt to create a concrete expectation for Langston before he attended the revival? Why or why not?

4. Why does Hughes cry in bed after his experience? How had he expected Jesus to help him? What does this reaction tell the reader about Langston?

5. Why do you think this event was so significant in Langston Hughes's life? Have you ever had a similar experience? If so, explain it.

QUESTIONS ON WRITING TECHNIQUE

1. How do the short, one-sentence paragraphs aid Hughes in telling his story?
2. How does Hughes's choice of words help to establish a realistic atmosphere for a religious revival meeting?
3. What does the title mean?
4. A great deal of dialogue is used in this reading. What is the effect of using dialogue?
5. Find three examples of Hughes's rich description with words and write them here.

PRE-READING QUESTIONS

1. Have you lived up to your parents' expectations? How? What were their expectations?
2. If you have children, will your expectations be similar to what your parents expected from you? Why or why not?
3. Do you believe that the United States is a place where anyone can be anything? Why or why not?

The Good Daughter

Caroline Hwang

Caroline Hwang, a Korean American, is a magazine editor and writer whose work has appeared in Glamour, Redbook, Self, Newsweek, *and other contemporary publications. She is a graduate of the University of Pennsylvania and has an MFA from New York University. Her novel* Full Bloom *fully explores her relationship with her mother.*

1 The moment I walked into the dry-cleaning store, I knew the woman behind the counter was from Korea, like my parents. To show her that we shared a heritage, and possibly get a fellow countryman's discount, I tilted my head forward, in shy imitation of a traditional bow.

2   "Name?" she asked, not noticing my attempted obeisance.

3   "Hwang," I answered.

4   "Hwang? Are you Chinese?"

5   Her question caught me off-guard. I was used to hearing such queries from non-Asians who think all Asians all look alike, but never from one of my own people. Of course, the only Koreans I knew were my parents and their friends, people who've never asked me where I came from, since they knew better than I.

6   I ransacked my mind for the Korean words that would tell her who I was. It's always struck me as funny (in a mirthless sort of way) that I can more readily say "I am Korean" in Spanish, German, and even Latin than I can in the language of my ancestry. In the end, I told her in English.

7   The dry-cleaning woman squinted as though trying to see past the glare of my strangeness, repeating my surname under her breath. "Oh, Fxuang," she said, doubling over with laughter. "You don't know how to speak your name."

8   I flinched. Perhaps I was particularly sensitive at the time, having just dropped out of graduate school. I had torn up my map for the future, the one that said not only where I was going but who I was. My sense of identity was already disintegrating.

9   When I got home, I called my parents to ask why they had never bothered to correct me. "Big deal," my mother said, sounding more flippant than I knew she intended. (Like many people who learn English in a classroom, she uses idioms that don't always fit the occasion.) "So what if you can't pronounce your name? You are American," she said.

10   Though I didn't challenge her explanation, it left me unsatisfied. The fact is, my cultural identity is hardly that clear-cut.

11   My parents immigrated to this country 30 years ago, two years before I was born. They told me often, while I was growing up, that, if I wanted to, I could be president someday, that here my grasp would be as long as my reach.

12   To ensure that I reaped all the advantages of this country, my parents saw to it that I became fully assimilated. So, like any American of my generation, I whiled away my youth strolling malls and talking on the phone, rhapsodizing over Andrew McCarthy's blue eyes or analyzing the meaning of a certain upper-classman's offer of a ride to the Homecoming football game.

13   To my parents, I am all American, and the sacrifices they made in leaving Korea—including my mispronounced name—pale in comparison to the opportunities those sacrifices gave me. They do not see that I straddle

two cultures, nor that I feel displaced in the only country I know. I identify with Americans, but Americans do not identify with me. I've never known what it's like to belong to a community—neither one at large, nor of an extended family. I know more about Europe than the continent my ancestors unmistakably come from. I sometimes wonder, as I did that day in the dry cleaner's, if I would be a happier person had my parents stayed in Korea.

14   I first began to consider this thought around the time I decided to go to graduate school. It had been a compromise: my parents wanted me to go to law school; I wanted to skip the starched- collar track and be a writer— the hungrier the better. But after 20-some years of following her wishes and meeting all of their expectations, I couldn't bring myself to disobey or disappoint. A writing career is riskier than the law, I remember thinking. If I'm a failure and my life is a washout, then what does that make my parents' lives?

15   I know that many of my friends had to choose between pleasing their parents and being true to themselves. But for children of immigrants, the choice seems more complicated, a happy outcome impossible. By making the biggest move of their lives for me, my parents indentured me to the largest debt imaginable—I owe them the fulfillment of their hopes for me.

16   It tore me up inside to suppress my dream, but I went to school for a Ph.D. in English literature, thinking I had found the perfect compromise. I would be able to write at least about books while pursuing a graduate degree. Predictably, it didn't work out. How could I labor for five years in a program I had no passion for? When I finally left school, my parents were disappointed, but since it wasn't what they wanted me to do, they weren't devastated. I, on the other hand, felt I was staring at the bottom of the abyss. I had seen the flaw in my life of halfwayness, in my planned life of compromises.

17   I hadn't thought about my love life, but I had a vague plan to make concessions there, too. Though they raised me as an American, my parents expect me to marry someone Korean and give them grandchildren who look like them. This didn't seem like such a huge request when I was 14, but now I don't know what I'm going to do. I've never been in love with someone I

dated, or dated someone I loved. (Since I can't bring myself even to enter-tain the thought of marrying the non-Korean men I'm attracted to, I've been dating only those I know I can stay clearheaded about.) And as I near the age when the question of marriage stalks every relationship, I can't help but wonder if my parents' expectations are responsible for the lack of passion in my life.

18   My parents didn't want their daughter to be Korean, but they don't want her fully American, either. Children of immigrants are living paradoxes. We are the first generation and the last. We are in this country for its opportu-nities, yet filial duty binds us. When my parents boarded the plane, they knew they were embarking on a rough trip. I don't think they imagined the rocks in the path of their daughter who can't even pronounce her own name.

COMPREHENSION QUESTIONS

1. What is the author's purpose in her essay? Who is her audience?
2. What did the dry-cleaning woman teach the author about herself?
3. Explain the line "my parents didn't want their daughter to be Korean, but they don't want her fully American, either."
4. How were the author's and her parents' dreams different? How did the author compromise with her parents' wishes? Has this ever happened to you?
5. What dreams will you have for your children?

QUESTIONS ON WRITING TECHNIQUE

1. How did the author organize her essay?
2. What is the significance of the title?
3. How is the use of dialogue effective between the author and the dry-cleaning lady?
4. How would you characterize the title "The Good Daughter"? Humorous? Ironic? How so?
5. How did the author conclude her essay? Is it effective? Why or why not?

PRE-READING QUESTIONS

1. What is the origin of your name? How did your parents choose it?
2. What would you name a son if you had one? What would you name a daughter? Why?
3. Do you like your name? Why or why not?

What's in a Name?

Deborah Work

Deborah Work is an American writer on contemporary social issues and is published in news magazines. Her writing often reflects her strong feelings on social issues and a call for change. Work currently resides in Fort Lauderdale, Florida.

1 LaFrances Trotter was talking about how she came to name her daughter.

2   She always knew a child of hers would be given a name that was unique, a name no other child would answer to when the teacher called roll or when a friend beckoned on a crowded street.

3   In her mind's eye, she had an image of a child who would be culturally conscious and always aware of her heritage.

4   She turned to some friends from Nigeria, who helped name her baby daughter, Akija. Akija Kalembre.

5   "I've studied African literature, and have always wanted to know more about the culture, the food, and the different celebrations. It seemed only natural that I would give my daughter an African name," says Trotter, who is African American.

6   But the name had to grow on her husband. "I don't like that," he said.

7   To help the name take root in his heart and mind, she left it around the house for him to see, spelled out in block letters on slips of paper.

8   It worked.

Deborah Work, "Name Calling: Michael, Khalid, Jamesha, Ashley, Ashaunte . . . The Names Parents Choose for Their Children Are Loaded with Cultural and Personal Significance," *Sun-Sentinel,* September 27, 1993, p. 1. Reprinted with permission from the South Florida Sun-Sentinel.

9   "I was determined she would have a connection to her African past," says Trotter, who lives in Sunrise, Florida. "It's like a present from her ancestors."

10   Names are important. A parent's gift, they establish identity and place, even if the name is too unusual to be found on a personalized dime-store mug.

11   Dee Catteneo, a Palm Beach County genealogist, says today's parents have all but given up the traditional naming methods of the past. For example, many families of European descent named their eldest son after the husband's father. The next son took his maternal grandfather's name, with the same pattern used for girls. The children who followed were given names that belonged to other relatives, so the same names were recycled throughout families over and over.

12   "It would take ten children before a new name popped up," says Cattaneo, a genealogist with Palm Beach Gardens Church of Latter Day Saints.

13   But none of this is true today, she says. "The way parents name their babies has changed drastically over the years. I feel sorry for genealogists 100 years from now. They won't be able to figure anything out."

14   Unlike the sixties, which spawned a surge of children named for social and environmental causes, like Harmony and Peace, the trend today is toward names that reflect ethnic roots or economic status, like Maxwell, Winthrop, and what else, Rich.

15   And while the Bible still remains a popular place for parents of all religions and nationalities to find a name, parents are also borrowing names from their favorite TV characters or simply making them up.

16   Daisy Camacho, who is Puerto Rican, named her son Hector, four, after his father. But her eight-year-old daughter, Christal, was named after the star of a Hispanic soap opera.

17   Camacho, of Coral Springs, Florida, says her mother-in-law didn't like the name at first because she was looking for something more traditionally Hispanic. But once she got hooked on the program, she came to love the name.

18   "Everyone is out for the unusual," Cattaneo says. "We are seeing more and more names that have no connection to family background or history."

19   In African-American communities, for example, parents are coming up with African-sounding names for their babies. Some are authentic, some are not.

20   The trend began during the Civil Rights and black power movements of the sixties, with black Americans choosing African or Islamic names, shunning names given to slaves by European masters.

21   Today, black parents are going one step further: they are using their imaginations to coin new names.

22   This practice has been criticized for burdening children with awkward names that are difficult to pronounce, while others see it as positive.

23   Samida Jones, who works with teenage girls through a civic organization, has witnessed firsthand the movement toward non-European names.

24   For every Helen and Sandra, there is a Saqauela and a Verlisha. There is a Zandra, Tamiya, Shenika, Zakia, Traveta, and Ashaunte. There is even a Lakrishaw.

25   "I said, boy, times sure have changed. Where are the Marys and Sues?" says Jones, whose own first name has Arabic roots. "Now it seems people just make them up."

26   Still, made-up names lose something in the translation, she says. "Parents should consider a name's true meaning, instead of merely trying to be different."

27   Altan Erskin named her baby daughter Jamesha not because she was searching for an identity, her roots, or anything remotely resembling ethnicity.

28   She just likes the name's exotic sound.

29   "I knew I didn't want a plain name like Jane or Susan. And I wasn't trying for anything that sounded African, either," says Erskin, twenty-one. "I just wanted something special. So I made her name up."

30   She liked the sound mesha, so she started at the beginning of the alphabet: Amesha, Bamesha, Camesha.

31   "When I hit the letter J, I knew that was the one," Erskin says. "It sounded just right.

32   Neither did Joni Sabri have any reservations when she named her two sons. Since her husband Hassan Sabri is Palestinian, she gave her sons Muslim names.

33   "My husband gave me a book of Muslim names, complete with meanings. I liked that they are many generations old; they go way back," says Sabri, who lives with her family in Pompano Beach.

34   Her four-year old is Ali, "a famous Islamic name, very simple," and the two-year-old is Khalid.

35   And Joni Sabri, raised Catholic but converted to Islam four years ago, is Fatima at home and at the Mosque.

36   Muslims are encouraged to give their children certain names, says Hassan Sabri, who has lived in this country for eight years.

37   For example, anything containing the verb hamad, which means 'to praise God' is good.

38   "Mohammed is good for boys, and for girls Hamida is very popular," Hassan Sabri says.

39   One of a child's first rights is to be given a good name, Sabri says. "Islam is a full way of life, and part of that way is naming your child."

40   Genealogist Cattaneo agrees that your name is your birthright, and an important one because it follows you through life.

41   But the quest for the unforgettable name was not popular several generations back, she says. And naming was as much about family as it was about the time in history.

42   "Back then, you didn't want to appear different or ethnic. Immigrants wanted to blend in; you wanted to be a part of where you lived," Cattaneo says.

43   "My husband's parents came over from Italy. They named him Herbert, after Herbert Hoover. But they tucked in an Italian middle name—Mansuetto," she says. "Later on, they decided they didn't like (President) Hoover. So they call him Dick."

44   But today it's not as important to blend into the melting pot. People are looking for individuality. For example, libraries are being deluged with people looking for information to help them prove they have Native-American ancestry, Cattaneo says.

45   "The number of people tracing a Native heritage has increased since the movie *Dances with Wolves*," she says.

46   Virginia Osceola, who is a Seminole Indian, named her new baby daughter Courtney. Her nine-year-old daughter Mercedes chose the name after hearing it in a local mall.

47   Osceola's other three youngsters are Tasha Kelly, Jo-Jo Dakota, and Joseph Daniel.

48   Those, however, are their Anglo names, the names they use to attend public school. But they also have Indian names.

49   What are they?

50   "They are only for Indians to know," Osceola says, taken aback that someone would ask. "They are not to be given out."

51   Seminoles are not the only people who present their children with two sets of names, one cultural.

52   In Franklin Tse's household, for example, his daughter Jennifer might answer to Tse Ying Wah, which connotes elegance and gratitude.

53   "At a Chinese gathering, I would use that name," Tse says. "Most parents, if they have hope and vision for their children, give them a name that will have impact. A dress you don't like you can throw away. But names always stick with you."

54   Many American Jews are turning back to traditional Hebrew names like Ari and Rebecca.

55   Rochelle Liederman says there is no trick to naming Jewish babies, that it's really quite basic.

56   "You want to name your first child after a deceased loved one," says Liederman.

57   Rochelle Liederman's experience illustrates how powerful a role assimilation plays in naming a child.

58   Is trying to fit in always the answer? Maybe not, she says.

59   Her husband Lee Liederman recalls being in a fistfight every day with public school kids who taunted those attending Hebrew school.

60   "It's difficult to retain your identity when there is prejudice. But it's a hurtful thing to lose your name, knowing most of your family was killed during World War II," he says. "You wonder about who you are, you try to find out."

61   "And that's why I love this movement to identify your roots. Everyone should push their children to name their offspring according to their ethnic background," says Rochelle Liederman.

COMPREHENSION QUESTIONS

1. Which different ethnic groups are discussed in this essay? What did you learn about each?
2. How has the naming of children changed over the last century? How has popular culture affected the naming of children?
3. Why do you think so many people are trying to find Native-American origins in their bloodlines?
4. What considerations will you make when you name your first child?
5. How might a person's name affect his or her life?

QUESTIONS ON WRITING TECHNIQUE

1. What is the effect of such short paragraphs in this essay?
2. Does the essay have a good title? Why or why not?
3. The essay uses short interviews to provide examples for the reader. Is that effective?
4. How did the essay conclude?
5. What was the author's purpose in writing this essay? Who is her audience?

Pre-reading Questions

1. Define the term "home."
2. What has "home" meant to you?
3. What are the advantages to living in different places when you are young? The disadvantages?
4. Despite living away from home, do you tend to revert to your childhood when you return to your parents' home? How?

No Place Like Home

Jennifer Crispin

Jennifer Crispin writes on contemporary American social issues and is published in news magazines. She began writing in her teens. In this essay, she writes about her varied geographic background.

1   "Where are you from?" my new co-worker asked. I loaded her brand-new, brand-name suitcase into the dark-blue air force van. "Where are you from?" I countered as I unlocked the passenger door for her. "Florida." She smiled brightly. The new enlistee was a tiny, cute blonde with a brand-new, brand-name suitcase and a hometown. Cute and tiny didn't bother me. Blonde and perky I could live with. What really made me jealous was that she knew where she was from.

2   "Are you excited to be here in Italy?" I asked as we headed for the snack bar on base. This was her first air force assignment, and, as her sponsor, I had to make sure she ate before I dropped her off at the dormitory. "Yeah," she said, bouncing a little in her seat like the teenager she was. "You didn't answer my question. Where are you from?"

3   I know where my roots are. My mom and dad were both born in the same South Jersey county. Mom "helped" Dad with his high school algebra homework. (She did it for him.) Unfortunately for them, her mom was their

algebra teacher. That sort of thing happens when you're from somewhere. Though my mother lives in California with her husband, she knows she's from New Jersey. My father and his wife live in Las Vegas now, but he, too, knows he's from New Jersey.

4   I've spent a total of three years in New Jersey. I can't say I'm from there, because that would imply an intimate knowledge of the area. Someone else from New Jersey would know right away that I'm an imposter.

5   Usually when I explain this, people give me a funny look and ask, "Where were you born?" They insist that wherever you were born is where you're from. I feel trapped, like they want to push me into a corner. I'm not from the state where I was born. Dad joined the air force after he left college. He was in technical school at Keesler Air Force Base in Mississippi when I was born. We lived in Mississippi for a few more months, then Dad got an assignment to Florida. My brother was born in Florida, but he's not from Florida any more than I'm from Mississippi.

6   We moved to bases in Nevada and California. Then Dad changed air force jobs, and we went overseas. We lived in Greece and Portugal. Whenever we moved, Dad would send us to live with his mother in New Jersey until he got settled. The kids didn't like me because I wasn't from there. Adults always said, "She's lived in Greece and Portugal. You should be impressed." Kids don't take well to adults' telling them they should be impressed. The kids reminded me that I wasn't from New Jersey. Just like I wasn't from Greece or Portugal.

7   When I was 11, we moved to Rhein-Main Air Base in Germany. I was a part of history there. The air force dedicated our school to two pilot heroes of the Berlin airlift, and my band class played at the ceremony. I felt connected to Germany. But there were American kids who were born there, who had been going to Halvorsen-Tunner school their whole lives. They knew I wasn't from Germany.

8   Three years after arriving at Rhein-Main, we moved again, against my very loud protests. I would hate Italy, I promised with every fiber of my 14-year-old being. I would not like anything about it.

9   Italy lived up to my grim expectations, at first. Vicenza High School depressed me, with its dimly lit hallways and garish red lockers. As I despaired of ever making a true friend, Heather came into my life. Heather was as rootless as I. She made it her mission to be my friend. She worked backstage at plays I acted in and always talked to me in computer class, even when I was rude and mean. I couldn't help being friends with her. We're still best friends, and Vicenza is our history. It's as close as we can get to a place we're from. Although I didn't like Vicenza at first, I grew to love it. But there

are always people who have lived there longer. Vicenza belongs to them. I can't really say I'm from Vicenza.

10   Heather and I came up with an answer for people who asked "Where are you from?" Our addresses in Italy ended with APO NY because all the mail was processed through New York. We thought we finally had a clever way to respond. We could say we were from APO, New York.

11   Not for long, though. The military postal system changed the addresses. The final line for Europe now reads APO AE for Area Europe. Well, I can't say I'm from APO AE because that's not the address I had growing up. Stumped again.

12   When I joined the air force at 18, my dad was stationed in Los Angeles. According to the government, your hometown is wherever you enlist. So for the five and a half years I served, my records said I was from Los Angeles. I had lived in Los Angeles for about eight months, but for official purposes it was my hometown.

13   The government sent me to South Korea for a year and the Azores for 15 months. My next assignment was Aviano Air Base in Italy. I was returning to the country I felt the most like home in. I worked with a talented air force news producer who loved Italy as much as I did. We got married a year and a half after we met. John is from Iowa. He went to school two blocks from his home. His family has been there so long that they're included in town-history books. When his folks asked me where I was from, I didn't have an answer.

14   Just like I didn't have an answer for my air force co-worker. Her bright face waited expectantly for an answer. I had to make up something on the spot because I didn't want to go through the speech again. "I'm not from anywhere," I said.

15   I'm not from anywhere. But that's as much a part of my identity as a hometown is for other people. I am a person who is not from anywhere, and after 26 years of mumbling, I can finally admit it with pride. I am from nowhere, and I am from everywhere. That's the way I like it.

COMPREHENSION QUESTIONS

1. What are some of the author's "homes"? What problems has the author had in defending her "homelessness"?
2. Can you think of other situations where individuals would have trouble determining their "homes"?

3. Is it easier for someone who has moved frequently as a child to move as an adult? Why or why not?
4. How is your life similar to and different from the author's?
5. What was the author's purpose in writing the essay?

QUESTIONS ON WRITING TECHNIQUE

1. The author uses many examples to explain the trouble she has had in determining a "home." Was this an effective strategy? Why or why not?
2. Is the conclusion effective? How might you have changed it?
3. What does the author mean when she states that she "wasn't from anywhere?" Would you characterize this as irony, sarcasm, humor?
4. The author uses a very conversational style. What effect does that have on you as the reader?
5. The author does not detail the places where she lived. Why not?

WRITING SUGGESTIONS

1. Create an essay in which you describe your life both before and after a significant event in your life.
2. Do you define yourself as part of a social or political group? What does it mean to be a part of that group? What are the values of that group?
3. What part of you is your source of power? Arms, legs, hands, eyes, other? Explain in an essay.
4. Write an essay about someone who unexpectedly made a difference in your life.
5. Langston Hughes vividly recounts his story of salvation. Recount an important event in your life that changed the way you view the world.
6. Write about a regret you have when you go home. Are you reminded of something from your past that you would change if you could? Tell the story.

IN-SIGHT

Matthew Cavanaugh/EPA/Corbis

Everyone has something in their lives that they do well. Everyone reading this book is an authority on something like giving a speech, making people laugh, procrastination, caring for children, playing an instrument, cooking a meal, or trouble-shooting a computer problem.

1. What is going on in the picture shown here?
2. What are you an authority on?
3. What do you wish you were an authority on?

In this next exercise you will explore the things you do well.

AUTHORITY PROJECT

1. List three things that you are an authority on.
2. Choose one of the three topics from your list and write three sentences that explain why you are an authority on that topic.
3. Write an essay that explains why you are an authority on that topic. Include relevant details. Give examples.
4. When your essay is finished, share it with your classmates.

PEER CRITIQUE

Your Name _____

The Author's Name _____

1. Read your partner's essay.

2. What is your immediate reaction to the essay?

3. Is there an explicit thesis statement? If so, write it here. If it is not explicit, was it clear? If so, put it in your own words here.

4. Does the essay include sufficient description? Make a suggestion where the writer could add more.

5. What additional information would you like to know as the reader?

6. Does everything in the essay support the thesis statement? Why or why not?

7. How did the author conclude his or her essay? What method was used (prediction, call for action, summary, question, etc.)? Is it effective? Why or why not?

8. Did you find any spelling errors or typos in this essay? If so, identify them here.

MECHANICS AND GRAMMAR
The Parts of Speech

When we bake a cake, we use ingredients in order to prepare a delicious, finished product. The same applies to a sentence. We need different ingredients in order to make a sentence understandable and interesting for our reader. These ingredients are called the parts of speech in English grammar.

There are eight basic parts of speech: nouns, pronouns, verbs, adjectives, adverbs, prepositions, conjunctions, and interjections. When you learn to recognize the parts of speech, you will be able to discuss your writing intelligently and accurately.

Noun

Simply put, a noun is a person, place, or thing. Let's expand the concept of "thing" to include ideas and concepts, and we should have an idea what a noun is.

Examples: John, kite, happiness, skiing, Jamaica

Pronoun

A pronoun takes the place of a noun. Instead of repeating a noun again and again, we replace it with a pronoun to allow our reader to flow through our reading.

Examples: he, she, it, we, they, their, mine, someone

Verbs

We cannot get along in a sentence without a verb. Every sentence will have one. Verbs either indicate action or link our subject with other information in our sentence. Thus, verbs show action or a state of being.

Examples: (action) begin, show, stain, direct, resolve, sing
(linking) is, were, was

Sometimes, to show more differences in meaning, verbs use helping words that suggest the time at which the action of the verb takes place and other kinds of meaning. These words are called helping or auxiliary verbs, and they always come before the main verb.

Examples: will, had, did, should

Adjectives

Adjectives help us describe people, places, and things more accurately. They give life and color to our writing and help our readers better visualize what we are attempting to describe. Thus, an adjective modifies or describes a noun or pronoun.

Examples: purple, six, this, many, interesting

Adverbs

An adverb will take some study, as it has several functions. An adverb is a word that modifies a verb, an adjective, or an adverb. Usually an adverb answers one of these questions: "How much?" "When?" "Where?" "How?"

Examples: When? I can go fishing *tomorrow*.
Where? I looked *everywhere* for my coat.
How? Ruth speaks *clearly*.
How much? I am *very* tired today.

Prepositions

Prepositions "direct" meaning. That is, they often show the relationship between one noun or pronoun to another noun or pronoun. They are connecting words. If you memorize a number of them, others will become more clear.

Examples: in, at, on, to, for, under, before, by, within

Conjunctions

Conjunctions are connectors. They link words and sometimes whole sentences together. There are two types of conjunctions: subordinating and coordinating.
Most of us are familiar with coordinating conjunctions.

Examples: and, but, or, nor, so, yet, for, although

We may be less familiar with subordinating conjunctions.

Examples: since, until

Interjections

An interjection is also known as an exclamation. It expresses emotion and exists independently from the rest of the sentence.
Interjections may be followed by either a comma or an exclamation mark. This depends on how strongly the speaker feels about the subject.

Examples: Yes, I would like to go.
Darn! I don't have any money left.
Ouch! That really hurt!

EXERCISES

Exercise 1

Indicate whether the bold words are adjectives or adverbs. Remember, an adjective modifies nouns (person, place, thing, idea), and an adverb modifies verbs as well as other adjectives and adverbs.

1. A **soft** answer turns away anger. _____

2. A little **red** cottage sat on the hilltop. _____

3. The sublime and ridiculous are **often** nearly related. _____

4. **Undoubtedly** he was a hero. _____

5. He sleeps **well** despite the fever. _____

6. This is my **best** work. _____

7. She lay on the roof as the **loud** rain fell. _____

8. The sentinels at the door **quickly** fled. _____

9. She wore a **very** long red sweater to the fair. _____

10. I served through the **enduring** war. _____

11. The wind bites **sharply**; it is a bitter cold. _____

12. The **little** playful streams hurry down the hillside. _____

Exercise 2

Tell the part of speech of the words in bold. They are either nouns, verbs, adjectives, or adverbs.

1. The **down** of the dandelion tells our fortune. _____

2. They **dance** very well. _____

3. I went to a square **dance** during the weekend._____

4. That **study** occupies all of their time. _____

5. I have had to **study** since last weekend for the test. _____

6. He often sits in his **study** chair._____

7. Did the goose **feather** its nest? _____

8. Since undertaking the Atkin's diet, she is light as a **feather**._____

9. Have you ever slept on a **feather** bed? _____

10. They **man** the boat and push from shore. _____

Exercise 3

Use the following words in a sentence as the parts of speech indicated:

1. work (noun) _____

2. work (verb) _____

3. work (adjective)_____

4. fall (noun)_____

5. fall (verb) _____

6. fall (adjective) _____

7. rain (noun) _____

8. rain (verb) _____

9. rain (adjective) _____

Exercise 4

List all of the pronouns found in each sentence.

(1) My friend Jane and I went Christmas shopping yesterday. (2) We found a lot of great deals. (3) First we went to the furniture store. (4) Jane found the perfect set of tables for her sister's living room, and I found a beautiful rug for my mom's kitchen. (5) Next we went to a department store where Jane found something for everyone on her list. (6) Usually it takes us weeks to get all of our shopping done, but this time we did almost all of it in one day.

Exercise 5

Add an appropriate pronoun for each sentence even if a word from a different part of speech would work as well.

(1)_____ asked my brother if (2)_____ could come over to do some repairs on (3)_____ car. (4)_____ said that (5)_____ would be happy to, but only if (6)_____ would agree to make dinner. (7)_____ went to the store with (8)_____ friend Ann, and (9)_____ bought all of the ingredients that (10)_____ would need to make a nice Italian dinner. (11)_____ bought lots of fresh tomatoes, some pasta, some Italian bread, and some wine. Together (12)_____ were able to create a wonderful dinner in no time. (13)_____ even gave some leftovers to (14)_____ dog that wagged (15)_____ tail the whole time we were cooking. Afterwards my brother and his partner said that (16)_____ had not had such a wonderful meal in a very long time. (17)_____ were happy to accommodate (18)_____.

Exercise 6

Label the underlined words as verbs, nouns, adverbs, or adjectives.

The (1)<u>controversy</u> over (2)<u>graphic</u> violence in video games (3)<u>has</u> continued to grow as video games (4)<u>become</u> more sophisticated and gamers (5)<u>demand</u> something new, different, and more exciting each year. Some experts say that violent video (6)<u>games</u> (7)<u>promote</u> violence in adults, while others say only adults who are likely to commit violent acts are (8)<u>adversely</u> affected by the violence in video games. Although some gamers have (9)<u>admitted</u> to some short-term (10)<u>aggressive</u> feelings after playing violent video games, or games that promote (11)<u>anti-social</u> behavior, most (12)<u>strongly</u> agree that their sense of right and wrong are not affected.

Exercise 7

Add the appropriate (N)ouns, (P)ronouns, (V)erbs, (Adj)ectives, or (Adv)erbs.

My friend and (1. P)___ were (2. Adv)___ excited to finally be going on (3. P)___ first cruise. We booked our reservations (4. N)___ in advance and only had to fly a short distance from Phoenix to Los Angeles, and then we would be on the boat and off to the Baja Peninsula. However, things were not that simple. When we (5. V)___ at the airport, we were told that there had been (6. Adj)___ thunderstorms in some other parts of the country that were causing (7. Adj)___ flight delays across the United States. Our flight was first delayed and then cancelled. We had to spend that (8. Adj)___ day in that (9. Adj)___ airport running from one gate to another as the airline tried to find us another flight. We were finally able to get another flight to Los Angeles at six o'clock that evening. Unfortunately, our boat had sailed at five. We decided to go ahead and (10. V)___ into Los Angeles and try to catch our boat the next day at its first port stop at Catalina Island. We stayed in a (11. N)___ in Long Beach that night and took a (12. N)___ to the ferry that would bring us to Catalina Island. While we waited for the next ferry, we went to the Queen Mary that was (13. V)___ nearby. We took a short tour and had a (14. Adj)___ lunch, then we (15. Adv)___ headed for the ferry docks. We were able to meet up with our cruise ship and had a lovely time. We will never forget that (16. Adj)___ and (17. Adj)___ adventure.

Exercise 8

List all of the prepositions in each sentence.

(1) Every year during the Fourth of July holiday, my family gets together for a family reunion. (2) We usually meet in Las Vegas to gamble and go to several shows. (3) Some of us only travel a few miles, but others come from as far away as Germany. (4) We spend the mornings and afternoons swimming and go out to the casinos after it gets dark because it is very hot during the day. (5) It is fun to walk through the casinos and see all of the attractions. (6) My favorite Las Vegas attraction is the garden in the Bellagio near the art museum. (7) The museum is above the garden. (8) It is wonderful to be with my family while vacationing. (9) I don't know what I would do without them.

Exercise 9

Rewrite the following paragraph. Circle the prepositions and underline the prepositional phrases.

Sometimes I am terribly absent minded. I often cannot remember where I put things from one minute to the next. The last thing I lost was my car keys. I looked everywhere for them. First, I looked on all of the tables and counters in the house. Then, I looked under the beds, the sofa, and the tables. Finally, I looked in strange places like in the oven and under the refrigerator. I finally decided to try again after work and got a ride with my sister. After looking everywhere for many hours that night, I decided the keys were gone for good. Before going to sleep that night, I went into the garage to take out the garbage. There, on the garbage can lid, were my keys!

Some Common Prepositions

About	Down	Out
Above	During	Over
Across	Except	Past
After	For	Since
Against	From	Through
Among	In	Throughout
Around	Inside	To
As	Into	Toward
At	Like	Under
Before	Near	Until
Behind	Next	Up
Below	Of	With
Beneath	Off	Without
Beside	On	
Between	Onto	

Multi-word Prepositions

According to	Because of	Except for
Along with	Due to	Up to
As well as		

ADDITIONAL EXERCISES

Exercise 1

In the following short paragraph, identify then abbreviate the part of speech above each word. Noun, n.; Verb, v.; Pronoun, pro.; Adjective, adj.; Adverb, adv.; Interjection, int.; Conjunction, con.; Preposition, prep.

Last Friday evening we had just left our biology lecture and held our class elections in our history class. The teacher called for nominations for president, and one of the bright pupils in the class stood up and said, "I nominate Arnold Schwarzenegger." The whole class and the teacher laughed.

Exercise 2

Try to identify the parts of speech in the following paragraph without referring back to your notes.

There was a dark lonely forest at the southern end of my father's farm. The forest was always a good place to go and play when my sister and I had finished our chores. One evening it began to get dark and my sister and I were still playing down in the forest. Then I saw strange shadows. A little chill ran up my spine. I heard a queer noise behind me and turned quickly around. There was a young rabbit. My sister and I laughed but we still ran home quickly.

Exercise 3

Practice one more time identifying the parts of speech in the following paragraph.

Snow began to fall early on that late February morning. I had set my alarm to ring two hours before it normally rang so that I could watch the snow fall. I was not disappointed. When I awoke, snow had already begun to accumulate. I spent the next two hours blissfully watching it fall and hoping that school would be cancelled for that day. Slowly, the household awoke. My mother got up and turned on the radio in the kitchen and we all listened to the list of school closings. My school was not on the first list of closings. My mother insisted that I get ready for school since it had not been cancelled. Just as I was leaving for the bus stop, Muncy (my home school) was on the list. Hurray! I had a free day to sled ride and make snowmen.

GROUP ACTIVITY

Students should get in groups of three. Each student should create a list of three things they enjoy doing in their free time over the weekend. The students will then put each of their sentences in grids on one sheet of paper. The grid should look like this:

I	like	to	go	to	The	park	with	my	dog

The students will place the words to each sentence in the bottom half of the grid.

After all the grids have the bottom half filled, then the students will work together to decide which part of speech is in the bottom half and will write that part of speech in the top space of the grid.

pronoun	verb	prep	verb	prep	article	noun	prep	pronoun	noun
I	like	to	go	to	the	park	with	my	dog

When the group is finished, they should have created nine grids in all.

Each group should then choose the sentence grid that has a good variety of the parts of speech. The group will then recreate the grid for that sentence on the board to share with the class.

4

FAMILY

The family unit takes many forms. Whom do you consider your family? The answer will be different for nearly everyone. In addition to the traditional nuclear family consisting of a mother, father, and children, we see many types of families today: single-parent households, same-gender parenting, multigenerational families, and grandparents raising their grandchildren.

This chapter illustrates family issues. Kaufman's "Just a Normal Girl" explores a differently abled student's triumphs and challenges in college. Tan's "Two Kinds" and Kincaid's "Girl" examine the difficult relationship between mothers and daughters. Smith-Yackel's "My Mother Never Worked" looks at the government's responsibility regarding families. Swanson's "The Turning Point" and Dorris's "Father's Day" both illustrate the way adults often look back at their childhoods and the roles that parents and other influential adults may have played in their journeys to adulthood.

PRE-READING QUESTIONS

1. What do you know about Down syndrome?
2. Should mentally challenged individuals attend college?
3. What experiences have you had with mentally challenged classmates either in high school or college?

Just a Normal Girl

Leslie Kaufman

Leslie Kaufman began her career as a freelance reporter writing for alternative newspapers. She has reported on the first female crew on an aircraft carrier, the suspicious death of a Navajo environmental activist, the 1996 sweatshops in El Salvador, the Wal-Mart chain, and e-commerce. Recently, she began covering the social services beat for the New York Times *and currently writes on homelessness, welfare, and child abuse in New York City.*

1   At 6:30 a.m. Katie Apostolides rises, showers and pulls and tugs at her long brown hair under the dryer until it is a shiny, luxuriant mane. She applies a little eye makeup and arrives on the Becker College campus for her course on principles of teaching at 8:20 a.m. She is more than an hour early.

2   She calls "Hello" and "How are you?" to all the students she passes—whether or not she knows them—and then gets a large Green Mountain coffee and listens to Latin rap on her iPod.

3   Forty-five minutes before class begins, she is in Nina Mazloff's office to pepper her with questions. She wants to know what they will cover for the day, whether she will have to take notes and if there will be any homework.

4   Professor Mazloff is patient but gently encourages her student not to spend the whole time waiting with her. "Katie really is a devoted student," she explains kindly.

5   Ms. Apostolides, 23, likes to say of herself, "I am just a normal girl with a lifelong story." But that is really just another way of explaining that she has Down syndrome, a genetic abnormality that has many side effects, including mental retardation that can range from severe to mild.

6   In her determined quest to have a normal college experience, she is at the forefront of a wave of cognitively challenged students who are demanding, and gaining, a place on campuses nationwide. Ms. Apostolides was accepted at Becker, a small liberal arts school with campuses in Leicester and Worcester, Mass., three years ago through regular admissions.

7   Of course, regular admissions at Becker is fairly gentle—almost 78 percent of applicants are accepted, and the average SAT score is 880, combined math and reading. Still, Ms. Apostolides had to produce a high school transcript and take the SAT (she doesn't remember her score).

8   She attends regular classes and lives in a coed dorm. She has her own room but shares common spaces with a diverse representation of the student body, including many members of the football team.

9   While she is among a small number of students with Down syndrome to have such a completely integrated education, there are dozens of others in programs that place cognitively disabled students in regular classrooms and sometimes in dormitories. The Web site ThinkCollege.net, a database on postsecondary schooling financed by the United States Department of Education, has information on 106 programs. "And the number is growing fast," says Nancy Hurley, an education specialist at the Institute for Community Inclusion, which collects information for the database.

10   The opening of college campuses comes as an outgrowth of the Individuals with Disabilities Education Act of 1975. That law mandated that public schools educate children of all intellectual abilities and, whenever possible, in regular classrooms with same-age peers.

11   Now, coming of age expecting full inclusion from kindergarten through 12th grade, students and their parents are asking to graduate to similar opportunities. By law, children with disabilities are entitled to a free public education until age 21. Until recently, that mostly meant an extended stay in special-education classrooms at a public high school, but recent clarifications of the law have allowed states to use money earmarked for lower education for appropriate postsecondary programs instead.

12   By now, colleges have had experience accommodating students with learning disabilities like dyslexia and attention deficit disorder. But teaching students with cognitive delays or mental retardation is the next frontier. These new students are far more challenging: colleges must struggle not just with how students learn but with the limits on what they can absorb.

13   "The students have intellectual disabilities, but their chronological age goes along normally, and they want the same kind of social experiences," says Linda Hickson, who coordinates programs on mental retardation and

autism at Teachers College at Columbia. "The challenge is to find age-appropriate experiences so that they are not totally held back by their childish intellectual limitations."

14   Parents and educators pressing for inclusion say they are committed out of practical concerns as well. People with cognitive disabilities have abysmal rates of participation in the workplace, and when they do get jobs, they tend to hold entry-level positions, like fast-food clerk and custodial aide. But studies commissioned by the National Down Syndrome Society have shown that the quality and quantity of jobs increase with postsecondary education.

15   As parents and advocates intensify efforts to get more access to mainstream colleges and to federal financing for these endeavors, the questions take on new public relevance: just what are Down syndrome children capable of learning? What does their presence suggest about the role of higher education? Is the college experience really the best way to enhance their lives—especially when their education can cost $10,000 a semester?

16   Postsecondary programs for the cognitively disabled vary substantially; some are more inclusive than others, some lead to a certificate or associate's degree, others don't. Community colleges offer vocational training in fields as diverse as child care, physical therapy, funeral services and hospitality services.

17   "Even though there are more than 100 programs, all of them developed separately," says Madeleine Will, vice president for public policy for the National Down Syndrome Society. "There has not been any overall coherent plan or nature to the programs. Many of them are lacking what we consider to be vital pieces. An awful lot of them, for example, do not have a residential component."

18   Ms. Will hopes that will soon change. Last year Laura Riggio and her husband, Steve, chief executive of Barnes & Noble, gave a grant of $300,000 through the Down syndrome society to enable two public colleges in New Jersey to develop models for cognitively disabled students on campus. The Riggios have a college-age child with Down syndrome.

19   The programs were designed to address four basic needs: employment training, socialization, independent-living skills and academic growth—through a mix of remedial reading and writing courses, exposure to creative experiences like drawing and acting and, eventually, more challenging coursework.

20   "We are trying to assess what works and what doesn't," Ms. Will says. "Ultimately, it will be a model that we can describe in more definitive ways and seek to replicate. Ideally, we would like a statewide system of programs like this."

21   The grant was split by the College of New Jersey, a four-year institution, and Mercer County Community College, both in the Trenton area. For this first year, the College of New Jersey accepted six applicants, who are learning

college study habits and focusing on career options. They are also enrolled in a seminar called "Abilities Unplugged" with 15 traditional freshmen. For this class, they are expected to read a book, participate in an online discussion board, produce an oral history and watch films and write critiques. Rebecca Daley, the program's administrator, says that with time the students are expected to be included in more and more classes with the rest of the student body.

22   At Mercer, participants in what it calls the Dream program are assigned student mentors. They take most of their classes with the general student body and can work toward an associate degree or certificate in any of the college's 66 fields. First, however, they must pass so-called foundation courses in math, reading and writing.

23   Although Mercer has open admissions for the general population, it requires applications for Dream so potential students can be screened for "ability to benefit and commitment," says Susan Onaitis, who administers the program and teaches the life and college skills class. For the first semester, this fall, Dream accepted nine students, one of them, John McCormack, with Down syndrome.

24   At student orientation in August, Mr. McCormack, a gregarious 24-year-old, got a hint of the struggle ahead. Even among his cognitively disabled peers, he was the last to finish a scavenger hunt meant to familiarize the students with the campus. At the college art gallery, where he was supposed to describe a painting, he needed help spelling "orange" on the form he was filling out. At the library, where he was discovering how to make a photocopy, he became confused by a sign on the change machine and thought it cost $1 instead of 10 cents. At the cafeteria, he was suddenly shy waiting in line to order a cheeseburger and asked for help. "I am afraid they won't understand me," he explained.

25   A get-to-know-you session with just the Dream group went much better. He hugged a girl he knew from high school and participated well in a game in which he was asked to describe what he had learned about the likes and dislikes of his mentor. In discussions between exercises, he told the other students about a vacation in Hawaii, and when one young man volunteered that he had recently broken up with his girlfriend because she wasn't "treating him right," Mr. McCormack was the first to offer sympathy. "You can do better, man," he said with a knowing pat on the back.

26   Asked why he is attending college, Mr. McCormack says it is because his sister "went there." He hopes to get a good job when he gets out. His ambition is to be a singer.

27   "He always wanted to go to college, and this new program was the perfect opportunity to get the support he needed," says his mother, Susan

McCormack. She doesn't think her goals for his education are unachievable. "My hope is that he will get a little out of an education and make some contacts," she says, "maybe get a job, make friends and have new experiences."

28   Since Mr. McCormack is not trying to earn a degree, he is not eligible for tuition assistance. The College of New Jersey charges $10,000 per term, but Mercer participants pay the same as other community college students: several thousand dollars a year. "He might not get the full value that a normal child would, but he still deserves the opportunity to get as much as he can and learn as much as he can," Mrs. McCormack says. "It is something we are willing to do to help him to get to his potential."

29   Classes have been tough, she acknowledges. There is a lot of reading to be done. So far he has been assigned a short story by Langston Hughes, "Thank You M'am," and "The Stolen Party," by the Argentine writer Liliana Heker. Mr. McCormack does not read the material himself. His mother reads to him and asks him questions. "It is amazing how much he is able to give back," she says, "but he would never be able to read it on his own."

30   Dr. William Cohen, director of the Down Syndrome Center of Western Pennsylvania at Children's Hospital of Pittsburgh, says that in general, people with Down syndrome exhibit I.Q.'s of 40 to 70, with below 70 considered mentally retarded. Scores on I.Q. tests correlate with an individual's ability to do abstract reasoning and absorb complicated information, tasks usually associated with college.

31   "The bind that we are in is that we want to support families' hopefulness about what their children want to achieve," he says. "But at the same time we are aware that there are likely to be limits."

32   Dr. Cohen cites research showing that children with I.Q.'s of 60 to 70 can read at fourth-grade level, sometimes higher; those with I.Q.'s below that can read at first-grade level. Math levels tend to be lower than reading, and writing correlates with reading but is also affected by fine motor skills. During early childhood, emotional and social development lags as well, but Down syndrome children eventually develop strong social skills and are perceptive about their relations with others.

33   In many ways, Katie Apostolides is not just a pioneer but also an avatar of all the potential and limits of students with Down syndrome. For starters, she was given extraordinary preparation for educational success by particularly driven parents.

34   Her mother, Paulette, was reading books on how to raise a gifted child while pregnant. Katie's disability came as shock. Paulette Apostolides was in her 20's, and there was no history of Down syndrome in the family.

35   But she decided quickly that she would not accept the limits of cognitive development that doctors were preparing her for. She started her daugh-

ter on a rigorous course of therapy at the age of three weeks, after consulting one of the country's foremost experts in Down syndrome, Siegfried M. Pueschel. She cut back her work as a marketing consultant. Two sons without Down syndrome, now 19 and 9, followed. Still, she devoted much of her time to managing her daughter's education and therapy. "I just didn't have friends," she explains.

36   Katie had language therapy from the time she could make sounds until she was 18 and has been in inclusion classes since kindergarten. Her mother says her I.Q. is on the high side for a Down syndrome child.

37   "I broke all the rules on how to raise the special child," Paulette Apostolides says. "We executed therapy goals every minute of the day. When she was in the bathtub, I would read her the *Wall Street Journal*. I couldn't let her just sit there. There was never a moment she wasn't stimulated."

38   In many ways, Katie Apostolides's achievements are amazing. She tried out for and made the high school cheerleading squad. Last semester at Becker she received two B's and an A without significant accommodation from the college. She receives large-type syllabuses, a note-taker for each class and extra time for exams, but she must still master the same material as her classmates. Madeleine Entel, the administrator of Becker's Centers for Academic Success, says, "This was no giveaway. Katie worked really hard."

39   Perhaps more astonishing, in classrooms Ms. Apostolides barely stands out. In a recent evening class on effective communications, she sits in the front row with a note-taker. During the three-hour class she does not participate, but she nods vigorously when the instructor discusses how to avoid bias in business communication and starts talking about the disabled.

40   Afterward, Ms. Apostolides explains that she does not like to ask a question in class unless she has prepared ahead or knows the subject well—for example, how a person with a disability might like to be addressed. But the next day, in Professor Mazloff's class, she is very verbal. The students sit in groups of four. Ms. Apostolides is next to a dorm-mate she describes as a break-dancer and friend, who whispers to her occasionally during the class. For an exercise in recalling their most vivid memories of childhood teachers, Ms. Apostolides has as many contributions as anyone.

41   Yet for all her accomplishments, her academic experience is limited. Her classes are introductory, even in her third year. There is no Shakespeare and no philosophy and nothing that involves math, which Ms. Apostolides has particular difficulty comprehending. She spends hours each week with a private tutor struggling to understand material that other students might find rote. The lack of advanced work means that, even though she has 36 credits at Becker, she will never graduate.

42   She has had to retreat from her original ambition, being a physical therapist, because she could not memorize medical terms.

43   Ms. Apostolides describes what she is learning in her "Principles of Education" class: "It has given me insight on observing children and on how we do assessments of children. When you are observing you are interacting, but you are basically recording stuff in a notebook. It is a really neat way to understand children." When asked to describe her best learning experience at college, she cites a computer class. "I learned how to use Microsoft Word, PowerPoint and the Internet. I got all A's."

44   And for all her effervescence, it is routine social interaction that most frustrates and confuses. With an understanding that has clearly been informed by numerous talks with her mother, she says she sometimes "can hang on too much and too quickly." Her tendency to misjudge a situation is all too evident. Traveling by campus shuttle bus, Ms. Apostolides makes all the students getting off give her a high five. They do it, but obviously without relish. She doesn't sense that she may have imposed.

45   One counselor, who asked not to be named because the comments might be perceived as insensitive, has a tragic view of Ms. Apostolides's time at Becker. "Katie thinks she has a million friends, but she is going to leave here and not one student is going to stay in touch," she says. "I can't help thinking if she was with other Down syndrome children, it would be better."

46   Paulette Apostolides calls that idea—that someone with Down syndrome cannot have true friends among the nondisabled—a prejudice that will be overcome in time. When her daughter is home, she says, her cellphone rings frequently—friends wanting to stay in touch.

47   Ken Cameron, dean of students at Becker, has been helping Ms. Apostolides navigate the social byways. "Some of the social boundaries just aren't there for her," he says. "But she has improved tremendously since she's been here. She is aware of not pushing too hard to be someone's friend or not. During her first year I'd see her every day, and she'd say, 'This is happening and this is happening.' Now she is much more independent. The staff hears from her a lot less. You can sense that she has matured."

48   In Mr. Cameron's estimation, that is one of the main purposes of a college education anyway.

COMPREHENSION QUESTIONS

1. In the introduction, what is unusual about Katie? What unusual thing does she do that might clue in the reader to her disability even before it is fully described?

2. Why are mentally challenged individuals entering college now more than ever before?
3. What are some of the problems these students often face? What are the benefits?
4. According to the text, what might have given Katie an advantage over some other young people with Down syndrome?
5. What questions are you left with after reading the essay? List at least three.

QUESTIONS ON WRITING TECHNIQUE

1. How did the essay begin? Was that beginning effective?
2. How did the author make the transition from telling Katie's story to a discussion about all young people with mental disabilities?
3. What was the tone of the essay? Was there any indication about how the author felt about students with mental disabilities attending college?
4. Was the essay easy to read and understand? Explain your answer.
5. What details do you think should have been added or could have been left out?

PRE-READING QUESTIONS

1. What is something that your parents forced you to do that you really did not want to do (e.g., practice the piano, play football)?
2. Did you do it anyway or did you resist? Why? Do you regret doing it or resisting it? Why or why not?
3. Do you believe your parents or caregivers influenced the choices you have made in your life? If so, how? If not, why not?
4. How will you try to influence your children?

Two Kinds

Amy Tan

Amy Tan was born in Oakland, California, in 1952, several years after her mother and father immigrated from China. She was raised in various cities in the San Francisco Bay area. When she was eight, her essay "What the Library

Means to Me" won first prize among elementary school participants, for which Tan received a transistor radio and publication in the local newspaper. Upon the deaths of her brother and father in 1967 and 1968 from brain tumors, the family began a haphazard journey through Europe, before settling in Montreux. Switzerland, where Tan graduated in her junior year in 1969.

For the next seven years, Tan attended five schools. She first went to Linfield College in McMinnville Oregon, and there, on a blind date, met her future husband Lou DeMattei. She followed him to San Jose, where she enrolled in San Jose City College. She next attended San Jose State University, and, while working two part-time jobs, she became an English honors student and a President's Scholar, while carrying a semester course load of 21 units. In 1972 she graduated with honors, receiving a B.A. with a double major in English and Linguistics. She was awarded a scholarship to attend the Summer Linguistics Institute at the University of California, Santa Cruz. In 1973, she earned her M.A. in Linguistics, also from San Jose State University, and was then awarded a Graduate Minority Fellowship under the affirmative action program at the University of California, Berkeley, where she enrolled as a doctoral student in linguistics.

1   My mother believed you could be anything you wanted to be in America. You could open a restaurant. You could work for the government and get good retirement. You could buy a house with almost no money down. You could become rich. You could become instantly famous.

2   "Of course, you can be a prodigy, too," my mother told me when I was nine. "You can be best anything. What does Auntie Lindo know? Her daughter, she is only best tricky."

3   America was where all my mother's hopes lay. She had come to San Francisco in 1949 after losing everything in China: her mother and father, her home, her first husband, and two daughters, twin baby girls. But she never looked back with regret. Things could get better in so many ways.

4   We didn't immediately pick the right kind of prodigy. At first my mother thought I could be a Chinese Shirley Temple. We'd watch Shirley's old movies on TV as though they were training films. My mother would poke my arm and say, "*Ni kan.* You watch." And I would see Shirley tapping her feet, or singing a sailor song, or pursing her lips into a very round O while saying "Oh, my goodness."

5   "*Ni kan,*" my mother said, as Shirley's eyes flooded with tears. "You already know how. Don't need talent for crying!"

6   Soon after my mother got this idea about Shirley Temple, she took me to the beauty training school in the Mission District and put me in the hands of a student who could barely hold the scissors without shaking. Instead of

getting big fat curls, I emerged with an uneven mass of crinkly black fuzz. My mother dragged me off to the bathroom and tried to wet down my hair.

7   "You look like a Negro Chinese," she lamented, as if I had done this on purpose. The instructor of the beauty training school had to lop off these soggy clumps to make my hair even again. "Peter Pan is very popular these days" the instructor assured my mother. I now had bad hair the length of a boy's, with curly bangs that hung at a slant two inches above my eyebrows. I liked the haircut, and it made me actually look forward to my future fame.

8   In fact, in the beginning I was just as excited as my mother, maybe even more so. I pictured this prodigy part of me as many different images, and I tried each one on for size. I was a dainty ballerina girl standing by the curtain, waiting to hear the music that would send me floating on my tiptoes. I was like the Christ child lifted out of the straw manger, crying with holy indignity. I was Cinderella stepping from her pumpkin carriage with sparkly cartoon music filling the air.

9   In all of my imaginings I was filled with a sense that I would soon become perfect: My mother and father would adore me. I would be beyond reproach. I would never feel the need to sulk, or to clamor for anything. But sometimes the prodigy in me became impatient. "If you don't hurry up and get me out of here, I'm disappearing for good," it warned. "And then you'll always be nothing."

10   Every night after dinner my mother and I would sit at the Formica topped kitchen table. She would present new tests, taking her examples from stories of amazing children that she read in *Ripley's Believe It or Not* or *Good Housekeeping, Reader's Digest,* or any of a dozen other magazines she kept in a pile in our bathroom. My mother got these magazines from people whose houses she cleaned. And since she cleaned many houses each week, we had a great assortment. She would look through them all, searching for stories about remarkable children.

11   The first night she brought out a story about a three-year-old boy who knew the capitals of all the states and even most of the European countries. A teacher was quoted as saying that the little boy could also pronounce the names of the foreign cities correctly. "What's the capital of Finland?" my mother asked me, looking at the story.

12   All I knew was the capital of California, because Sacramento was the name of the street we lived on in Chinatown. "Nairobi!" I guessed, saying the most foreign word I could think of. She checked to see if that might be one way to pronounce *Helsinki* before showing me the answer.

13   The tests got harder—multiplying numbers in my head, finding the queen of hearts in a deck of cards, trying to stand on my head without using

my hands, predicting the daily temperatures in Los Angeles, New York, and London. One night I had to look at a page from the Bible for three minutes and then report everything I could remember. "Now Jehoshaphat had riches and honor in abundance and . . . that's all I remember, Ma," I said.

14   And after seeing, once again, my mother's disappointed face, something inside me began to die. I hated the tests, the raised hopes and failed expectations. Before going to bed that night I looked in the mirror above the bathroom sink, and I saw only my face staring back—and understood that it would always be this ordinary face—I began to cry. Such a sad, ugly girl! I made high-pitched noises like a crazed animal, trying to scratch out the face in the mirror.

15   And then I saw what seemed to be the prodigy side of me—a face I had never seen before. I looked at my reflection, blinking so that I could see more clearly. The girl staring back at me was angry, powerful. She and I were the same. I had new thoughts, willful thoughts—or rather, thoughts filled with lots of won'ts. I won't let her change me, I promised myself. I won't be what I'm not. So now when my mother presented her tests, I performed listlessly, my head propped on one arm. I pretended to be bored. And I was. I got so bored that I started counting the bellows of the foghorns out on the bay while my mother drilled me in other areas. The sound was comforting and reminded me of the cow jumping over the moon. And the next day I played a game with myself, seeing if my mother would give up on me before eight bellows. After a while I usually counted only one below, maybe two at most. At last she was beginning to give up hope.

16   Two or three months went by without any mention of my being a prodigy. And then one day my mother was watching *The Ed Sullivan Show* on TV. The TV was old and the sound kept shorting out. Every time my mother got halfway up from the sofa to adjust the set, the sound would come back on and Sullivan would be talking. As soon as she sat down, Sullivan would go silent again. She got up—the TV broke into loud piano music. She sat down—silence. Up and down, back and forth, quiet and loud. It was like a stiff, embraceless dance between her and the TV set. Finally, she stood by the set with her hand on the sound dial.

17   She seemed entranced by the music, a frenzied little piano piece with a mesmerizing quality, which alternated between quick, playful passages and teasing, lilting ones.

18   "*Ni kan*," my mother said, calling me over with hurried hand gestures. "Look here."

19   I could see why my mother was fascinated by the music. It was being pounded out by a little Chinese girl, about nine years old, with a Peter Pan haircut. The girl had the sauciness of a Shirley Temple. She was proudly modest, like a proper Chinese child. And she also did a fancy sweep of a

curtsy, so that the fluffy skirt of her white dress cascaded to the floor like petals of a large carnation.

20   In spite of these warning signs, I wasn't worried. Our family had no piano and we couldn't afford to buy one, let alone reams of sheet music and piano lessons. So I could be generous in my comments when my mother badmouthed the little girl on TV.

21   "Play note right, but doesn't sound good!" my mother complained "No singing sound."

22   "What are you picking on her for?" I said carelessly. "She's pretty good. Maybe she's not the best, but she's trying hard." I knew almost immediately that I would be sorry I had said that.

23   "Just like you," she said. "Not the best. Because you not trying." She gave a little huff as she let go of the sound dial and sat down on the sofa.

24   The little Chinese girl sat down also, to play an encore of "Anitra's Dance," by Grieg. I remember the song, because later on I had to learn how to play it.

25   Three days after watching *The Ed Sullivan Show* my mother told me what my schedule would be for piano lessons and piano practice. She had talked to Mr. Chong, who lived on the first floor of our apartment building. Mr. Chong was a retired piano teacher, and my mother had traded housecleaning services for weekly lessons and a piano for me to practice on every day, two hours a day, from four until six.

26   When my mother told me this, I felt as though I had been sent to hell. I whined, and then kicked my foot a little when I couldn't stand it anymore.

27   "Why don't you like me the way I am?" I cried. "I'm *not* a genius! I can't play the piano. And even if I could, I wouldn't go on TV if you paid me a million dollars!"

28   My mother slapped me. "Who ask you to be genius?" she shouted. "Only ask you be your best. For your sake. You think I want you to be genius? Hnnh! What for! Who ask you!"

29   "So ungrateful," I heard her mutter in Chinese. "If she had as much talent as she has temper, she'd be famous now."

30   Mr. Chong, whom I secretly nicknamed Old Chong, was very strange, always tapping his fingers to the silent music of an invisible orchestra. He looked ancient in my eyes. He had lost most of the hair on the top of his head, and he wore thick glasses and had eyes that always looked tired. But he must have been younger than I thought, since he lived with his mother and was not yet married.

31   I met Old Lady Chong once, and that was enough. She had a peculiar smell, like a baby that had done something in its pants, and her fingers felt like a dead person's, like an old peach I once found in the back of the refrigerator: its skin just slid off the flesh when I picked it up.

32   I soon found out why Old Chong had retired from teaching piano. He was deaf. "Like Beethoven!" he shouted to me. "We're both listening only in our head!" And he would start to conduct his frantic silent sonatas.

33   Our lessons went like this. He would open the book and point to different things, explaining, their purpose: "Key! Treble! Bass! No sharps or flats! So this is C major! Listen now and play after me!"

34   And then he would play the C scale a few times, a simple cord, and then, as if inspired by an old unreachable itch, he would gradually add more notes and running trills and a pounding bass until the music was really something quite grand.

35   I would play after him, the simple scale, the simple chord, and then just play some nonsense that sounded like a cat running up and down on top of garbage cans. Old Chong would smile and applaud and say "Very good! But now you must learn to keep time!"

36   So that's how I discovered that Old Chong's eyes were too slow to keep up with the wrong notes I was playing. He went through the motions in half-time. To help me keep rhythm, he stood behind me and pushed down on my right shoulder for every beat. He balanced pennies on top of my wrists so that I would keep them still as I slowly played scales and arpeggios. He had me curve my hand around an apple and keep that shape when playing chords. He marched stiffly to show me how to make each finger dance up and down, staccato, like an obedient little soldier.

37   He taught me all these things, and that was how I also learned I could be lazy and get away with mistakes, lots of mistakes. If I hit the wrong notes because I hadn't practiced enough, I never corrected myself, I just kept playing in rhythm. And Old Chong kept conducting his own private reverie.

38   So maybe I never really gave myself a fair chance. I did pick up the basics pretty quickly, and I might have become a good pianist at that young age. But I was so determined not to try, not to be anybody different, that I learned to play only the most ear-splitting preludes, the most discordant hymns.

39   Over the next year I practiced like this, dutifully in my own way. And then one day I heard my mother and her friend Lindo Jong both talking in a loud bragging tone of voice so others could hear. It was after church, and I was leaning against a brick wall, wearing a dress with stiff white petticoats. Auntie Lindo's daughter, Waverly, who was my age, was standing farther down the wall, about five feet away. We had grown up together and shared all the closeness of two sisters, squabbling over crayons and dolls. In other words, for the most part, we hated each other. I thought she was snotty. Waverly Jong had gained a certain amount of fame as "Chinatown's Littlest Chinese Chess Champion."

40   "She bring home too many trophy." Auntie Lindo lamented that Sunday. "All day she play chess. All day I have no time do nothing but dust off her winnings." She threw a scolding look at Waverly, who pretended not to see her.

41   "You lucky you don't have this problem," Auntie Lindo said with a sigh to my mother.

42   And my mother squared her shoulders and bragged: "Our problem worser than yours. If we ask Jing-mei wash dish, she hear nothing but music. It's like you can't stop this natural talent." And right then I was determined to put a stop to her foolish pride.

43   A few weeks later Old Chong and my mother conspired to have me play in a talent show that was to be held in the church hall. By then my parents had saved up enough to buy me a secondhand piano, a black Wurlitzer spinet with a scarred bench. It was the showpiece of our living room.

44   For the talent show I was to play a piece called "Pleading Child," from Schumann's *Scenes from Childhood*. It was a simple, moody piece that sounded more difficult than it was. I was supposed to memorize the whole thing. But I dawdled over it, playing a few bars and then cheating, looking up to see what notes followed. I never really listened to what I was playing. I daydreamed about being somewhere else, about being someone else.

45   The part I liked to practice best was the fancy curtsy: right foot out, touch the rose on the carpet with a pointed foot, sweep to the side, bend left leg, look up, and smile.

46   My parents invited all the couples from their social club to witness my debut. Auntie Lindo and Uncle Tin were there. Waverly and her two older brothers had also come. The first two rows were filled with children either younger or older than I was. The littlest ones got to go first. They recited simple nursery rhymes, squawked out tunes on miniature violins, and twirled hula hoops in pink ballet tutus, and when they bowed or curtsied, the audience would sigh in unison, "Awww, and then clap enthusiastically.

47   When my turn came, I was very confident. I remember my childish excitement. It was as if I knew, without a doubt, that the prodigy side of me really did exist. I had no fear whatsoever, no nervousness. I remember thinking, This is it! This is it! I looked out over the audience, at my mother's blank face, my father's yawn, Auntie Lindo's stiff-lipped smile, Waverly's sulky expression. I had on a white dress, layered with sheets of lace, and a pink bow in my Peter Pan haircut. As I sat down, I envisioned people jumping to their feet and Ed Sullivan rushing up to introduce me to everyone on TV.

48   And I started to play. Everything was so beautiful. I was so caught up in how lovely I looked that I wasn't worried about how I would sound. So I was surprised when I hit the first wrong note. And then I hit another

and another. A chill started at the top of my head and began to trickle down. Yet I couldn't stop playing, as though my hands were bewitched. I kept thinking my fingers would adjust themselves back, like a train switching to the right track. I played this strange jumble through to the end, the sour notes staying with me all the way.

49   When I stood up, I discovered my legs were shaking. Maybe I had just been nervous, and the audience, like Old Chong had seen me go through the right motions and had not heard anything wrong at all. I swept my right foot out, went down on my knee, looked up, and smiled. The room was quiet, except for Old Chong, who was beaming and shouting "Bravo! Bravo! Well done!" By then I saw my mother's face, her stricken face. The audience clapped weakly, and I walked back to my chair, with my whole face quivering as I tried not to cry, I heard a little boy whisper loudly to his mother. "That was awful," and mother whispered "Well, she certainly tried."

50   And now I realized how many people were in the audience—the whole world, it seemed. I was aware of eyes burning into my back. I felt the shame of my mother and father as they sat stiffly through the rest of the show.

51   We could have escaped during intermission. Pride and some strange sense of honor must have anchored my parents to their chairs. And so we watched it all. The eighteen-year-old boy with a fake moustache who did a magic show and juggled flaming hoops while riding a unicycle. The breasted girl with white make-up who sang an aria from *Madame Butterfly* and got an honorable mention. And the eleven-year-old boy who was first prize playing a tricky violin song that sounded like a busy bee.

52   After the show the Hsus, the Jongs, and the St. Clairs, from the Joy Luck Club, came up to my mother and father.

53   "Lots of talented kids," Auntie Lindo said vaguely, smiling broadly. "That was somethin' else," my father said, and I wondered if he was referring to me in a humorous way, or whether he even remembered what I had done.

54   Waverly looked at me and shrugged her shoulders. "You aren't a genius like me," she said matter-of-factly. And if I hadn't felt so bad, I would have pulled her braids and punched her stomach. But my mother's expression was what devastated me: a quiet, blank look that said she had lost everything. I felt the same way, and everybody seemed now to be coming up, like gawkers at the scene of an accident to see what parts were actually missing.

55   When we got on the bus to go home, my father was humming the busy-bee tune and my mother kept silent. I kept thinking she wanted to wait until we got home before shouting at me. But when my father unlocked the door

to our apartment, my mother walked in and went straight to the back, into the bedroom. No accusations. No blame. And in a way, I felt disappointed. I had been waiting for her to start shouting, so that I could shout back and cry and blame her for all my misery.

56   I had assumed that my talent-show fiasco meant that I would never have to play the piano again. But two days later, after school, my mother came out of the kitchen and saw me watching TV.

57   "Four clock," she reminded me, as if it were any other day. I was stunned, as though she were asking me to go through the talent-show torture again. I planted myself more squarely in front of the TV.

58   "Turn off TV," she called from the kitchen five minutes later. I didn't budge. And then I decided, I didn't have to do what mother said anymore. I wasn't her slave. This wasn't China. I had listened to her before, and look what happened. She was the stupid one.

59   She came out of the kitchen and stood in the arched entryway of the living room. "Four clock," she said once again, louder.

60   "I'm not going to play anymore," I said nonchalantly. "Why should I? I'm not a genius."

61   She stood in front of the TV. I saw that her chest was heaving up and down in an angry way.

62   "No!" I said, and I now felt stronger, as if my true self had finally emerged. So this was what had been inside me all along.

63   "No! I won't!" I screamed. She snapped off the TV, yanked me by the arm and pulled me off the floor. She was frighteningly strong, half pulling, half carrying me towards the piano as I kicked the throw rugs under my feet. She lifted me up onto the hard bench. I was sobbing by now, looking at her bitterly. Her chest was heaving even more and her mouth was open, smiling crazily as if she were pleased that I was crying.

64   "You want me to be something that I'm not!" I sobbed. " I'll never be the kind of daughter you want me to be!"

65   "Only two kinds of daughters," she shouted in Chinese. "Those who are obedient and those who follow their own mind! Only one kind of daughter can live in this house. Obedient daughter!"

66   "Then I wish I weren't your daughter, I wish you weren't my mother," I shouted. As I said these things I got scared. It felt like worms and toads and slimy things crawling out of my chest, but it also felt good, that this awful side of me had surfaced, at last.

67   "Too late to change this," my mother said shrilly.

68   And I could sense her anger rising to its breaking point. I wanted see it spill over. And that's when I remembered the babies she had lost in China,

the ones we never talked about. "Then I wish I'd never been born!" I shouted. "I wish I were dead! Like them."

69   It was as if I had said magic words. Alakazam!—her face went blank, her mouth closed, her arms went slack, and she backed out of the room, stunned, as if she were blowing away like a small brown leaf, thin, brittle, lifeless.

70   It was not the only disappointment my mother felt in me. In the years that followed, I failed her many times, each time asserting my will, my right to fall short of expectations. I didn't get straight As. I didn't become class president. I didn't get into Stanford. I dropped out of college.

71   Unlike my mother, I did not believe I could be anything I wanted to be, I could only be me.

72   And for all those years we never talked about the disaster at the recital or my terrible declarations afterward at the piano bench. Neither of us talked about it again, as if it were a betrayal that was now unspeakable. So I never found a way to ask her why she had hoped for something so large that failure was inevitable.

73   And even worse, I never asked her about what frightened me the most: Why had she given up hope? For after our struggle at the piano, she never mentioned my playing again. The lessons stopped. The lid to the piano was closed shutting out the dust, my misery, and her dreams.

74   So she surprised me. A few years ago she offered to give me the piano, for my thirtieth birthday. I had not played in all those years. I saw the offer as a sign of forgiveness, a tremendous burden removed. "Are you sure?" I asked shyly. "I mean, won't you and Dad miss it?" "No, this your piano," she said firmly. "Always your piano. You only one can play."

75   "Well, I probably can't play anymore," I said. "It's been years." "You pick up fast," my mother said, as if she knew this was certain. "You have natural talent. You could be a genius if you want to." "No, I couldn't." "You just not trying," my mother said. And she was neither angry nor sad. She said it as if announcing a fact that could never be disproved. "Take it," she said.

76   But I didn't at first. It was enough that she had offered it to me. And after that, every time I saw it in my parents' living room, standing in front of the bay window, it made me feel proud, as if it were a shiny trophy that I had won back.

77   Last week I sent a tuner over to my parent's apartment and had the piano reconditioned, for purely sentimental reasons. My mother had died a few months before and I had been getting things in order for my father a little bit at a time. I put the jewelry in special silk pouches. The sweaters I put in mothproof boxes. I found some old Chinese silk dresses, the kind with

little slits up the sides. I rubbed the old silk against my skin, then wrapped them in tissue and decided to take them home with me.

78   After I had the piano tuned, I opened the lid and touched the keys. It sounded even richer than I remembered. Really, it was a very good piano. Inside the bench were the same exercise notes with handwritten scales, the same secondhand music books with their covers held together with yellow tape. I opened up the Schumann book to the dark little piece I had played at the recital. It was on the left-hand page, "Pleading Child." It looked more difficult than I remembered. I played a few bars, surprised at how easily the notes came back to me.

79   And for the first time, or so it seemed, I noticed the piece on the right-hand side. It was called "Perfectly Contented." I tried to play this one as well. It had a lighter melody but with the same flowing rhythm and turned out to be quite easy. "Pleading Child" was shorter but slower; "Perfectly Contented" was longer but faster. And after I had played them both a few times, I realized they were two halves of the same song.

COMPREHENSION QUESTIONS

1. Why did the mother believe that her daughter was a prodigy? What were some of the tests that the mother devised for her daughter?
2. What are the "Two Kinds" indicated in the title?
3. What was the mother's history?
4. What was the rivalry between Auntie Lindo and Jing-mei's mother?
5. When the mother died, what happened to the piano?

QUESTIONS ON WRITING TECHNIQUE

1. What is the significance of the song title?
2. How is the story organized?
3. Why is the girl's father barely mentioned in the story?
4. This is a story taken from a collection of stories that make up the novel *The Joy Luck Club* by Amy Tan. Do you think you would have a greater understanding of the story if you read the entire novel, or does the story stand on its own? Explain.
5. How does the story conclude? Is the conclusion effective?

PRE-READING QUESTIONS

1. What were your parents' goals for you when you were a child?
2. Were these the same as your goals? How were they the same, or how were they different?
3. Do you think you have lived up to your parents' expectations? How? Or why not?
4. What have you learned from your experiences with your parents that you will apply to your own children?

Girl

Jamaica Kincaid

Born Elaine Potter Richardson in St. John's, Antigua, in the West Indies, Jamaica Kincaid (1949–) left Antigua for New York when she was seventeen, took classes at a community college, studied photography at the New School for Social Research, and attended Franconia College. She has been a staff writer for The New Yorker *and has published her work in* Rolling Stone, The Village Voice, *and* The Paris Review. *Her first book* At the Bottom of the River *(1983) won an award from the American Academy and Institute of Arts and Letters. Her more recent works include* The Autobiography of My Mother *(1996) and* My Brother *(1997). The following selection originally appeared in* The New Yorker *and was included in* At the Bottom of the River. *It vividly narrates a relationship between a powerful mother and her young daughter and confronts us with the advice the daughter must listen to.*

1   Wash the white clothes on Monday and put them on the stone heap; wash the color clothes on Tuesday and put them on the clothesline to dry; don't walk barehead in the hot sun; cook pumpkin fritters in very hot sweet oil; soak your little cloths right after you take them off; when buying cotton to make yourself a nice blouse, be sure that it doesn't have gum on it, because that way it

won't hold up well after a wash; soak salt fish overnight before you cook it; is it true that you sing benna in Sunday school?; always eat your food in such a way that it won't turn someone else's stomach; on Sundays try to walk like a lady and not like the slut you are so bent on becoming; don't sing benna in Sunday school; you mustn't speak to wharf-rat boys, not even to give directions; don't eat fruits on the street—flies will follow you; *but I don't sing benna on Sundays at all and never in Sunday school*; this is how to sew on a button; this is how to make a button-hole for the button you have just sewed on; this is how to hem a dress when you see the hem coming down and so to prevent yourself from looking like the slut I know you are so bent on becoming; this is how you iron your father's khaki shirt so that it doesn't have a crease; this is how you iron your father's khaki pants so that they don't have a crease; this is how you grow okra—far from the house, because okra tree harbors red ants; when you are growing dasheen, make sure it gets plenty of water or else it makes your throat itch when you are eating it; this is how you sweep a corner; this is how you sweep a whole house; this is how you sweep a yard; this is how you smile to someone you don't like too much; this is how you smile to someone you don't like at all; this is how you smile to someone you like completely; this is how you set a table for tea; this is how you set a table for dinner; this is how you set a table for dinner; this is how you set a table for dinner with an important guest; this is how you set a table for lunch; this is how you set a table for breakfast; this is how to behave in the presence of men who don't know you very well, and this way they won't recognize immediately the slut I have warned you against becoming; be sure to wash every day, even if it is with your own spit; don't squat down to play marbles—you are not a boy, you know; don't pick people's flowers—you might catch something; don't throw stones at blackbirds, because it might not be a blackbird at all; this is how to make a bread pudding; this is how to make doukona; this is how to make pepper pot; this is how to make a good medicine for a cold; this is how to make a good medicine to throw away a child before it even becomes a child; this is how to catch a fish; this is how to throw back a fish you don't like, and that way something bad won't fall on you; this is how to bully a man; this is how a man bullies you; this is how to love a man, and if this doesn't work there are other ways, and if they don't work don't feel too bad about giving up; this is how to spit up in the air if you feel like it, and this is how to move quick so that it doesn't fall on you; this is how to make ends meet; always squeeze bread to make sure it's fresh; *but what if the baker won't let me feel the bread?*; you mean to say that after all you are really going to be the kind of woman who the baker won't let near the bread?

COMPREHENSION QUESTIONS

1. Who is speaking in the story, and to whom? Describe their relationship.
2. Is this a typical mother/daughter relationship? Why or why not?
3. What effect do you think the repeated phrase "this is how you . . ." has on the listener in the story? What effect does it have on you as the reader?
4. What is your understanding of "the kind of woman who the baker won't let near the bread?" With what tone do you think these words are delivered?
5. Is love expressed anywhere in this story?

QUESTIONS ON WRITING TECHNIQUE

1. What writing techniques does the author use? Are they effective?
2. What do the italicized words indicate in this story?
3. How would you characterize the mother's speech in the story? Were you surprised or shocked by anything the mother said?
4. What is the effect on the reader of the continuous text without paragraphing?
5. What are three of the descriptive images in the text?

PRE-READING QUESTIONS

1. Has one of your parents ever lost a job? What effect did it have on the family?
2. Have you ever made crafts? What kind of crafts, and how did this activity affect your personal development?
3. What was a turning point in your own life? How did it affect you?

The Turning Point

Craig Swanson

Craig Swanson is a writer and humorist born in 1961 in Ridgewood, New Jersey. He enjoys games and puzzles and graphics programming, and he is teaching himself to play the piano. Swanson's writing often reflects his own experiences, what he has observed in life, and his appreciation for his family.

1   Dad lost his job last summer. They say that it was due to political reasons. After twenty years in the government it was a shock to us all. Dad never talked much about what he did at work, although it took up enough of his time. All I really know was his position: Deputy Assistant Commissioner of the State Department of Education. I was impressed by his title, though he rarely seemed to enjoy himself. Just the same, it was a job. These days it's hard enough to support a family without being out of work.

2   Apparently his co-workers felt so badly about the situation that they held a large testimonial dinner in his honor. People came from all over the east coast. I wish I could have gone. Everyone who went said it was really nice. It's a good feeling to know that your Dad means a lot to so many people. As a farewell present they gave Dad a potter's wheel. Dad says it's the best wheel he's ever seen, and to come from someone who's done pottery for as long as he has, that's saying a lot. Over the years Dad used to borrow potter's wheels from friends. That's when I learned how to "throw" a pot.

Craig Swanson, "The Turning Point" (1982). www.perspicuity.com. Reprinted by permission of the author.

3   When I came home for Thanksgiving vacation the first thing I did was rush down to the basement to check it out. I was quite surprised. Dad had fixed the whole corner of the basement with a big table top for playing with the clay; an area set up for preparing the clay, including a plaster bat and a wedging board; the kiln Walt built for Dad one Christmas; one hundred and fifty pounds of clay; nine different glazes; hand tools for sculpting, and the brand new potter's wheel. It had a tractor seat from which you work the clay. It could be turned manually or by motor, and it offered lots of surface area, which always comes in handy. Dad was right, it was beautiful. He had already made a couple dozen pots. I couldn't wait to try it.

4   The next day I came down into the basement to find Dad in his old gray smock preparing the clay. I love to watch Dad do art, whether it's drawing, painting, lettering, or pottery. I stood next to him as he wedged a ball of clay the size of a small cantaloupe. He'd slice it in half on the wire and slam one half onto the wedging board, a canvas-covered slab of plaster; then he'd slam the other half on top of the first. He did this to get all the air bubbles out of the clay. You put a pot with air bubbles in the kiln, the pot'll explode in the heat and you've got yourself one heck of a mess to clean up. Dad wedged the clay, over and over.

5   When he was finished he sat down, wet the wheelhead, and pressed the clay right in the center of the wheel. Dad hit the accelerator and the clay started turning. He wet his hands and leaned over the clay. Bracing his elbows on his knees he began centering the clay. Steady right hand on the sides of the clay. Steady left hand pushing down on the clay. Centering the clay is the toughest part for me. The clay spins around and around and you have to shape it into a perfectly symmetric form in the center by letting the wheel do all the moving. Your hands stay motionless until the clay is centered. It takes me ten or fifteen minutes to do this. It takes Dad two. I shake my head and smile in amazement.

6   Dad's hands cup the clay, thumbs together on top. He wets his hands again and pushes down with his thumbs. Slowly, steadily. Once he's as far down as he wants to go he makes the bottom of the pot by spreading his thumbs. His hands relax and he pulls them out of the pot. Every motion is deliberate. If you move your hands quickly or carelessly you can be sure you will have to start again. Dad wipes the slip, very watery clay, off his hands with a sponge. It is extremely messy.

7   To make the walls Dad hooks his thumbs and curls all of his fingers except for his index fingers. Holding them like forceps, he reaches into the pot to mold the walls to just the right thickness. He starts at the bottom and

brings them up slowly, making the walls of the pot thin and even all the way up, about twelve inches.

8   Dad sponges off his hands, wets them, and then cups his hands around the belly of the pot. Slowly, as the pot spins around, he squeezes his hands together, causing it to bevel slightly. Dad spends five minutes on the finishing touches. He's got himself a real nice skill.

9   It is a rare treat to watch Dad do something that he enjoys so much.

COMPREHENSION QUESTIONS

1. What additional information would Swanson need to provide to complete his explanation of the making of a pot?
2. What life benefits do hobbies provide?
3. How is the essay organized? Is the method effective?
4. What is the meaning of the title "The Turning Point"?
5. What is the essay's main topic?

QUESTIONS ON WRITING TECHNIQUE

1. What is the author's purpose in writing this essay?
2. What is the tone of this essay?
3. Why has Swanson chosen understatement rather than a more emotional means to make his point?
4. What elements would you have added to make this essay more effective?
5. How does the essay conclude? How effective is the conclusion?

PRE-READING QUESTIONS

1. Describe your father. What are his greatest strengths and weaknesses?
2. What are the principal characteristics of being a good caregiver?
3. Are fathers undervalued in American society? Why or why not?

Father's Day

Michael Dorris

Michael Dorris, born in 1945, was a prominent Native American novelist and scholar. His most famous books include the nonfiction work The Broken Cord *and the novel* A Yellow Raft in Blue Water. *In 1971 he was the first unmarried man in the United States to adopt a child. He was later married to author Louise Erdrich. He committed suicide in 1997.*

1   My father, a career army officer, was twenty-seven when he was killed. . . .

2   . . . I was a few months old the last time he saw me, and a single photograph of me in his arms is the only hard evidence that we ever met. . . .

3   There was a children's book in the 1950s—perhaps it still exists—titled *The Happy Family*, and it was a piece of work. Dad toiled at the office, Mom baked in the kitchen, and brother and sister always had neighborhood friends sleeping over. The prototype of "Leave It to Beaver" and "Father Knows Best," this little text reflects a midcentury standard, a brightly illustrated reproach to my own unorthodox household, but luckily that wasn't the way I heard it. As read to me by my Aunt Marion—her acid delivery was laced with sarcasm and punctuated with many a sidelong glance—it turned into hilarious irony.

4   Compassionate and generous, irreverent, simultaneously opinionated and open-minded, iron-willed and ever optimistic, my aunt was the one who pitched a baseball with me in the early summer evenings, who took me horseback riding, who sat by my bed when I was ill. A fierce, lifelong Democrat—a precinct captain even—she helped me find my first jobs and arranged

among her friends at work for my escorts to the father-son dinners that closed each sports season. When the time came, she prevailed upon the elderly man next door to teach me how to shave.

5   "Daddy" Tingle, as he was known to his own children and grandchildren, was a man of many talents. He could spit tobacco juice over the low roof of his garage, gum a sharpened mumbly-peg twig from the ground even without his false teeth, and produce, from the Bourbon Stockyards where he worked, the jewel-like cornea of a cow's eye—but he wasn't much of a shaver. After his instruction, neither am I.

6   Aunt Marion, on the other hand, was a font of information and influence. When I was fifteen, on a series of tempestuous Sunday mornings at a deserted River Road park, she gave me lessons in how to drive a stick shift. A great believer in the efficacy of the *World Book Encyclopedia*—the major literary purchase of my childhood—she insisted that I confirm any vague belief by looking it up. To the then-popular tune of "You, You, You," she counted my laps in the Crescent Hill pool while I practiced for a life-saving certificate. Operating on the assumption that anything out of the ordinary was probably good for me, she once offered to mortgage the house so that I could afford to go to Mali as a volunteer participant in Operation Crossroads Africa. She paid for my first Smith-Corona typewriter in thirty-six $4-a-week installments.

7   For over sixty years Aunt Marion was never without steady employment: telegraph operator for Western Union, budget officer for the city of Louisville, "new girl" at a small savings and loan (when, after twenty-five years in a patronage job, the Democrats lost the mayor's race), executive secretary for a nationally renowned attorney.

8   Being Aunt Marion, she didn't and doesn't give herself much credit. Unless dragged to center stage, she stands at the periphery in snapshots, minimizes her contributions. Every June for forty years I've sent her a Father's Day card.

COMPREHENSION QUESTIONS

1. List the things that Aunt Marion did for the author that inspire him to send her a Father's Day card every June.
2. Why does the author begin his short essay with a description of the book *The Happy Family*?
3. Describe Aunt Marion's character. Describe the Aunt Marion in your life.

4. Explain a time when someone was very generous to you. What happened? This person may be a relative or not.
5. Is the essay what you expected after reading the title? Why or why not?

QUESTIONS ON WRITING TECHNIQUE

1. Read the first three sentences of the essay and comment on them.
2. What was the author's purpose in writing the essay?
3. What is the significance of the title?
4. How is the essay organized?
5. What is the strongest image in the essay?

PRE-READING QUESTIONS

1. What does your mother or primary caretaker do for a living?
2. Do you believe that a mother should stay at home with her children rather than work outside the home?
3. Should the government lend some support to stay-at-home moms? Why or why not?
4. Do you think that the Social Security system is a good one in this country? Why or why not?

My Mother Never Worked

Bonnie Smith-Yackel

Bonnie Smith-Yackel is a contemporary author who writes on social issues. She writes for various popular magazines and newspapers. She uses her experiences in life to inform her writing and she asks questions about American society.

1 "Social Security Office." (The voice answering the telephone sounds very self-assured.)

Bonnie Smith-Yackel, "My Mother Never Worked," *Women: A Journal of Liberation* (1975). Reprinted by permission of the author.

2   "I'm calling about . . . my mother just died . . . I was told to call you and see about a . . . death-benefit check, I think they call it . . ."

3   "I see. Was your mother on Social Security? How old was she?"

4   "Yes . . . she was seventy-eight . . . "

5   "Do you know her number?"

6   "No . . . I, ah . . . don't you have a record?"

7   "Certainly. I'll look it up. Her name?"

8   "Smith. Martha Smith. Or maybe she used Martha Ruth Smith? . . . Sometimes she used her maiden name . . . Martha Jerabek Smith?"

9   "If you'd care to hold on, I'll check our records—it'll be a few minutes."

10   "Yes . . ."

11   Her love letters—to and from Daddy—were in an old box, tied with ribbons and stiff, rigid-with-age leather thongs: 1918 through 1920; hers written on stationery from the general store she had worked in full-time and managed, single-handed, after her graduation from high school in 1913; and his, at first, on YMCA or Soldiers and Sailors Club stationery dispensed to the fighting men of World War I. He wooed her thoroughly and persistently by mail, and though she reciprocated all his feelings for her, she dreaded marriage. . . .

12   "It's so hard for me to decide when to have my wedding day—that's all I've thought about these last two days. I have told you dozens of times that I won't be afraid of married life, but when it comes down to setting the date and then picturing myself a married woman with half a dozen or more kids to look after, it just makes me sick. . . . I am weeping right now—I hope that some day I can look back and say how foolish I was to dread it all."

13   They married in February, 1921, and began farming. Their first baby, a daughter, was born in January, 1922, when my mother was 26 years old. The second baby, a son, was born in March, 1923. They were renting farms; my father, besides working his own fields, also was a hired man for two other farmers. They had no capital initially, and had to gain it slowly, working from dawn until midnight every day. My town-bred mother learned to set hens and raise chickens, feed pigs, milk cows, plant and harvest a garden, and can every fruit and vegetable she could scrounge. She carried water nearly a quarter of a mile from the well to fill her wash boilers in order to do her laundry on a scrub board. She learned to shock grain, feed threshers, shock and husk corn, feed corn pickers. In September, 1925, the third baby came, and in June, 1927, the fourth child—both daughters. In 1930, my parents had enough money to buy their own farm, and that March they moved all the livestock and belongings themselves, 55 miles over rutted, muddy roads.

14   In the summer of 1930 my mother and her two eldest children reclaimed a 40-acre field from Canadian thistles, by chopping them all out with a hoe. In the other fields, when the oats and flax began to head out, the green and blue of the crops were hidden by the bright yellow of wild mustard. My mother walked the fields day after day, pulling each mustard plant. She raised a new flock of baby chicks—500—and she spaded up, planted, hoed, and harvested a half-acre garden.

15   During the next spring their hogs caught cholera and died. No cash that fall.

16   And in the next year the drought hit. My mother and father trudged from the well to the chickens, the well to the calf pasture, the well to the barn, and from the well to the garden. The sun came out hot and bright, endlessly, day after day. The crops shriveled and died. They harvested half the corn, and ground the other half, stalks and all, and fed it to the cattle as fodder. With the price at four cents a bushel for the harvested crop, they couldn't afford to haul it into town. They burned it in the furnace for fuel that winter.

17   In 1934, in February, when the dust was still so thick in the Minnesota air that my parents couldn't always see from the house to the barn, their fifth child—a fourth daughter—was born. My father hunted rabbits daily, and my mother stewed them, fried them, canned them, and wished out loud that she could taste hamburger once more. In the fall the shotgun brought prairie chickens, ducks, pheasant, and grouse. My mother plucked each bird, carefully reserving the breast feathers for pillows.

18   In the winter she sewed night after night, endlessly, begging cast-off clothing from relatives, ripping apart coats, dresses, blouses, and trousers to remake them to fit her four daughters and son. Every morning and every evening she milked cows, fed pigs and calves, cared for chickens, picked eggs, cooked meals, washed dishes, scrubbed floors, and tended and loved her children. In the spring she planted a garden once more, dragging pails of water to nourish and sustain the vegetables for the family. In 1936 she lost a baby in her sixth month.

19   In 1937 her fifth daughter was born. She was 42 years old. In 1939 a second son, and in 1941 her eighth child—and third son.

20   But the war had come, and prosperity of a sort. The herd of cattle had grown to 30 head; she still milked morning and evening. Her garden was more than a half acre—the rains had come, and by now the Rural Electricity Administration and indoor plumbing. Still she sewed—dresses and jackets for the children, housedresses and aprons for herself, weekly patching of jeans, overalls, and denim shirts. She still made pillows, using feathers she had plucked, and quilts every year—intricate patterns as well as patchwork,

stitched as well as tied—all necessary bedding for her family. Every scrap of cloth too small to be used in quilts was carefully saved and painstakingly sewed together in strips to make rugs. She still went out in the fields to help with the haying whenever there was a threat of rain.

21   In 1959 my mother's last child graduated from high school. A year later the cows were sold. She still raised chickens and ducks, plucked feathers, made pillows, baked her own bread, and every year made a new quilt—now for a married child or for a grandchild. And her garden, that huge, undying symbol of sustenance, was as large and cared for as in all the years before. The canning, and now freezing, continued.

22   In 1969, on a June afternoon, mother and father started out for town so that she could buy sugar to make rhubarb jam for a daughter who lived in Texas. The car crashed into a ditch. She was paralyzed from the waist down.

23   In 1970 her husband, my father, died. My mother struggled to regain some competence and dignity and order in her life. At the rehabilitation institute, where they gave her physical therapy and trained her to live usefully in a wheelchair, the therapist told me: "She did fifteen pushups today—fifteen! She's almost seventy-five years old! I've never known a woman so strong!"

24   From her wheelchair she canned pickles, baked bread, ironed clothes, wrote dozens of letters weekly to her friends and her "half dozen or more kids," and made three patchwork housecoats and one quilt. She made balls and balls of carpet rags—enough for five rugs. And kept all her love letters.

25   "I think I've found your mother's records—Martha Ruth Smith; married to Ben F. Smith?"

26   "Yes, that's right."

27   "Well, I see that she was getting a widow's pension . . ."

28   "Yes, that's right."

29   "Well, your mother isn't entitled to our $225 death benefit."

30   "Not entitled! But why?"

31   The voice on the telephone explains patiently:

32   "Well, you see—your mother never worked."

COMPREHENSION QUESTIONS

1. What is the effect of opening the essay with a phone conversation? What is the outcome of the phone conversation?
2. What was the mother's background before she got married? Was it difficult for the mother to adapt to farm life? Why or why not?

3. What had the mother done in her life? List five significant events.
4. How does the government define "work"?
5. The essay was first published in 1975. Is it still relevant today?

QUESTIONS ON WRITING TECHNIQUE

1. What is the effect of the use of dialogue at the beginning of the essay?
2. Why do we return to the phone call at the end of the essay? What effect does this have on the reader?
3. How is irony used in this essay?
4. What does the author hope to bring about through writing this essay?
5. How are the descriptions of the mother's chores made memorable by the author?

WRITING SUGGESTIONS

1. Write a descriptive essay of what you envision as a "traditional" family. Explain how your family is or is not a "traditional" family.
2. Interview a member of your family, preferably an older relative. Tell the story of this person's life. Intertwine historic events with the telling of your narrative.
3. Parents and caregivers are not always right about everything. Write an essay describing some bad advice that you received from a parent or caregiver and what you learned from that bad advice.
4. Do you believe that the role of the traditional housewife is undervalued? Write an essay detailing why you believe or do not believe this is so.
5. Write a descriptive essay of your most colorful family member.
6. Compare and contrast the family life of your parents with that of your grandparents. Describe the similarities and differences.

IN-SIGHT

Sharon L. Jonz/Jupiter.

Couples sometimes meet at a young age and stay together throughout their lives.

1. With the current divorce rate remaining at around 50 percent in the United States, what is the secret to long-lasting loving relationships?
2. How many people do you know with two birth parents who are still married to each other?
3. How many people do you know who are divorced? What caused those couples to decide on divorce instead of working things out?

GROUP ACTIVITY

Take a few minutes to think in writing about the following question:

In your opinion, why is the divorce rate so high in the United States?

1. Share the thoughts you have written with a classmate. How were your ideas the same as your partner's and how were they different?
2. Discuss your ideas with the teacher and class.

PEER CRITIQUE

Your Name _____

The Author's Name _____

1. Read your partner's essay.

2. What is your immediate reaction to the essay? Is the essay clear? Passionate? Organized?

3. How does the author introduce the essay? Did it grab your attention ? Why ?

4. Is there an explicit thesis statement? If so, write it here. If it is not explicit, is it clear? If so, put it in your own words here.

5. Is the essay well organized? What suggestions do you have to improve the organization of this essay?

6. Does the author use sufficient descriptive language, including adjectives and adverbs? Can you list some that you especially liked?

7. Did you find any typos, spelling errors, or grammatical mistakes? If so, list them:

MECHANICS AND GRAMMAR

Verbs

Verbs are the one absolutely essential element to every English sentence. Therefore, it is important to learn verb forms correctly. Usually, native speakers of English are able to produce the correct form without thinking because it is used so often. Sometimes, however, a form may have been learned or used incorrectly. In these cases, we must self-monitor and consciously make an effort to use the correct form in speech and writing.

The principal forms of a verb are the base form, past tense, and past participle. If we can master these three forms, we will be well on our way to good academic English.

> Examples: break – broke – broken (irregular)
> walk – walked – walked (regular)

As you can see by the examples above, we have both irregular verbs (e.g., break) and regular verbs (e.g., walk). The regular verbs cause us little concern, but the irregular forms need careful study. These verb forms are critical to our using tenses correctly in English. Tenses show time.

Theoretically, verbs are inflected (or changed) to show the time at which an action occurs. In practice, however, the tense of an English verb sometimes has little relation to the time of the action. This is especially true of the present tense that may refer to past, present, or future actions. It is best to think of the present tense as more of an indicator of facts, habits, and commonalities about a person, place, or thing.

Problems occur when a writer shifts tenses during writing without a reason. This confuses the reader. Once writers commit themselves to a tense, they must stay with it unless there is a reason to shift tenses.

The three time periods in English grammar are past, present, and future. These time periods exist in several aspects; the most important are simple, continuous, and perfect. We combine time periods with aspects and create tenses.

Simple tenses in all three time periods emphasize facts and outcomes. Progressive tenses emphasize ongoing actions. Perfect tenses combine two different (nonsimultaneous) actions or different chronological time periods.

> Examples:
>
> Simple present: Martha goes to the market on
>   Saturdays. (a general statement of fact
>   about Martha's life)

| Present continuous: | Martha is cooking dinner. (the action is now) |
| Present perfect: | Martha has cooked dinner every night this week. (an action that began in the past and continues in the present) |

EXERCISES

To recognize the importance of tenses, correct the following paragraphs for tense errors.

Exercise 1

Last winter we took a trip to Quebec, a region in eastern Canada which bordered the United States. The name Quebec is French and referred to the fact that it was the first province which retained French as its provincial language. Today, Quebec still contained most of its original structures originally built by the French hundreds of years ago. While there were a few provinces in eastern Canada, Quebec was famous for its European charm and beautiful scenery. Quebec was especially known for its wonderful skiing in the winter months. Skiing was important for Quebec's economy these days.

Exercise 2

I truly enjoyed my summer vacation this year. It isn't long enough, of course, but I made the most of the time I have. My chemistry club took a trip to Puerto Vallarta. We didn't pack enough to eat, but the incredible beaches takes my breath away. Once I'm back home, I always play a lot of basketball with my college fraternity brothers. One night we stayed at the basketball court until after it closes. We are just shooting hoops in the dark with only the moon to guide us. It was an unplanned event, and we could barely see the basketball. It's fun to relax with my friends on a summer evening. Overall, the trip to Puerto Vallarta and the after-hours basketball match are the highlights of my summer vacation.

Exercise 3

I watched a documentary on the Amish of Pennsylvania last night. I am amazed to find out that they only wear white, black, and gray clothing. The Amish enjoyed activities that deal with the family, like cooking, carpentry, and gardening. They mostly live in the south central part of Pennsylvania, with Lancaster the largest city with a large Amish population. They had lived there since the 1800s. Ohio, West Virginia, and Virginia also have large Amish populations. The Amish are mostly of German derivation and settle in Pennsylvania at the same time as the Lutherans and Catholics of Germany did in the mid-1800s.

USES OF THE SIX MAIN VERB TENSES IN ENGLISH

Simple Present

The chief uses of the simple present tense are to indicate present action, action that occurs at all times (the timeless present), and past action that, for dramatic purposes, is described as occurring in the present (historical present).

Present time:	John is alone; his wife is at work.
Timeless present:	The rain falls into the wash and ends up in the Colorado River.
Historical present:	Finally, Grant makes his decision. He gives the order, and his troops begin their long march through South Carolina.

Present Perfect

The present perfect tense indicates that the action has recently been completed or that the action of the past is tied to action in the present time.

I have lost my watch! (the action occurred very recently)

She has eaten three apples today. (today has not yet ended, so perhaps she will have another)

Walter has taught at the university since May. (he was teaching in May and still is)

Simple Past

The simple past tense is used to indicate an action that may have occurred at any time in the past. The action is complete, with no residual action in the present time.

She broke the vase yesterday. (action completed)

He read the Bronte novel last summer. (he completed the action though not all at once in the past)

Past Perfect

The past perfect is used to indicate that, of two past actions, one took place before the other. The oldest action would use the past perfect, and the newer action would take the simple present tense.

Tom had been sick only a few days when he died.

Before 1999, Oprah had worked as a television newscaster. (there are not two actions here, but two time period indicators)

We had left the party before the Queen arrived.

Simple Future

The simple future is used to indicate an action still to occur.

He will attend the game tomorrow.

She shall go to work in the morning.

The mostly common indicator of the simple future is the use of "will"; however, "shall" is still occasionally used, especially more formally.

Future Perfect

The future perfect is used to indicate that, of two future actions, one will occur before the other.

By the time you get there, your mother will have left.

REGULAR AND IRREGULAR VERBS

As mentioned earlier, English verbs are categorized as regular and irregular. Regular verbs usually form the past tense with-d or-ed, but irregular verbs have no formula for formation. Therefore, we must memorize the forms of irregular verbs. Sometimes, through habit, we might use the wrong form. We may need to unlearn an incorrect form and learn the correct form to suit academic standards.

Exercise

In the table of common irregular verbs, cover the past and past participle forms with a sheet of paper and give yourself a test to see which verb forms you must commit to memory.

COMMON IRREGULAR VERBS

Present (Base)	Past	Past Participle
arise	arose	arisen
be	was	been
bear	bore	borne
become	became	become
begin	began	begun
break	broke	broken
bring	brought	brought
build	built	built
burst	burst	burst
catch	caught	caught
buy	bought	bought
choose	chose	chosen
cling	clung	clung
come	came	come
dive	dove	dived
do	did	done
draw	drew	drawn
drink	drank	drunk
drive	drove	driven
fall	fell	fallen
feed	fed	fed
eat	ate	eaten

(continued)

COMMON IRREGULAR VERBS *(continued)*

feed	fed	fed
feel	felt	felt
flee	fled	fled
fight	fought	fought
fly	flew	flown
forgive	forgave	forgiven
freeze	froze	frozen
get	got	gotten
give	gave	given
go	went	gone
grow	grew	grown
hang (clothes)	hung	hung
hang (execute)	hanged	hanged
have	had	had
hear	heard	heard
hide	hid	hidden
hold	held	held
hurt	hurt	hurt
keep	kept	kept
know	knew	known
lay	laid	laid
lie	lay	lain
lose	lost	lost
make	made	made
mean	meant	meant
meet	met	met
pay	paid	paid
put	put	put
read	read	read
ride	rode	ridden
ring	rang	rung
rise	rose	risen
run	ran	run
say	said	said
see	saw	seen
seek	sought	sought

COMMON IRREGULAR VERBS *(continued)*

sell	sold	sold
set	set	set
shake	shook	shaken
shine (light)	shone	shone
shine (polish)	shined	shined
sing	sang	sung
sink	sank	sunk
sleep	slept	slept
speak	spoke	spoken
spend	spent	spent
spin	spun	spun
spring	sprang	sprung
stand	stood	stood
steal	stole	stolen
strike	struck	struck (or stricken)
stink	stank	stunk
strive	strove	striven
swear	swore	sworn
swim	swam	swum
take	took	taken
teach	taught	taught
tear	tore	torn
tell	told	told
think	thought	thought
throw	threw	thrown
understand	understood	understood
wake	woke	woken
weave	wove	woven
wear	wore	worn
win	won	won
wring	wrung	wrung
write	wrote	written

ADDITIONAL EXERCISES

Exercise 1

How we speak with our friends and how we write in a college English class can sometimes be a little different. Most students have to work on learning the proper Standard English forms in college. Give yourself a quiz to see if you know the standard forms for each of the following verbs in the given sentences. Fill in the appropriate form of the verb in each sentence.

1. Have you _____ the lesson? (begin)

2. We have _____ for success. (strive)

3. Have you often _____ in the Mandalay Resort pool? (swim)

4. Last week, the man _____ my shoes in the lobby of the hotel. (shine)

5. The state of Utah _____ Gary Gilmore for murder. (hang)

6. Have you _____ all of your milk? (drink)

7. My shirt _____ in the laundry this morning. (shrink)

8. She _____ into action yesterday. (spring)

9. My books _____ on the table yesterday. (lie)

10. We _____ pictures of farm animals in kindergarten. (draw)

11. The teacher has _____ us all that he knows. (teach)

12. The thief _____ the diamonds last week. (steal)

13. The ladies _____ the bamboo into baskets last Christmas. (weave)

14. The sun _____ on us yesterday. (shine)

15. Have you _____ of an answer? (think)

16. We have been _____ all we need to see. (show)

17. I _____ into the mud last August during the flood. (sink)

18. The gambler _____ all of his money playing the nickel slots! (lose)

19. I have _____ my sweater. (tear)

20. The water _____ into ice last winter. (freeze)

Exercise 2

Supply the two missing verb forms—past tense and past participle—for each of the present tense forms below.

Example:

Present (Base)	Past	Past Participle
build	built	built

1. bring
2. sleep
3. keep
4. creep
5. cost
6. catch
7. teach
8. bet
9. dive
10. hit
11. hurt
12. cut

Present (Base)	Past	Past Participle
13. seek		
14. think		
15. bleed		
16. bend		
17. lend		
18. spread		
19. come		
20. become		
21. buy		
22. write		
23. rise		
24. stride		
25. ride		
26. drive		
27. hide		
28. bite		
29. swim		
30. spring		
31. sing		
32. sink		
33. shrink		
34. ring		
35. drink		
36. begin		
37. throw		
38. know		
39. grow		
40. fly		

Present (Base)	Past	Past Participle
41. blow		
42. sweep		
43. stink		
44. keep		
45. be		
46. sit		

5

LIFE EXPERIENCES

We live in a country of many cultures. Many of our grandparents or great-grandparents were born in other countries. This has led to an exciting and dynamic America with many ethnicities and religions. These cultures have blended to form an interesting and unique country in the world. Despite the differences, Americans respect and learn from their fellow Americans. While identifying as Americans, many individuals respect the culture of their ancestors, and many families and communities continue to practice traditions from generations past.

As a nation, America has its own unique culture and identity. This may not be immediately obvious to those who have lived in the United States all of their lives. However, visitors from other countries quickly notice commonalities among diverse groups of Americans. For example, the American love of fast food has led to the belief in some other countries that Americans only eat hamburgers, hot dogs, and pizza! This says a great deal about the power of American advertising.

The following essays examine some of America's diverse people and places. Menkel's "I Saw Anne Frank Die" shows a difficult life experience and its catharsis. Geok-lin Lim examines the imposition of culture in "Pomegranates and English Education." Wright's "Black Boy" takes the reader along on a young man's journey to freedom and enlightenment through literacy. Nanda's "Arranging a Marriage in India" looks at arranged marriages. Gonsales's "I'm Afraid to Look, Afraid to Turn Away" considers the family of a soldier at war.

PRE-READING QUESTIONS

1. What do you know about Anne Frank?
2. What have you heard about the Holocaust?
3. What do you know about the concentration camps in World War II?
4. Is it important to think about terrible events? Why or why not?

I Saw Anne Frank Die

Irma Sonnenberg Menkel

Irma Sonnenberg Menkel was born in Germany in 1897. When Hitler came to power, she was sent to the Westerbork transit camp and later to Bergen-Belsen. Her husband and brother both died there. She was liberated in the spring of 1945.

1 I turned 100 years old in April and had a beautiful birthday party surrounded by my grandchildren, great-grandchildren and other family members. I even danced a little. Willard Scott mentioned my name on television. But such a time is also for reflection. I decided to overcome my long reluctance to revisit terrible times. Older people must tell their stories. With the help of Jonathan Alter of *Newsweek*, here's a bit of mine:

2 I was born in Germany in 1897, got married and had two children in the 1920s. Then Hitler came to power, and like many other Jews, we fled to Holland. As the Nazis closed in, we sent one daughter abroad with

relatives and the other into hiding with my sister and her children in The Hague. My husband and I could not hide so easily, and in 1941 we were sent first to Westerbork, a transit camp where we stayed about a year, and later to Bergen-Belsen, a work and transit camp, from where thousands of innocent people were sent to extermination camps. There were no ovens at Bergen-Belsen; instead the Nazis killed us with starvation and disease. My husband and brother both died there. I stayed for about three years before I was liberated in the spring of 1945. When I went in, I weighed more than 125 pounds. When I left, I weighed 78.

3   After I arrived at the Bergen-Belsen barracks, I was told I was to be the barracks leader. I said, "I'm not strong enough to be barracks leader." They said that would be disobeying a command. I was terrified of this order, but had no choice. It turned out that the Nazi commandant of the camp was from my home town in Germany and had studied with my uncle in Strasbourg. This coincidence probably helped save my life. He asked to talk to me privately and wanted to know what I had heard of my uncle. I said I wanted to leave Bergen-Belsen, maybe go to Palestine. The commandant said, "If I could help you, I would, but I would lose my head." About once every three weeks, he would ask to see me. I was always afraid. It was very dangerous. Jews were often shot over nothing. After the war, I heard he had committed suicide.

4   There were about 500 women and girls in my barracks. Conditions were extremely crowded and unsanitary. No heat at all. Every morning, I had to get up at 5 and wake the rest. At 6 a.m., we went to roll call. Often we had to wait there for hours, no matter the weather. Most of the day, we worked as slave labor in the factory, making bullets for German soldiers. When we left Holland, I had taken only two changes of clothes, one toothbrush, no books or other possessions. Later I had a few more clothes, including a warm jacket, which came from someone who died. Men and women lined up for hours to wash their clothes in the few sinks. There were no showers in our barracks. And no bedding. The day was spent working and waiting. At 10 p.m., lights out. At midnight, the inspection came—three or four soldiers. I had to say everything was in good condition when, in fact, the conditions were beyond miserable. Then up again at 5 a.m.

5   One of the children in my barracks toward the end of the war was Anne Frank, whose diary became famous after her death. I didn't know her family beforehand, and I don't recall much about her, but I do remember her as a quiet child. When I heard later that she was 15 when she was in the camps, I was surprised. She seemed younger to me. Pen and paper were hard to find,

but I have a memory of her writing a bit. Typhus was a terrible problem, especially for the children. Of 500 in my barracks, maybe 100 got it, and most of them died. Many others starved to death. When Anne Frank got sick with typhus, I remember telling her she could stay in the barracks—she didn't have to go to roll call.

6   There was so little to eat. In my early days there, we were each given one roll of bread for eight days, and we tore it up, piece by piece. One cup of black coffee a day and one cup of soup. And water. That was all. Later there was even less. When I asked the commandant for a little bit of gruel for the children's diet, he would sometimes give me some extra cereal. Anne Frank was among those who asked for cereal, but how could I find cereal for her? It was only for the little children, and only a little bit. The children died anyway. A couple of trained nurses were among the inmates, and they reported to me. In the evening, we tried to help the sickest. In the morning, it was part of my job to tell the soldiers how many had died the night before. Then they would throw the bodies on the fire.

7   I have a dim memory of Anne Frank speaking of her father. She was a nice, fine person. She would say to me, "Irma, I am very sick." I said, "No, you are not so sick." She wanted to be reassured that she wasn't. When she slipped into a coma, I took her in my arms. She didn't know that she was dying. She didn't know that she was so sick. You never know. At Bergen-Belsen, you did not have feelings anymore. You became paralyzed. In all the years since, I almost never talked about Bergen-Belsen. I couldn't. It was too much.

8   When the war was over, we went in a cattle truck to a place where we stole everything out of a house. I stole a pig, and we had a butcher who slaughtered it. Eating this—was bad for us. It made many even sicker. But you can't imagine how hungry we were. At the end, we had absolutely nothing to eat. I asked an American soldier holding a piece of bread if I could have a bite. He gave me the whole bread. That was really something for me.

9   When I got back to Holland, no one knew anything. I finally found a priest who had the address where my sister and daughter were. I didn't know if they were living or not. They were. They had been hidden by a man who worked for my brother. That was luck. I found them and began crying. I was so thin that at first they didn't recognize me.

10   There are many stories like mine, locked inside people for decades. Even my family heard only a little of this one until recently. Whatever stories you have in your family, tell them. It helps.

COMPREHENSION QUESTIONS

1. Why is Menkel telling her story now? Why was the author reluctant to tell her story?
2. What is the central idea of this essay?
3. Where was the author sent? Describe it.
4. How and when did the author work for the Nazis?
5. Why was the author ordered to be a barracks leader?

QUESTIONS ON WRITING TECHNIQUE

1. How does the author organize her essay?
2. Why are the details about Anne Frank introduced gradually?
3. How does the author end her essay? Why?
4. What is the author's purpose in telling her story?
5. Will this essay be important in 100 years? Why or why not?

WRITING SUGGESTIONS

1. Who in your life would you characterize as a hero? Write an essay explaining why.
2. Do you know someone who has faced special challenges? Tell that person's story.
3. Have you known someone very young, like Anne Frank, who had a great influence on your life or someone else's? Write an essay telling the story.
4. What direct impact has 9/11 had on your life? Write an essay detailing this impact.
5. Has a famous person affected your life? Describe how.
6. Have you or anyone you know had "15 minutes of fame"? Tell the story.

IN-SIGHT

Anthony Correia/Getty.

PRE-READING QUESTIONS

1. What was your elementary school like? Can you describe it?
2. Did your school have a diverse population?
3. Was there a poem or song that you had to learn in elementary school? Can you still sing or recite it today?

Pomegranates and English Education

Shirley Geok-lin Lim

Shirley Geok-lin Lim, currently a professor in the English Department at the University of California, Santa Barbara, is an award-winning Malaysian-born American writer of poetry, fiction, and criticism, and one of Hong

From *Among the White Moon-Faces: An Asian-American Memoir of Homelands* by Shirley Geok-lin Lim. Copyright © 1996 by Shirley Geok-lin Lim. Reprinted by permission of The Feminist Press at the City University of New York.

Kong's most published authors. Her first collection of poems, "Crossing the Peninsula," was published in 1980. She was born into a life of poverty, deprivation, parental violence, and abandonment in a culture that, at that time, rarely recognized girls as individuals. Reading was a huge retreat for her.

1   A pomegranate tree grew in a pot on the open-air balcony at the back of the second floor. It was a small skinny tree, even to a small skinny child like me. It had many fruits, marble-sized, dark green, shiny like overwaxed coats. Few grew to any size. The branches were sparse and graceful, as were the tear-shaped leaves that fluttered in the slightest breeze. Once a fruit grew round and large, we watched it every day. It grew lighter, then streaked with yellow and red. Finally we ate it, the purple and crimson seeds bursting with a tart liquid as we cracked the dry tough skin into segments to be shared by our many hands and mouths.

2   We were many. Looking back it seems to me that we had always been many. Beng was the fierce brother, the growly eldest son. Chien was the gentle second brother, born with a squint eye. Seven other children followed after me: Jen, Wun, Wilson, Hui, Lui, Seng, and Marie, the last four my half-siblings. I was third, the only daughter through a succession of eight boys and, as far as real life goes, measured in rice bowls and in the bones of morning, I have remained an only daughter in my memory.

3   We were as many as the blood-seeds we chewed, sucked, and spat out, the indigestible cores pulped and gray while their juice ran down our chins and stained our mouths with triumphant color. I still hold that crimson in memory, the original color of Chinese prosperity and health, now transformed to the berry shine of wine, the pump of blood in test tubes and smeared on glass plates to prophesy one's future from the wriggles of a virus. My Chinese life in Malaysia up to 1969 was a pomegranate, thickly seeded.

. . .

4   When Beng and Chien began attending the Bandar Hilir Primary School, they brought home textbooks, British readers with thick linen-rag covers, strong slick paper, and lots of short stories and poems accompanied by colorful pictures in the style of Aubrey Beardsley. The story of the three Billy Goats Gruff who killed the Troll under the bridge was stark and compressed, illustrated by golden kids daintily trotting over a rope bridge and a dark squat figure peering from the ravine below. Wee Willie Winkie ran through a starry night wearing only a white night cap and gown. The goats, the troll, and Willie Winkie were equally phantasms to me, for who ever saw anything like a flowing white gown on a boy or a pointy night cap in Malaya?

5   How to explain the disorienting power of story and picture? Things never seen or thought of in Malayan experience took on a vividness that ordinary life could not possess. These British childhood texts materialized for me, a five- and six-year-old child, the kind of hyper-reality that television images hold for a later generation, a reality, moreover, that was consolidated by colonial education.

6   At five, I memorized the melody and lyrics to "The Jolly Miller" from my brother's school rendition:

> There lived a jolly miller once
> Along the River Dee.
> He worked and sang from morn till night,
> No lark more blithe than he.
> And this the burden of his song
> As always used to be,
> I care for nobody, no not I,
> And nobody cares for me.

7   It was my first English poem, my first English song, and my first English lesson. The song ran through my head mutely, obsessively, on hundreds of occasions. What catechism did I learn as I sang the words aloud? I knew nothing of millers or of larks. As a preschool child, I ate bread, that exotic food, only on rare and unwelcome occasions. The miller working alone had no analogue in the Malayan world. In Malacca, everyone was surrounded by everyone else.

8   A hawker needed his regular customers, a store-front the stream of pedestrians who shopped on the move. Caring was not a concept that signified. Necessity, the relations between and among many and diverse people, composed the bonds of Malaccan society. Caring denoted a field of choice, of individual voluntary action, that was foreign to family, the place of compulsory relations. Western ideological subversion, cultural colonialism, whatever we call those forces that have changed societies under forced political domination, for me began with something as simple as an old English folk song.

9   The pomegranate is a fruit of the East, coming originally from Persia. The language of the West, English, and all its many manifestations in stories, songs, illustrations, films, school, and government, does not teach the lesson of the pomegranate. English taught me the lesson of the individual, the miller who is happy alone, and who affirms the principle of not caring for community. Why was it so easy for me to learn that lesson? Was it because within the pomegranate's hundreds of seeds is also contained the drive for singularity that will

finally produce one tree from one seed? Or was it because my grandparents'
Hokkien and *nonya* societies had become irremediably damaged by British
colonial domination, their cultural confidence never to be recovered intact, so
that Western notions of the individual took over collective imaginations, making of us, as V. S. Naipaul has coined it, "mimic" people?

10   But I resist this reading of colonialist corruption of an original pure culture. Corruption is inherent in every culture, if we think of corruption as a
will to break out, to rupture, to break down, to decay, and thus to change.
We are all mimic people, born to cultures that push us, shape us, and pum-
mel us; and we are all agents, with the power of the subject, no matter how
puny or inarticulate, to push back and to struggle against such shaping. So
I have seen myself not so much sucking at the teat of British colonial culture as actively appropriating those aspects of it that I needed to escape that
other familial/gender/native culture that violently hammered out only one
shape for self. I actively sought corruption to break out of the pomegranate
shell of being Chinese and girl.

. . .

11   It was the convent school that gave me the first weapons with which to
wreck my familial culture. On the first day, Ah Chan took me, a six-year-
old, in a trishaw to the Convent of the Holy Infant Jesus. She waited outside the classroom the entire day with a *chun*, a tiffin carrier, filled with
steamed rice, soup, and meat, fed me this lunch at eleven-thirty, then took
me home in a trishaw at two. I wore a starched blue pinafore over a white
cotton blouse and stared at the words, *See Jane run. Can Jane run? Jane can
run.* After the first week, I begged to attend school without Ah Chan present. Baba drove me to school after he dropped my older brothers at their
school a mile before the convent; I was now, like my brothers, free of domestic female attachment.

12   The convent school stood quiet and still behind thick cement walls that
hid the buildings and its inhabitants from the road and muffled the sounds
of passing traffic. The high walls also served to snuff out the world once you
entered the gates, which were always kept shut except at the opening and
closing of the school day. Shards of broken bottles embedded in the top of
the walls glinted in the hot tropical sunshine, a provocative signal that the
convent women were daily conscious of dangers intruding on their seclu-
sion. For the eleven years that I entered through those gates, I seldom met
a man on the grounds, except for the Jesuit brought to officiate at the annual
retreat. A shared public area was the chapel, a small low dark structure made
sacred by stained glass windows, hard wooden benches, and the sacristy oil
lamp whose light was never allowed to go out. The community was allowed

into the chapel every Sunday to attend the masses held for the nuns and the orphans who lived in the convent.

13   But if the convent closed its face to the town of men and unbelievers, it lay open at the back to the Malacca Straits. Every recess I joined hundreds of girls milling at the canteen counters for little plates of noodles, curry puffs stuffed with potatoes, peas and traces of meat, and vile orange-colored sugared drinks. The food never held me for long. Instead I spent recess by the sea wall, a stone barrier free of bristling glass. Standing before the sandy ground that separated the field and summer house from the water, I gazed at high tide as the waves threw themselves against the wall with the peculiar repeated whoosh and sigh that I never wearied of hearing. Until I saw the huge pounding surf of the Atlantic Ocean, I believed all the world's water to be dancing, diamond bright surfaced, a hypnotic meditative space in which shallow and deep seemed one and the same. Once inside the convent gates, one was overtaken by a similar sense of an overwhelming becalmedness, as if one had fallen asleep, out of worldliness, and entered the security of a busy dream.

14   During recess the little girls sang, "In and out the window, in and out the window, as we have done before," and skipped in and out of arching linked hands, in a mindless pleasure of repeated movement, repeating the desire for safety, for routine, and for the linked circular enclosure of the women's community that would take me in from six to seventeen.

· · ·

15 I also learned to write the alphabet. At first, the gray pencil wouldn't obey my fingers. When the little orange nub at the end of the pencil couldn't erase the badly made letter, I wetted a finger with spit, rubbed hard, and then blubbered at the hole I had made in the paper. Writing was fraught with fear. I cried silently as I wrestled with the fragile paper that wouldn't sit still and that crushed and tore under my palm.

16   My teacher was an elderly nun of uncertain European nationality, perhaps French, who didn't speak English well. She spoke with a lisp, mispronounced my name, called me "chérie" instead of "Shirley," and, perhaps accordingly, showed more affection to me than to the other children in her class. Sister Josie was the first European I knew. Even in her voluminous black robes and hood, she was an image of powder-white and pink smiles. Bending over my small desk to guide my fingers, and peering into my teary eyes, she spoke my name with a tender concern. She was my first experience of an enveloping, unconditional, and safe physical affection. She smelled sweet, like fresh yeast, and as I grew braver each day and strayed from my desk, she would upbraid me in the most remorseful of tones, "Chérie," which carried with it an approving smile.

17   In return I applied myself to Jane and Dick and Spot and to copying the alphabet letter by letter repeatedly. Sister Josie couldn't teach anything beyond the alphabet and simple vocabulary. In a few years, she was retired to the position of gatekeeper at the chapel annex. When I visited her six years later, as a child of twelve, at the small annex in which a store of holy pictures, medals, and lace veils were displayed for sale, Sister Josie's smile was still as fond. But to my mature ears, her English speech was halting, her grammar and vocabulary fractured. It was only to a six-year-old new to English that dear Sister Josie could have appeared as a native speaker of the English language.

18   It was my extreme good fortune to have this early missionary mother. Her gentle, undemanding care remains memorialized as a type of human relation not found in the fierce self-involvements of my family. My narrowly sensory world broadened not only with the magical letters she taught that spelled lives beyond what my single dreaming could imagine, but differently with her gentle greetings, in her palpable affection.

. . .

19 Nurturing is a human act that overleaps categories, but it is not free of history. It is not innocent. For the next eleven years nuns like Sister Josie broke down the domain of my infancy. Leaving the Bata shop and entering the jagged-glass-edged walls of the convent, I entered a society far removed from Baba and Emak.

20   The nuns wore the heavy wool habit of the missionary, full black blouses with wide sleeves like bat wings, long voluminous black skirts, black stockings, and shoes. Deep white hoods covered their heads and fell over their shoulders, and a white skull cap came down over their brows. Inexplicably they were collectively named "the French Convent," like a French colony or the foreign legion, but they were not chiefly white or European. Even in the early 1950s, some were Chinese and Eurasian "sisters."

21   Yet, despite their uniform habits and sisterly titles, a ranking regulated by race was obvious, even to the youngest Malayan child. Mother Superior was always white. A few white sisters, Sister Sean, Sister Patricia, and Sister Peter, taught the upper grades; or they performed special duties, like Sister Maria, who gave singing lessons, or Sister Bernadette, who taught cooking and controlled the kitchen and the canteen.

22   Sister Maria was the only woman who was recognizably French. Her accent was itself music to us as she led us through years of Scottish and Irish ballads. No one asked why "Ye Banks and Braes of Bonnie Doon" or "The Minstrel Boy" formed our music curriculum, why Indian, Eurasian, Malay, and Chinese children should be singing, off-key, week after week in a faintly

French-accented manner the melancholic attitudes of Celtic gloom. What was the place of Celt ballads in a Malayan future? What did they instruct of a history of feelings, of British bloodshed and patriotism? Or were the curriculum setters in the Colonial Office in London reproducing in fortissimo an imperial narrative—the tragedy of failed Scottish and Irish nationalism, the first of England's colonies—in the physical pulses of the newly colonized?

• • •

23 Of the nonmissionary teachers from Malacca, many were Eurasian, and a few were Indian, and Chinese. The sole Malay teacher appeared only after the British ceded independence to the Federation of Malaya in 1957. Chik Guru taught us the Malay language in my last two years at the convent, just as now in the United States in many colleges and universities, the only African-American or Latino or Asian-American professor a student may meet teaches African-American or Latino or Asian-American studies. Up to the end of the 1950s, and perhaps right up to the violence of the May 13 race riots in 1969, the educational structure in Malaya was British colonial.

24   My first inkling of race preference was formed by these earliest teachers. In primary school, my teachers were almost all European expatriates or native-born Eurasian Catholics bearing such Hispanic and Dutch names as De Souza, De Witt, Minjoot, Aerea, and De Costa. They were the descendants of Portuguese soldiers and sailors who had captured Malacca from the Malay Sultanate in 1511, when Portugal was a small, poorly populated state. Expanding into the Spice Islands in the East, the Governor-Generals of the Indies encouraged intermarriage between Portuguese males and native women, thus seeding the loyal settler population with Portuguese mestizos. The Portuguese governed Malacca for 130 years. When the forces of the Dutch East India Company captured the port and its fortress in 1641, they found a garrison there of some 260 Portuguese soldiers, reinforced with a mestizo population of about two to three thousand fighting men. For over four hundred years, the mestizos of Malacca had identified themselves as Portuguese.

25   The Eurasian teachers were physically distinguished from me. I learned this in Primary Two with Mrs. Damien, a white-haired, very large woman whose fat dimpled arms fascinated me. While she demonstrated how to embroider a daisy stitch as we crowded around her chair, I poked my finger into the dimples and creases that formed in the pale flesh that flowed over her shoulders and sagged in her upper arms. She was a fair Eurasian who dressed as a British matron, in sleeveless flowered print frocks with square-cut collars for coolness. Her exposed arms and chest presented dazzling mounds of white flesh that aroused my ardent admiration. I do not remember learning anything else in her class.

26   A few Eurasian girls were among my classmates. While they were not as coddled as the white daughters of plantation managers, they had an air of ease and inclusion that I envied. Their hair, which often had a copper sheen to it, was braided, while we Chinese girls had black, pudding-bowl cropped hair. By the time we were twelve and thirteen, and still flat-chested, they had budded into bosomy women whose presence in Sunday masses attracted the attention of young Catholic males. The royal blue pleated pinafores that covered our prim skinny bodies like cardboard folded teasingly over their chests and hips. The difference between us and the early maturity of Eurasian girls was a symptom of the difference between our Chinese Malaccan culture and that dangerous Western culture made visible in their lushness. They were overtly religious, controlled by their strict mothers and the Ten Commandments that we had all memorized by preadolescence. But their breasts and hips that made swing skirts swing pronounced them ready for that unspoken but pervasive excitement we knew simply as "boys."

. . .

27 The convent held a number of orphans, girls abandoned as babies on the convent doorsteps, or given over to the nuns to raise by relatives too poor to pay for their upkeep. During school hours these "orphaned" girls were indistinguishable from the rest of us. They wore the school uniforms, white short-sleeved blouses under sleeveless blue linen smocks that were fashioned with triple over-pleats on both sides so that burgeoning breasts were multiply overlayered with folds of starched fabric. But once school hours were over they changed into pink or blue gingham dresses that buttoned right up to the narrow Peter Pan collars. Those loose shapeless dresses, worn by sullen girls who earned their keep by helping in the kitchen and laundry, formed some of my early images of a class to be shunned.

28   Instead I longed to be like the privileged boarders, almost all of whom were British, whose parents lived in remote and dangerous plantations or administrative outposts in the interior. These girls wore polished black leather shoes and fashionable skirts and blouses after school. In our classes, they sang unfamiliar songs, showed us how to dance, jerking their necks like hieroglyphic Egyptians. In the convent classroom where silence and stillness were enforced as standard behavior, they giggled and joked, shifting beams of sunshine, and were never reprimanded. To every schoolgirl it was obvious that something about a white child made the good nuns benevolent.

COMPREHENSION QUESTIONS

1. Who were the orphaned girls in the convent and how were they treated?
2. Why were Chinese children in a Malaysian Catholic school run by French nuns educated in British culture about things never experienced by Malaysians?
3. What effect did British education have on the author?
4. How did Geok-lin Lim's education in various cultures affect her self-esteem?
5. Many Americans are descendents of colonial peoples, either the colonizers or the colonized. What connections might readers make between Geok-lin Lim's experience of a colonial education and their own life history or cultural history?

QUESTIONS ON WRITING TECHNIQUE

1. What do you believe Geok-lin Lim's use of the pomegranate tree is meant to symbolize?
2. In what language was the author educated? In what culture? For what purposes? How did this affect the essay?
3. In what language and for what readers does the author write about her education? For what purposes?
4. What is the author's purpose in writing this essay?
5. List three phrases that show rich description in this essay.

PRE-READING QUESTIONS

1. Define censorship.
2. In this information age, can you imagine living in a world where all information you receive is censored?
3. Have you ever experienced a life-changing event? Describe it.

Black Boy

Richard Wright

Richard Wright was born in 1908 on a plantation near Natchez, Missis-sippi. He was among the first African American writers to achieve literary fame and fortune. Though he spent only a few years of his life in Mississippi, those years would play a key role in his two most important works: Native Son, *a novel, and his autobiography,* Black Boy. *First published in 1937,* Black Boy *tells the compelling story of Wright's life in the racially segregated South. Throughout the book, Wright describes in stark detail the racism, poverty, and fear that dominated the lives of blacks in the South and his own emotional, spiritual, and intellectual development.*

1 I entered the library as I had always done when on errands for whites, but I felt that I would somehow slip up and betray myself. I doffed my hat, stood a respectful distance from the desk, looked as unbookish as possible, and waited for the white patrons to be taken care of. When the desk was clear of people, I still waited. The white librarian looked at me.

2 "What do you want, boy?"

3 As though I did not possess the power of speech, I stepped forward and simply handed her the forged note, not parting my lips.

4 "What books by Mencken does he want?" she asked.

5 "I don't know, ma'am," I said, avoiding her eyes.

6 "Who gave you this card?"

7 "Mr. Falk," I said.

8   "Where is he?"

9   "He's at work, at the M——— Optical Company," I said. "I've been in here for him before."

10   "I remember," the woman said. "But he never wrote notes like this."

11   Oh, God, she's suspicious. Perhaps she would not let me have the books? If she had turned her back at that moment, I would have ducked out the door and never gone back. Then I thought of a bold idea.

12   "You can call him up, ma'am," I said, my heart pounding.

13   "You're not using these books, are you?" she asked pointedly.

14   "Oh, no, ma'am. I can't read."

15   "I don't know what he wants by Mencken," she said under her breath.

16   I knew now that I had won; she was thinking of other things and the race question had gone out of her mind. She went to the shelves. Once or twice she looked over her shoulder at me, as though she was still doubtful. Finally she came forward with two books in her hand.

17   "I'm sending him two books," she said. "But tell Mr. Falk to come in next time, or send me the names of the books he wants. I don't know what he wants to read."

18   I said nothing. She stamped the card and handed me the books. Not daring to glance at them, I went out of the library, fearing that the woman would call me back for further questioning. A block away from the library I opened one of the books and read a title: *A Book of Prefaces*. I was nearing my nineteenth birthday and I did not know how to pronounce the word "preface." I thumbed the pages and saw strange words and strange names. I shook my head, disappointed. I looked at the other book; it was called *Prejudices*. I knew what that word meant; I had heard it all my life. And right off I was on guard against Mencken's books. Why would a man want to call a book *Prejudices*? The word was so stained with all my memories of racial hate that I could not conceive of anybody using it for a title. Perhaps I had made a mistake about Mencken? A man who had prejudices must be wrong.

19   When I showed the books to Mr. Falk, he looked at me and frowned.

20   "That librarian might telephone you," I warned him.

21   "That's all right," he said. "But when you're through reading those books, I want you to tell me what you get out of them."

22   That night in my rented room, while letting the hot water run over my can of pork and beans in the sink, I opened *A Book of Prefaces* and began to read. I was jarred and shocked by the style, the clear, clean, sweeping sentences. Why did he write like that? And how did one write like that? I pictured the man as a raging demon, slashing with his pen, consumed with

hate, denouncing everything American, extolling everything European or German, laughing at the weaknesses of people, mocking God, authority. What was this? I stood up, trying to realize what reality lay behind the meaning of the words . . . Yes, this man was fighting, fighting with words. He was using words as a weapon, using them as one would use a club. Could words be weapons? Well, yes, for here they were. Then, maybe, perhaps, I could use them as a weapon? No. It frightened me. I read on and what amazed me was not what he said, but how on earth anybody had the courage to say it.

23   Occasionally I glanced up to reassure myself that I was alone in the room. Who were these men about whom Mencken was talking so passionately? Who was Anatole France? Joseph Conrad? Sinclair Lewis, Sherwood Anderson, Dostoyevsky, George Moore, Gustave Flaubert, Maupassant, Tolstoy, Frank Harris, Mark Twain, Thomas Hardy, Arnold Bennett, Stephen Crane, Zola, Norris, Gorky, Bergson, Ibsen, Balzac, Bernard Shaw, Dumas, Poe, Thomas Mann, O. Henry, Dreiser, H. G. Wells, Gogol, T. S. Eliot, Gide, Baudelaire, Edgar Lee Masters, Stendhal, Turgenev, Huneker, Nietzsche, and scores of others? Were these men real? Did they exist or had they existed? And how did one pronounce their names?

24   I ran across many words whose meanings I did not know, and I either looked them up in a dictionary or, before I had a chance to do that, encountered the word in a context that made its meaning clear. But what strange world was this? I concluded the book with the conviction that I had somehow overlooked something terribly important in life. I had once tried to write, had once reveled in feeling, had let my crude imagination roam, but the impulse to dream had been slowly beaten out of me by experience. Now it surged up again and I hungered for books, new ways of looking and seeing. It was not a matter of believing or disbelieving what I read, but of feeling something new, of being affected by something that made the look of the world different.

25   As dawn broke I ate my pork and beans, feeling dopey, sleepy. I went to work, but the mood of the book would not die; it lingered, coloring everything I saw, heard, did. I now felt that I knew what the white men were feeling. Merely because I had read a book that had spoken of how they lived and thought, I identified myself with that book. I felt vaguely guilty. Would I, filled with bookish notions, act in a manner that would make the whites dislike me?

26   I forged more notes and my trips to the library became frequent. Reading grew into a passion. My first serious novel was Sinclair Lewis's *Main Street*. It made me see my boss, Mr. Gerald, and identify him as an American type. I would smile when I saw him lugging his golf bags into the office. I had always felt a vast distance separating me from the boss, and now I felt

closer to him, that I could feel the very limits of his narrow life. And this had happened because I had read a novel about a mythical man called George F. Babbitt.

27   The plots and stories in the novels did not interest me so much as the point of view revealed. I gave myself over to each novel without reserve, without trying to criticize it; it was enough for me to see and feel something different. And for me, everything was something different. Reading was like a drug, a dope. The novels created moods in which I lived for days. But I could not conquer my sense of guilt, my feeling that the white men around me knew that I was changing, that I had begun to regard them differently.

28   Whenever I brought a book to the job, I wrapped it in newspaper—a habit that was to persist for years in other cities and under other circumstances. But some of the white men pried into my packages when I was absent and they questioned me.

29   "Boy, what are you reading those books for?"

30   "Oh, I don't know, sir."

31   "That's deep stuff you're reading, boy."

32   "I'm just killing time, sir."

33   "You'll addle your brains if you don't watch out."

34   I read Dreiser's *Jennie Gerhardt* and *Sister Carrie* and they revived in me a vivid sense of my mother's suffering; I was overwhelmed. I grew silent, wondering about the life around me. It would have been impossible for me to have told anyone what I derived from these novels, for it was nothing less than a sense of life itself. All my life had shaped me for the realism, the naturalism of the modern novel, and I could not read enough of them.

35   Steeped in new moods and ideas, I bought a ream of paper and tried to write; but nothing would come, or what did come was flat beyond telling. I discovered that more than desire and feeling were necessary to write and I dropped the idea. Yet I still wondered how it was possible to know people sufficiently to write about them? Could I ever learn about life and people? To me, with my vast ignorance, my Jim Crow station in life, it seemed a task impossible of achievement. I now knew what being a Negro meant. I could endure the hunger. I had learned to live with hate. But to feel that there were feelings denied me, that the very breath of life itself was beyond my reach, that more than anything else, hurt, wounded me. I had a new hunger.

36   In buoying me up, reading also cast me down, made me see what was possible, what I had missed. My tension returned, new, terrible, bitter, surging, almost too great to be contained. I no longer *felt* that the world about me was hostile, killing; I *knew* it. A million times I asked myself what I could

do to save myself, and there were no answers. I seemed forever condemned, ringed by walls.

37   I did not discuss my reading with Mr. Falk, who had lent me his library card; it would have meant talking about myself and that would have been too painful. I smiled each day, fighting desperately to maintain my old behavior, to keep my disposition seemingly sunny. But some of the white men discerned that I had begun to brood.

38   "Wake up there, boy!" Mr. Olin said one day.

39   "Sir!" I answered for the lack of a better word.

40   "You act like you've stolen something," he said.

41   I laughed in the way I knew he expected me to laugh, but I resolved to be more conscious of myself, to watch my every act, to guard and hide the new knowledge that was dawning within me.

42   If I went north, would it be possible for me to build a new life then? But how could a man build a life upon vague, unformed yearnings? I wanted to write and I did not even know the English language. I bought English grammars and found them dull. I felt that I was getting a better sense of the language from novels than from grammars. I read hard, discarding a writer as soon as I felt that I had grasped his point of view. At night the printed page stood before my eyes in sleep.

43   Mrs. Moss, my landlady, asked me one Sunday morning:

44   "Son, what is this you keep on reading?"

45   "Oh, nothing. Just novels."

46   "What you get out of 'em?"

47   "I'm just killing time," I said.

48   "I hope you know your own mind," she said in a tone which implied that she doubted if I had a mind.

49   I knew of no Negroes who read the books I liked and I wondered if any Negroes ever thought of them. I knew that there were Negro doctors, lawyers, newspapermen, but I never saw any of them. When I read a Negro newspaper I never caught the faintest echo of my preoccupation in its pages. I felt trapped and occasionally, for a few days, I would stop reading. But a vague hunger would come over me for books, books that opened up new avenues of feeling and seeing, and again I would forge another note to the white librarian. Again I would read and wonder as only the naïve and unlettered can read and wonder, feeling that I carried a secret, criminal burden about with me each day.

COMPREHENSION QUESTIONS

1. How did Wright feel in the library? Why?
2. How did Wright obtain his books?
3. What kind of books did Wright prefer? Why?
4. What effect did H. L. Mencken's words have on Wright?
5. What did Wright mean when he said "The plots and stories in the novels did not interest me so much as the point of view revealed."

QUESTIONS ON WRITING TECHNIQUE

1. Why does the author use so much dialogue in this essay?
2. From what point of view is the story written?
3. Why did the author choose the title "Black Boy"?
4. What point is the author trying to make in the conclusion?
5. Why are so many authors listed in paragraph 23? What is the effect on the reader?

PRE-READING QUESTIONS

1. Where is India? What do you know about the country?
2. Are there advantages to an "arranged marriage"? Are there disadvantages?
3. Have you ever had a "blind date"? If so, what were the advantages and disadvantages of the event?

Arranging a Marriage in India

Serena Nanda

Serena Nanda was educated at New York University and taught cultural anthropology at City University of New York in the John Jay College of Criminal Justice. Her books include Cultural Anthropology *(1998),* American Cultural Pluralism and Law *(1996),* Neither Man nor Woman: The Hijras of India *(1999), and* Gender Diversity: Cross-Cultured Variations *(2000). Nanda's current research focuses on non-European representations of Europeans in art and performance. In "Arranging a Marriage in India," reprinted from* The Naked Anthropologist: Tales from Around the World *(1992), Nanda contrasts the Indian and American processes of getting married.*

Sister and doctor brother-in-law invite correspondence from North Indian professionals only, for a beautiful, talented, sophisticated, intelligent sister, 5'3", slim, M.A. in textile design, father a senior civil officer. Would prefer immigrant doctors, between 26–29 years. Reply with full details and returnable photo. A well-settled uncle invites matrimonial correspondence from slim, fair, educated South Indian girl, for his nephew, 25 years, smart, M.B.A., green card holder, 5'6". Full particulars with returnable photo appreciated.

Matrimonial Advertisements, India Abroad

Serena Nanda, "Arranging a Marriage in India," in *Stumbling Toward Truth: Anthropologists at Work*, ed. Philip R. Devita, Prospect Heights, IL: Waveland Press, 2000, pp. 196–204. Reprinted by permission of Serena Nanda.

In India, almost all marriages are arranged. Even among the educated middle classes in modern, urban India, marriage is as much a concern of the families as it is of the individuals. So customary is the practice of arranged marriage that there is a special name for a marriage which is not arranged: it is called a "love match."

On my first field trip to India, I met many young men and women whose parents were in the process of "getting them married." In many cases, the bride and groom would not meet each other before the marriage. At most they might meet for a brief conversation, and this meeting would take place only after their parents had decided that the match was suitable. Parents do not compel their children to marry a person who either marriage partner finds objectionable. But only after one match is refused will another be sought.

As a young American woman in India for the first time, I found this custom of arranged marriage oppressive. How could any intelligent young person agree to such a marriage without great reluctance? It was contrary to everything I believed about the importance of romantic love as the only basis of a happy marriage. It also clashed with my strongly held notions that the choice of such an intimate and permanent relationship could be made only by the individuals involved. Had anyone tried to arrange my marriage, I would have been defiant and rebellious!

At the first opportunity, I began, with more curiosity than tact, to question the young people I met on how they felt about this practice. Sita, one of my young informants, was a college graduate with a degree in political science. She had been waiting for over a year while her parents were arranging a match for her. I found it difficult to accept the docile manner in which this well-educated young woman awaited the outcome of a process that would result in her spending the rest of her life with a man she hardly knew, a virtual stranger, picked out by her parents.

"How can you go along with this?" I asked her, in frustration and distress. "Don't you care who you marry?"

"Of course I care," she answered. "This is why I must let my parents choose a boy for me. My marriage is too important to be arranged by such an inexperienced person as myself. In such matters, it is better to have my parents' guidance."

I had learned that young men and women in India do not date and have very little social life involving members of the opposite sex. Although I could not disagree with Sita's reasoning, I continued to pursue the subject.

8   "But how can you marry the first man you have ever met? Not only have you missed the fun of meeting a lot of different people, but you have not given yourself the chance to know who is the right man for you."

9   "Meeting with a lot of different people doesn't sound like any fun at all," Sita answered. "One hears that in America the girls are spending all their time worrying about whether they will meet a man and get married. Here we have the chance to enjoy our life and let our parents do this work and worrying for us."

10   She had me there. The high anxiety of the competition to "be popular" with the opposite sex certainly was the most prominent feature of life as an American teenager in the late fifties. The endless worrying about the rules that governed our behavior and about our popularity ratings sapped both our self-esteem and our enjoyment of adolescence. I reflected that absence of this competition in India most certainly may have contributed to the self-confidence and natural charm of so many of the young women I met.

11   And yet, the idea of marrying a perfect stranger, whom one did not know and did not "love," so offended my American ideas of individualism and romanticism, that I persisted with my objections.

12   "I still can't imagine it," I said. "How can you agree to marry a man you hardly know?"

13   "But of course he will be known. My parents would never arrange a marriage for me without knowing all about the boy's family background. Naturally we will not rely only on what the family tells us. We will check the particulars out ourselves. No one will want their daughter to marry into a family that is not good. All these things we will know beforehand."

14   Impatiently, I responded, "Sita, I don't mean know the family, I mean, know the man. How can you marry someone you don't know personally and don't love? How can you think of spending your life with someone you may not even like?"

15   "If he is a good man, why should I not like him?" she said. "With you people, you know the boy so well before you marry, where will be the fun to get married? There will be no mystery and no romance. Here we have the whole of our married life to get to know and love our husband. "This way is better, is it not?"

16   Her response made further sense, and I began to have second thoughts on the matter. Indeed, during months of meeting many intelligent young Indian people, both male and female, who had the same ideas as Sita, I saw arranged marriages in a different light. I also saw the importance of the family in Indian life and realized that a couple who took their marriage into

their own hands was taking a big risk, particularly if their families were irreconcilably opposed to the match. In a country where every important resource in life—a job, a house, a social circle—is gained through family connections, it seemed foolhardy to cut oneself off from a supportive social network and depend solely on one person for happiness and success.

17   Six years later I returned to India to again do fieldwork, this time among the middle class in Bombay, a modern, sophisticated city. From the experience of my earlier visit, I decided to include a study of arranged marriages in my project. By this time I had met many Indian couples whose marriages had been arranged and who seemed very happy. Particularly in contrast to the fate of many of my married friends in the United States who were already in the process of divorce, the positive aspects of arranged marriages appeared to me to outweigh the negatives. In fact, I thought I might even participate in arranging a marriage myself. I had been fairly successful in the United States in "fixing up" many of my friends, and I was confident that my matchmaking skills could be easily applied to this new situation, once I learned the basic rules. "After all," I thought, "how complicated can it be? People want pretty much the same things in a marriage whether it is in India or America."

18   An opportunity presented itself almost immediately. A friend from my previous Indian trip was in the process of arranging for the marriage of her eldest son. In India there is a perceived shortage of "good boys," and since my friend's family was eminently respectable and the boy himself personable, well educated, and nice looking, I was sure that by the end of my year's fieldwork, we would have found a match.

19   The basic rule seems to be that a family's reputation is most important. It is understood that matches would be arranged only within the same caste and general social class, although some crossing of subcastes is permissible if the class positions of the bride's and groom's families are similar. Although dowry is now prohibited by law in India, extensive gift exchanges took place with every marriage. Even when the boy's family do not "make demands," every girl's family nevertheless feels the obligation to give the traditional gifts, to the girl, to the boy, and to the boy's family. Particularly when the couple would be living in the joint family—that is, with the boy's parents and his married brothers and their families, as well as with unmarried siblings—which is still very common even among the urban, upper-middle class in India, the girls' parents are anxious to establish smooth relations between their family and that of the boy. Offering the proper gifts, even when not called "dowry," is often an important factor in influencing the relationship

between the bride's and groom's families and perhaps, also, the treatment of the bride in her new home.

20   In a society where divorce is still a scandal and where, in fact, the divorce rate is exceedingly low, an arranged marriage is the beginning of a lifetime relationship not just between the bride and groom but between their families as well. Thus, while a girl's looks are important, her character is even more so, for she is being judged as a prospective daughter-in-law as much as a prospective bride. Where she would be living in a joint family, as was the case with my friend, the girls' ability to get along harmoniously in a family is perhaps the single most important quality in assessing her suitability.

21   My friend is a highly esteemed wife, mother, and daughter-in-law. She is religious, soft-spoken, modest, and deferential. She rarely gossips and never quarrels, two qualities highly desirable in a woman. A family that has the reputation for gossip and conflict among its womenfolk will not find it easy to get good wives for their sons. Parents will not want to send their daughter to a house in which there is conflict.

22   My friend's family were originally from North India. They had lived in Bombay, where her husband owned a business, for forty years. The family had delayed in seeking a match for their eldest son because he had been an Air Force pilot for several years, stationed in such remote places that it had seemed fruitless to try to find a girl who would be willing to accompany him. In their social class, a military career, despite its economic security, has little prestige and is considered a drawback in finding a suitable bride. Many families would not allow their daughters to marry a man in an occupation so potentially dangerous and which requires so much moving around.

23   The son had recently left the military and joined his father's business. Since he was a college graduate, modern, and well traveled, from such a good family, and, I thought, quite handsome, it seemed to me that he, or rather his family, was in a position to pick and choose. I said as much to my friend.

24   While she agreed that there were many advantages on their side, she also said, "We must keep in mind that my son is both short and dark; these are drawbacks in finding the right match." While the boy's height had not escaped my notice, "dark" seemed to me inaccurate. I would have called him "wheat" colored perhaps, and in any case, I did not realize that color would be a consideration. I discovered, however, that while a boy's skin color is a less important consideration than a girl's, it is still a factor.

25   An important source of contacts in trying to arrange her son's marriage was my friend's social club in Bombay. Many of the women had daughters of the right age, and some had already expressed an interest in my friend's

son. I was most enthusiastic about the possibilities of one particular family who had five daughters, all of whom were pretty, demure, and well educated. Their mother had told my friend, "You can have your pick for your son, whichever one of my daughters appeals to you most."

26   I saw a match in sight. "Surely," I said to my friend, "we will find one there. Let's go visit and make our choice." But my friend held back; she did not seem to share my enthusiasm, for reasons I could not then fathom.

27   When I kept pressing for an explanation of her reluctance, she admitted, "See, Serena, here is the problem. The family has so many daughters, how will they be able to provide nicely for any of them? We are not making any demands, but still, with so many daughters to marry off, one wonders whether she will even be able to make a proper wedding. Since this is our eldest son, it's best if we marry him to a girl who is the only daughter, then the wedding will truly be a gala affair." I argued that surely the quality of the girls themselves made up for any deficiency in the elaborateness of the wedding. My friend admitted this point but still seemed reluctant to proceed.

28   "Is there something else," I asked her, "some factor I have missed?" "Well," she finally said, "there is one other thing. They have one daughter already married and living in Bombay. The mother is always complaining to me that the girl's in-laws don't let her visit her own family often enough. So it makes me wonder, will she be that kind of mother who always wants her daughter at her own home? This will prevent the girl from adjusting to our house. It is not a good thing." And so, this family of five daughters was dropped as a possibility.

29   Somewhat disappointed, I nevertheless respected my friend's reasoning and geared up for the next prospect. This was also the daughter of a woman in my friend's social club. There was clear interest in this family and I could see why. The family's reputation was excellent; in fact, they came from a sub-caste slightly higher than my friend's own. The girl, who was an only daughter, was pretty and well educated and had a brother studying in the United States. Yet, after expressing an interest to me in this family, all talk of them suddenly died down and the search began elsewhere.

30   "What happened to that girl as a prospect?" I asked one day. "You never mention her any more. She is so pretty and so educated, what did you find wrong?"

31   "She is too educated. We've decided against it. My husband's father saw the girl on the bus the other day and thought her forward. A girl who 'roams about' the city by herself is not the girl for our family." My disappointment this time was even greater, as I thought the son would have liked the girl very

much. But then I thought, my friend is right, a girl who is going to live in a joint family cannot be too independent or she will make life miserable for everyone. I also learned that if the family of the girl has even a slightly higher social status than the family of the boy, the bride may think herself too good for them, and this too will cause problems. Later my friend admitted to me that this had been an important factor in her decision not to pursue the match.

32   The next candidate was the daughter of a client of my friend's husband. When the client learned that the family was looking for a match for their son, he said, "Look no further, we have a daughter." This man then invited my friends to dinner to see the girl. He had already seen their son at the office and decided that "he liked the boy." We all went together for tea, rather than dinner—it was less of a commitment—and while we were there, the girl's mother showed us around the house. The girl was studying for her exams and was briefly introduced to us.

33   After we left, I was anxious to hear my friend's opinion. While her husband liked the family very much and was impressed with his client's business accomplishments and reputation, the wife didn't like the girl's looks. "She is short, no doubt, which is an important plus point, but she is also fat and wears glasses." My friend obviously thought she could do better for her son and asked her husband to make his excuses to his client by saying that they had decided to postpone the boy's marriage indefinitely.

34   By this time almost six months had passed and I was becoming impatient. What I had thought would be an easy matter to arrange was turning out to be quite complicated. I began to believe that between my friend's desire for a girl who was modest enough to fit into her joint family, yet attractive and educated enough to be an acceptable partner for her son, she would not find anyone suitable. My friend laughed at my impatience: "Don't be so much in a hurry," she said. "You Americans want everything done so quickly. You get married quickly and then just as quickly get divorced. Here we take marriage more seriously. We must take all the factors into account. It is not enough for us to learn by our mistakes. This is too serious a business. If a mistake is made we have not only ruined the life of our son or daughter, but we have spoiled the reputation of our family as well. And that will make it much harder for their brothers and sisters to get married. So we must be very careful."

35   What she said was true and I promised myself to be more patient, though it was not easy. I had really hoped and expected that the match would be made before my year in India was up. But it was not to be. When I left India my friend seemed no further along in finding a suitable match for her son than when I had arrived.

36   Two years later, I returned to India and still my friend had not found a
girl for her son. By this time, he was close to thirty, and I think she was a
little worried. Since she knew I had friends all over India, and I was going
to be there for a year, she asked me to "help her in this work" and keep an
eye out for someone suitable. I was flattered that my judgment was
respected, but knowing now how complicated the process was, I had lost
my earlier confidence as a matchmaker. Nevertheless, I promised that I
would try.

37   It was almost at the end of my year's stay in India that I met a family
with a marriageable daughter whom I felt might be a good possibility for
my friend's son. The girl's father was related to a good friend of mine and
by coincidence came from the same village as my friend's husband. This new
family had a successful business in a medium-sized city in central India and
were from the same subcaste as my friend. The daughter was pretty and chic:
in fact, she had studied fashion design in college. Her parents would not
allow her to go off by herself to any of the major cities in India where she
could make a career, but they had compromised with her wish to work by
allowing her to run a small dress-making boutique from their home. In spite
of her desire to have a career, the daughter was both modest and home-
loving and had had a traditional, sheltered upbringing. She had only one
other sister, already married, and a brother who was in his father's business.

38   I mentioned the possibility of a match with my friend's son. The girl's
parents were most interested. Although their daughter was not eager to
marry just yet, the idea of living in Bombay—a sophisticated, extremely
fashion-conscious city where she could continue her education in clothing
design—was a great inducement. I gave the girl's father my friend's address
and suggested that when they went to Bombay on some business or whatever, they look up the boy's family.

39   Returning to Bombay on my way to New York, I told my friend of this
newly discovered possibility. She seemed to feel there was potential but, in
spite of my urging, would not make any moves herself. She rather preferred
to wait for the girl's family to call upon them. I hoped something would come
of this introduction, though by now I had learned to rein in my optimism.

40   A year later I received a letter from my friend. The family had indeed
come to visit Bombay, and their daughter and my friend's daughter, who
were near in age, had become very good friends. During that year, the two
girls had frequently visited each other. I thought things looked promising.

41   Last week I received an invitation to a wedding: my friend's son and the
girl were getting married. Since I had found the match, my presence was

particularly requested at the wedding. I was thrilled. Success at last! As I prepared to leave for India, I began thinking, "Now, my friend's younger son, who do I know who has a nice girl for him . . . ?"

. . .

Further Reflections on Arranged Marriage . . .

42   This essay was written from the point of view of a family seeking a daughter-in-law. Arranged marriage looks somewhat different from the point of view of the bride and her family. Arranged marriage continues to be preferred, even among the more educated, Westernized sections of the Indian population. Many young women from these families still go along, more or less willingly, with the practice, and also with the specific choices of their families. Young women do get excited about the prospects of their marriage, but there is also ambivalence and increasing uncertainty, as the bride contemplates leaving the comfort and familiarity of her own home, where as a "temporary guest" she had often been indulged, to live among strangers. Even in the best situation she will now come under the close scrutiny of her husband's family. How she dresses, how she behaves, how she gets along with others, where she goes, how she spends her time, her domestic abilities—all of this and much more—will be observed and commented on by a whole new set of relations. Her interaction with her family of birth will be monitored and curtailed considerably. Not only will she leave their home, but with increasing geographic mobility, she may also live very far from them, perhaps even on another continent. Too much expression of her fondness for her own family, or her desire to visit them, may be interpreted as an inability to adjust to her new family, and may become a source of conflict. In an arranged marriage the burden of adjustment is clearly heavier for a woman than for a man. And that is in the best of situations.

43   In less happy circumstances, the bride may be a target of resentment and hostility from her husband's family, particularly her mother-in-law or her husband's unmarried sisters, for whom she is now a source of competition for the affection, loyalty, and economic resources of their son or brother. If she is psychologically, or even physically abused, her options are limited, as returning to her parents' home, or divorce, are still very stigmatized. For most Indians, marriage and motherhood are still considered the only suitable roles for a woman, even for those who have careers, and few women can comfortably contemplate remaining unmarried. Most families still consider "marrying off" their daughters as a compelling religious duty and social

necessity. This increases a bride's sense of obligation to make the marriage a success, at whatever cost to her own personal happiness.

44   The vulnerability of a new bride may also be intensified by the issue of dowry, which although illegal, has become a more pressing issue in the consumer conscious society of contemporary urban India. In many cases, where a groom's family is not satisfied with the amount of dowry a bride brings to her marriage, the young bride will be constantly harassed to get her parents to give more. In extreme cases, the bride may even be murdered, and the murder disguised as an accident or suicide. This also offers the husband's family an opportunity to arrange another match for him, thus bringing in another dowry. This phenomenon, called dowry death, calls attention not just to the "evils of dowry" but also to larger issues of the powerlessness of women as well.

Serena Nanda
March 1998

Comprehension Questions

1. How does the essay begin? Is this a good way to introduce this topic?
2. How does Nanda's conversation with Sita help illustrate her thesis that in India marriage is a family, not an individual decision?
3. How does Sita's criticism of American marriages help to clarify the author's purpose?
4. What did you learn about Indian culture from this essay?
5. How are American marriages similar to those in India?

Questions on Writing Technique

1. Who is the audience addressed here? If it were written for an Indian audience, how would it be different?
2. How does the audience learn about the criteria for a good marriage? Is this technique effective? Why or why not?
3. What techniques does the author use to provide the evidence in the essay?
4. How does the essay conclude? Is the conclusion effective?
5. What is the author's thesis? Where is it located?

PRE-READING QUESTIONS

1. Have you or someone in your family ever served overseas in the military? If so, when?
2. What are the stresses that military families go through when someone in the family goes overseas?
3. Are people in the military treated fairly in the United States? What would fair treatment be?

I'm Afraid to Look, Afraid to Turn Away

Denise Gonsales

Denise Gonsales is a military wife living in Rincon, Georgia. While her husband was stationed overseas, waiting for the war in Iraq to begin, she found out firsthand what a mixed blessing twenty-four-hour news coverage can be. She reminds us of the anxiety military families face while separated from their loved ones.

1 It's a stressful time for my family: I'm eight months pregnant and my husband, Martin, a Black Hawk pilot based in Savannah, Ga., has been in Kuwait for more than two months. Not surprisingly, I have been glued to the television, watching events unfold in this latest conflict, praying for my husband's safe return. As hard as it is to wait, it's not the first time I've done it and I suspect it won't be the last.

2 My first husband, who died three and a half years ago, was part of the 160th Special Operations unit deployed in 1993 to Somalia, where two Black Hawk helicopters were downed. Five of our dearest friends were killed during that mission. To my everlasting horror, I watched on CNN as the bodies of two of them were dragged through the streets of Mogadishu by a riotous crowd. My then 8-year-old daughter went to school the next day and saw a picture of one of the soldiers on the front page of our local paper. She

told me that she would have been worried except that the soldier had blond hair and her daddy's was black. Once the military officially declared the soldiers' deaths, I had to deliver the terrible news to two of their wives.

3   While Army families are prepped to expect stresses and strains of military service on their family life, I never thought the realities of war would affect me firsthand. Maybe I was in denial, maybe I just believed no nation in its right mind would take on America.

4   Martin was supposed to retire last February but he was caught in the stop-loss that the military put on select jobs in the wake of September 11. He is now expected to retire in November of 2004. Even during peacetime, our family is on tenterhooks, wondering if he might be deployed to another far-flung region of the world. While I am certain we can endure his absence, I have seen many families fall apart from the constant separations.

5   It pains me that the American public doesn't fully comprehend the sacrifices being made by soldiers during war, deployments and rotations. Incredibly, enlisted soldiers earn so little money that they qualify for food stamps. Many of them live in substandard military housing. Even so, they're willing to stick it out in the desert, where just having toilet paper is a luxury.

6   Their families sacrifice, too. Soldiers miss out on birthdays, anniversaries, children's sports events and summer vacations. There's a good chance Martin may miss the birth of our son next month. But I've learned over the years to have a backup plan so my family can have a sense of normalcy. Two of my best friends, Dan and Jennifer, will take Martin's place in the delivery room.

7   My access to Martin has been limited, but I keep thinking about the wives of soldiers who fought in World War II. Their husbands were away for years on end with little communication, so I try and keep a stiff upper lip and remain grateful for the contact I do have. Other wives have not been so fortunate—their husbands don't write home. This creates more stress for their families.

8   I've received about 10 letters from my husband since he's been gone. It takes them about 20 days to get to me. He's a charismatic kind of guy, very funny. Even in his letters he makes a valiant attempt to keep me uplifted. Between us we renamed this conflict "Operation Enduring Loneliness." I've gotten probably four or five phone calls. We had a three-minute conversation last Tuesday. He said, "D, I've been trying for 45 minutes to get through to you. There's a meeting and I have to go. Please don't worry, I love you and I'm really sorry I can't talk longer." I said "Martin, I don't care if it's 20 seconds, I'm just glad to hear your voice."

9   Being able to watch events unfold in real time has been a mixed blessing. I'm terrified of what I might see and yet I find it impossible to turn the television off while my husband is fighting this war. I can't help but worry that the Somalia experience will play out in living rooms across the country. My children, in their teens now, are equally interested in watching the coverage. They know that Martin's unit, the Third Infantry Division, is leading the push to Baghdad. They constantly ask questions about his location and whether he is in harm's way. No doubt they sense my fear.

10   As nerve-racking as it was when President Bush announced that the war had begun, it was in some ways a relief. My biggest fear was that our troops would sit over there all summer and morale would suffer. My heart just pours out to Iraqi families; as a mother, I can't imagine living with my two kids in a neighborhood that's being bombed. I can't even fathom that. And as terrified as I am for Martin, I can't imagine being an Iraqi wife whose husband is leaving to go fight the Americans. At least I know my husband has a fighting chance.

COMPREHENSION QUESTIONS

1. What is the author's topic?
2. Why was it a relief when the war began, according to the author?
3. What are some of the sacrifices that soldiers make, according to the author?
4. What is the effect on the military family when events unfold in real time on TV?
5. How does the author feel about Iraqi families? How do you know?

QUESTIONS ON WRITING TECHNIQUE

1. Who is the author's audience?
2. What description do you remember most vividly from the essay?
3. What point is the author trying to make, and how does she go about doing that?
4. How did the author organize the essay?
5. What writing techniques did the author use?

WRITING SUGGESTIONS

1. Write an essay describing how you have changed since starting college, if you have.

2. What is your reaction to arranged marriages? Do you believe it is possible to have a happy marriage without the consent of your immediate family. Write an essay detailing your explanation.

3. Do you believe that it is possible to have friends of the opposite sex when you are married? Why or why not?

4. Describe a significant event that happened during elementary school. Why was the event significant and how has it affected your life?

5. Interview your grandmother or grandfather and ask the person to tell you a story about your family. Write that story in an essay format.

6. Even in the twenty-first century, some societies chose to promote illiteracy among certain groups such as women in lower castes. Does this still happen in the United States?

IN-SIGHT

Tim Boyle/Getty.

Fast food has become a way of life for most Americans. In fact, some would describe fast food as a part of American culture.

1. Why do you think fast food has become so much a part of American culture?
2. How often do you eat fast food?
3. Are some types of fast food healthier choices than others? What types of fast food items would you consider unhealthy?

GROUP ACTIVITY

In groups of three or four, discuss whether you believe fast food companies should be held accountable if frequent patrons become ill from eating a steady diet of their products. Should fast food companies post warning labels explaining the dangers of eating certain types of foods too often? Decide on a response that all group members agree on and prepare an answer to share with the class.

PEER CRITIQUE

Your Name _____

The Author's Name_____

1. Read your partner's essay.

2. What is your immediate reaction to the essay? Did it interest you? In what way?

3. Is there an explicit thesis statement? If so, write it here. If it is not explicit, was it clear? If so, put it in your own words here.

4. Do the verb tenses follow an orderly pattern with the sequence of events (e.g., past, present, future tense)?

5. Did the writer use examples, stories, or other techniques to effectively uphold his or her thesis?

6. Is there sufficient description? Where might the writer add more?

7. Did you find any spelling or grammatical errors? If so, list them here:

MECHANICS AND GRAMMAR
Commonly Confused Words

We sometimes confuse certain words because some words sound alike but are spelled differently. It is difficult for a computer spell-checker to identify these problems because they are not spelling errors; they are misused words. For example, "aisle" in the following sentence is incorrect:

My wife lives on the lovely *aisle* of Manhattan.

The word needed above is "isle."

Below is a list of commonly confused words. Commit them to memory.

Word	Meaning	Example
a	An article used before consonant sounds	He had a student assist him.
an	An article used before vowel sounds	She ate an apple after class.
accept	To approve	I accept your money.
except	Excluding	She kept everything except her phone.
advice	Noun—a suggestion	Her advice was needed.
advise	Verb—to give a suggestion	She advised me of my rights.
affect	To influence or alter	The pills didn't affect her.
effect	A result	The effect was death.
aisle	The space between rows	The bride walked down the aisle.
isle	An island	The man lived alone on the isle.
already	Previously	I have already finished my homework.
all ready	Completely prepared	Tom is all ready for the exam.
brake	A device for stopping	My car's brakes are ruined.
break	To destroy	She breaks many men's hearts.
breath	An inhalation or exhalation	Her breath was short.
breathe	To inhale or exhale	She breathes deeply in Montana.

(continued)

Word	Meaning	Example *(continued)*
capital	A city recognized as the home of government	The capital of Hawaii is Honolulu.
capitol	The building where lawmakers meet	Governor Guinn makes frequent visits to the capitol building.
choose	To select	Please choose your dress.
chose	Past tense of choose	She chose her dress yesterday.
complement	To go well with	This cheese complements the meal.
compliment	To praise	We complimented his new suit.
coarse	Of inferior quality, rough	Her hands are coarse from field work.
course	A class of studies	A writing course is required here.
dessert	A sweet after a meal	We had shortcake for dessert.
desert	A dry geographical area	Nevada is largely a desert.
device	A mechanism	The device was not working.
devise	To arrange	She devised the plan.
good	An adjective	He is a good cook!
well	An adverb (usually)	She certainly cooks well.
immigrant	One entering	She is an immigrant to the United States.
emigrant	One exiting	She is an emigrant from Russia.
its	Possessive	The dog and its bone lay contentedly.
it's	Contraction for it is	It's just between us, okay?
later	Subsequently	I went to the party later than was customary.
latter	The last thing mentioned	Can we discuss the latter topic in detail?
lead	A metallic element	They used lead paint on those windows.
led	Past tense of lead	The teacher led us through the school.
loose	Not snug	Your pants are loose!
lose	To misplace; to fail to win	Did she lose her wallet?

(continued)

Word	Meaning	Example *(continued)*
passed	Past tense of pass	I passed her on the way to church.
past	Previous time	In the past, I owned a tape recorder.
principle	A basic truth	The principle of gravity makes us stable on Earth.
principal	Head of a school, or main	The principal is a lovely fellow. Her principal fear was loneliness.
quiet	Little or no sound	It was quiet on the streets of Manhattan.
quite	Very	She is quite nervous about the exam.
set	To put	She set the glasses on the table.
sit	To be seated (only people and animals)	We sit where we want to in class.
suppose	To assume or guess	We suppose that it is true.
supposed	Past tense of suppose	He supposed it happened on Monday.
than	As compared to	My sister is taller than my brother.
then	After	Let's eat! Then let's sleep!
their	Possessive of they	The players lost their last game.
there	Adverb indicating place	I may not go there yet.
they're	A contraction for they are	They're among friends in Holland.
through	In one side and out the other; finished; by means of	He walked through the screen door.
though	Although	Though he doesn't speak well, he speaks quickly.
to	A preposition	She went to the party.
too	Very or also	She is too fat for the party dress.
two	The number	She has two dresses to choose from.
weak	Not strong	He felt weak after his illness.
week	Seven days	The week is only seven days.

LOOK-ALIKES, SOUND-ALIKES

In each of the following paragraphs, cross out the incorrect word and place the correct word above it.

Exercise 1

Advertising is old: some advertisements on paper go back farther than two thousand years. In ancient Greece, it was quiet common to see signs advertising different kinds of services, but it was not until printing was invented that modern advertising was born. In Europe, in the seventeenth century, they use to place ads in newspapers; some of these ads were personnel messages, but most were for business. When many emigrants came to the United States, they used advertisements to get jobs; we can only imagine them going thorough each newspaper very carefully. Today, advertising is all around us, special on television. If we are not careful, we can loose our focus when we watch some programs. For example, when a flashy commercial interrupts a chef who is giving us a receipt for a complicated new dish, we are likely to remember the flashy commercial better then the chef's directions.

Exercise 2

One of the best ways to identify people is the use of fingerprints. Each set of fingers has it's unique pattern of ridges and designs. In the passed, this knowledge was not recognized as useful, but one hundred years ago, during the rein of Queen Victoria, an Englishman named Sir Edward Henry devised a hole system of identifying whose prints belong to whom. During the coarse of his investigation, he discovered that we really have two layers of skin, and where their joined, the upper layer of skin forms a number of ridges. These ridges are divided by type, into loops, double loops, and arches. Buy studying these different patterns,

we are able to match people with they're prints.

Exercise 3

Most of the following sentences contain sound-alike or other errors.
Some sentences are correct. If the sentence is correct, mark a C next to it. If it
is not correct, make the correction. A few sentences have more than one error.

1. My parents laid on the beach. _____

2. The carpenters raised the roof when they got to the house.
_____

3. My pencil is laying on the floor. _____

4. The sun rose at 5 a.m. this morning. _____

5. The candy was lose in the basket. _____

6. You must go to personnel to see about an increase in salary.
_____

7. Five is greater then four. _____

8. The heat had no effect on the whether. _____

9. What did you eat for desert in the dessert? _____

10. She is a very vain girl. _____

11. His waist is 30 inches. _____

12. Do you have the rite to vote in your state? _____

13. The car was stationery on the plain. _____

14. What is the capitol of Nevada? _____

15. I want to compliment you on your good taste. _____

16. The capital building in the capitol of Wyoming is lovely. _____

17. Jack ran past the barn. _____

18. Who's coat is that? _____

19. It's a wonderful life! _____

20. I excepted your advise for desert at the council meeting. _____

There are many types of heroes. Certainly September 11, 2001, made Americans conscious that we live in a great country with many heroes. Some heroes we encounter every day.

1. Where were you on 9/11?
2. How has 9/11 affected life in the United States?
3. Do you feel safe in your home? Why or why not?

PAIRED ACTIVITY

Working with one other student, create a complete extended definition of the term "hero." There is no wrong way to create this definition. Simply use your own experiences and examples of situations you are familiar with. Present your definition to the class.

PEER CRITIQUE

Your name_____

The author's name_____

1. Read your partner's essay.

2. What is your immediate reaction to the essay? Did you enjoy it? What did you like best about it?

3. Did it have a good title that grabbed your interest? Can you suggest an alternate title?

4. Is there an explicit thesis statement? If so, write it here. If it is not explicit, was it clear? If so, put it in your own words here.

5. Were there any commonly confused words that should be corrected?

6. Are any sentences worded in an imprecise or awkward manner? If so, write them here and correct them.

7. Were there any grammar or spelling errors? List them here.

MECHANICS AND GRAMMAR

Subject–Verb Agreement

A verb should agree with its subject in number and person. To make a verb agree with its subject, we need (1) to find the subject and (2) to discover whether the subject is singular or plural.

Examples:

The leaves _____ a valuable part of celery. (are, is)
The subject is leaves, and "are" is the correct verb because it is plural.

On Sundays, John and Susan _____ worship services. (attend, attends)
The subject is compound (John and Susan) so the verb is "attend."

There _____ many students in class today. (is, are)
The subject is students so the verb is "are."

Caution: Don't be fooled by a prepositional phrase between the subject and the verb. Find the subject and make the verb agree with it.

Example:

One of the boys (has, have) gone home.
"Of the boys" is a prepositional phrase, therefore "One" is the subject. The correct verb is "has."

Caution: Beware of words and phrases such as each, every, either, neither, anyone, anybody, everyone, everybody, someone, somebody, no one, nobody, one, many a, and a person. They are all singular.

Example:

Neither of the boys _____ going to come to the party. (is, are)
The correct answer is "is" as "Neither" is the subject of the sentence.

Exercise 1

There are errors in subject–verb agreement in the following paragraph. Make the corrections.

I belongs to a wonderful school drama club that puts on at least 10 pro-

ductions per school year. All pupils in my drama club has chosen the play *Cyrano de Bergerac* for the next production. There is actually two famous Cyrano de Bergeracs. One of them is the title character of the drama, and the other is the real person who had that name. Both of these men is famous for their large noses and for their writing. But only the fictional Cyrano loves Roxane. The tragic story of Cyrano and Roxane were written by Rostand. In it, Cyrano believe that Roxane could never love an ugly man. She thinks that she love Christian, Cyrano's fellow soldier who is extremely handsome. But she really love Cyrano, who writes all of the fine love letters that Christian gives Roxane. In those letters are the soul that Roxane admire, but she finds out too late. It's a very sad and dramatic story, and I hope that either my friend Cindy or I gets the part of Roxane.

Exercise 2

Again, there are errors in subject–verb agreement. Find and correct the errors.

Everyone in my art class are supposed to finish a painting per week. But each of us have a different way of starting. One of my classmates always starts by humming and rocking back and forth in front of her easel. Another one just put dots in the places where she want her figures and main characters to go. Velma, my best friend, likes to draw really light ovals wherever the faces will be. In the past, I have usually started by drawing a continuous line until it look like something. In other words, I let the drawing tell me what it wants. But Velma and my other classmates has taught me something. It help to have a plan; their drawings often turns out better than mine. Either they or I are right, but I don't know which it is yet.

6

POPULAR CULTURE

Some aspects of popular culture stay the same for many years while others change with the speed of technological advances. Today's Baby Boomers can remember a time when televisions had four channels, no remote controls, and only a handful of shows broadcast in color. Most mothers worked at home, and fathers carried the burden of earning enough money to support a family that often included a large number of children. Divorce was a rare occurrence. The roles of men and women were clearly defined, and fundamental American values included honesty, high moral standards, and a day's work for a day's pay.

Some of those standards still hold true today. Many Americans still consider themselves to be honest, hard-working individuals; however, although women used to work very hard-keeping house and caring for their husbands and families, today's women are more likely to be juggling marriage, child care, and a career. While many people still consider themselves to have high moral standards, underhanded corporate practices, violent crime stories, and sex as a commodity fill the hundreds of television channels now available in living color, at the touch of a remote control, in almost every living room in the United States. The divorce rate in our country, as well as in many industrialized countries, is very high.

Whether art imitates life, or life imitates art, popular culture is a reflection of society, for good or ill. The essays in this chapter are a reflection of society as well. Winn Miller describes ways in which television viewing habits could be a national addiction that undermines families. Pollitt looks at gender identity and ways in which the expectations of male and female children have remained the same while the world has changed. Sullivan questions the meaning of marriage in the twenty-first century. Ericsson examines the ways in which modern men and women tell acceptable lies. Netburn looks at unusual teenage behavior. Ogunnaike illustrates how a simple good-bye may be scrutinized in cyberspace.

1. Who was Andy Warhol?
2. Have you had your fifteen minutes of fame yet? Tell us about it.
3. Do you have a MySpace site? Describe the experience.

Andy Was Right

Josh Tyrangiel

Josh Tyrangiel is the editor of Time.com. In addition to writing and editing national and international cover stories, Tyrangiel was Time's music critic for five years. He has also worked at Vibe *and* Rolling Stone *magazines, produced the news at MTV, and received a master's degree in American Studies from Yale University.*

1   Nostradamus looked into the future and saw plagues, earthquakes, wars, floods and droughts. In the prediction game, this is known as covering your ass. In 1968 Andy Warhol was more precise. He squinted ahead and declared that "in the future, everyone will be world famous for 15 minutes." Warhol nailed it. Not only has his prophecy eclipsed his fame, but as a cultural observation, 15 minutes has had its 15 minutes.

2   We forget that it took a man at the nexus of art and self-promotion to figure out that as cameras shrank and screens multiplied, the barriers to fame would someday be eradicated. Call it Warhol's Theorem. Anyone who has uploaded a video to YouTube or posted a MySpace profile might be considered a child of Warhol—except that Warhol's vision of fame was very different from how he actually lived. "Oh, he was impossible," says Dr. Robert B. Millman, a psychiatrist and Warhol acquaintance who, not coincidentally, invented the term acquired situational narcissism. "When you were with him, you'd feel as if he didn't have the slightest interest in knowing you. All he wanted to know was what you thought of him—or *that* you thought of him."

3   From the son of an immigrant Czech coal miner in Pittsburgh, Pa., to the bleached dandy at the center of Studio 54's human carnival, Warhol willed himself into a celebrated object of others' imaginings—a blank slate on which culture writers, semioticians and hipsters projected themselves. It's not an accident that the Velvet Underground recorded *I'll Be Your Mirror* while he was their manager, or that his most famous self-portrait is of him putting his finger to his lips. As the art critic Harold Rosenberg put it, he was "the figure of the artist as nobody, though a nobody with a resounding signature."

4   There's something admirable and uniquely American in the act of self-creation—but it helps if you actually create something. In a conceptual artist, cultivating emptiness falls within the acceptable bounds of shtick. (Even Warhol's originals were reproductions.) But Warhol also put his blankness behind a series of conspicuous velvet ropes, turning a democratic notion—we're all stars, or at least we all could be—into something slightly toxic.

5   YouTube and MySpace and all the other Web 2.0 tools out there haven't eliminated exclusivity or narcissism. You've still got to think you're pretty damned interesting to post a video of yourself talking to a computer screen in your bedroom. But they have changed the way the fame game is played. A blank slate is not enough. To get fame—in the form of page views, comments and friend tags—you have to put yourself out there in a way that allows others to relate. "[YouTube] is narcissistic to the extent that you're thinking about yourself," says Millman. "But to get ahead, you need some empathy. It's weird, but it's a lot better to be famous this way than to covet the fame of others by reading *Us* magazine."

6   If Warhol were living in the Web 2.0 era, it would be interesting to see if he would use the medium as a chance to reveal something about himself or to obfuscate even more effectively. He'd probably do both—as lonelyboy15. But YouTube is Pop art in a form far closer to Warhol's original, uncorrupted vision than he could ever have imagined. And 15 minutes has been replaced by a new prophecy: "On the Web, everyone is famous to 15 people." Appropriately enough, many people share authorship of that one.

COMPREHENSION QUESTIONS

1. Was Andy right? Explain your answer.
2. Why do you think Andy Warhol made the statement "everyone will be world famous for 15 minutes"? Does everyone have 15 minutes of fame?

3. What is a conceptual artist?
4. How does YouTube and MySpace fit into the idea of conceptual art?
5. From the context clues, what is narcissism? Do you believe we have become more narcissistic since 1968? How?

QUESTIONS ON WRITING TECHNIQUE

1. Why does the author begin by discussing Nostradamus?
2. What is the article's thesis?
3. Is the thesis implied or explicit?
4. How is the article concluded? Is the conclusion effective?
5. Does the article entice you to know more about Andy Warhol?

1. How would you define marriage?
2. What are the characteristics of a good marriage?
3. Do you approve of gay marriage? Why or why not?
4. Do you believe gays face discrimination in today's society? How?

The "M Word": Why It Matters to Me

Andrew Sullivan

Andrew Sullivan, born in 1963 in South Godstone, England, is an author and political activist. He is HIV-positive, gay, a conservative, and a practicing Roman Catholic. The former editor of The New Republic *and the author of several books, he currently resides in Washington, D.C., and makes frequent television appearances on news and talk shows.*

1   What's in a name?

2   Perhaps the best answer is a memory.

3   As a child, I had no idea what homosexuality was. I grew up in a traditional home—Catholic, conservative, middle class. Life was relatively simple: education, work, family. I was brought up to aim high in life, even though my parents hadn't gone to college. But one thing was instilled in me. What matters is not how far you go in life, how much money you make, how big a name you make for yourself. What really matters is family, and the love you have for one another. The most important day of your life was not graduation from college or your first day at work or a raise or even your first house. The most important day of your life was when you got married. It was on that day that all your friends and all your family got together to celebrate the most important thing in life: your happiness, your ability to make a new home, to form a new but connected family, to find love that puts everything else into perspective.

4   But as I grew older, I found that this was somehow not available to me. I didn't feel the things for girls that my peers did. All the emotions and social rituals and bonding of teenage heterosexual life eluded me. I didn't know why. No one explained it. My emotional bonds to other boys were one-sided; each time I felt myself falling in love, they sensed it, pushed it away. I didn't and couldn't blame them. I got along fine with my buds in a non-emotional context; but something was awry, something not right. I came to know almost instinctively that I would never be a part of my family the way my siblings one day might be. The love I had inside me was unmentionable, anathema—even, in the words of the Church I attended every Sunday, evil. I remember writing in my teenage journal one day: "I'm a professional human being. But what do I do in my private life?"

5   So, like many gay men of my generation, I retreated. I never discussed my real life. I couldn't date girls and so immersed myself in school-work, in the debate team, school plays, anything to give me an excuse not to confront reality. When I looked toward the years ahead, I couldn't see a future. There was just a void. Was I going to be alone my whole life? Would I ever have a "most important day" in my life? It seemed impossible, a negation, an undoing. To be a full part of my family I had to somehow not be me. So like many gay teens, I withdrew, became neurotic, depressed, at times close to suicidal. I shut myself in my room with my books, night after night, while my peers developed the skills needed to form real relationships, and loves. In wounded pride, I even voiced a rejection of family and marriage. It was the only way I could explain my isolation.

6   It took years for me to realize that I was gay, years later to tell others, and more time yet to form any kind of stable emotional bond with another man. Because my sexuality had emerged in solitude—and without any link to the idea of an actual relationship—it was hard later to reconnect sex to love and self-esteem. It still is. But I persevered, each relationship slowly growing longer than the last, learning in my twenties and thirties what my straight friends found out in their teens. But even then, my parents and friends never asked the question they would have asked automatically if I were straight: so when are you going to get married? When is your relationship going to be public? When will we be able to celebrate it and affirm it and support it? In fact, no one—no one—has yet asked me that question.

7   When people talk about "gay marriage," they miss the point. This isn't about gay marriage. It's about marriage. It's about family. It's about love. It isn't about religion. It's about civil marriage licenses—available to atheists as well as believers. These family values are not options for a happy and stable

life. They are necessities. Putting gay relationships in some other category—civil unions, domestic partnerships, civil partnerships, whatever—may alleviate real human needs, but, by their very euphemism, by their very separateness, they actually build a wall between gay people and their own families. They put back the barrier many of us have spent a lifetime trying to erase.

8   It's too late for me to undo my own past. But I want above everything else to remember a young kid out there who may even be reading this now. I want to let him know that he doesn't have to choose between himself and his family any more. I want him to know that his love has dignity, that he does indeed have a future as a full and equal part of the human race. Only marriage will do that. Only marriage can bring him home.

COMPREHENSION QUESTIONS

1. According to Sullivan, why do people get married?
2. According to Sullivan, why do homosexual couples want to marry—what motivates them?
3. Do heterosexual couples marry for the same reasons as homosexual couples?
4. Why did Sullivan write this essay?
5. How do you think gay marriage will be handled in your state? How do you know?

QUESTIONS ON WRITING TECHNIQUE

1. What does Sullivan's title mean?
2. How does the title work with the essay's premise?
3. Why does he begin his essay with a question and an answer? What effect does this have on the reader?
4. Do media images of gay men and women portray couples who are looking for marriage? Give examples.
5. What is Sullivan's thesis?

PRE-READING QUESTIONS

1. How often do you send or receive e-mail? Do the e-mails look like formal letters, or are they more like encrypted messages without capital letters and lots of abbreviated words?
2. How might audience and purpose play a part in sending or receiving e-mail?
3. Have you ever been in a situation where you misinterpreted an e-mail, or someone else misinterpreted what you were trying to say in an e-mail?

'Yours Truly,' the E-Variations

Lola Ogunnaike

Lola Ogunnaike, who joined CNN in May 2007, reports on pop culture and entertainment news. She has also covered culture and entertainment for the New York Times, *the* New York Daily News, *and* Vibe *magazine. Her work has been published in* Rolling Stone, New York, Glamour, *the* New York Observer, *and* V Magazine. *Ogunnaike received a master's degree in journalism from New York University and a bachelor's degree in English literature from the University of Virginia.*

1   Chad Troutwine, an entrepreneur in Malibu, Calif., was negotiating a commercial lease earlier this year for a building he owns in the Midwest. Though talks began well, they soon grew rocky. The telltale sign that things had truly devolved? The sign-offs on the e-mail exchanges with his prospective tenant.

2   "As negotiations started to break down, the sign-offs started to get decidedly shorter and cooler," Mr. Troutwine recalled. "In the beginning it was like, 'I look forward to speaking with you soon' and 'Warmest regards,' and by the end it was just 'Best.' " The deal was eventually completed, but Mr. Troutwine still felt as if he had been snubbed.

3   What's in an e-mail sign-off? A lot, apparently. Those final few words above your name are where relationships and hierarchies are established, and where what is written in the body of the message can be clarified or undermined. In the days before electronic communication, the formalities of a letter, either business or personal, were taught to every third-grader; sign-offs—from "Sincerely" to "Yours truly" to "Love"—came to mind without much effort.

4   But e-mail is a casual medium, and its conventions are scarcely a decade old. They are still evolving, often awkwardly. It is common for business messages to appear entirely in lower case, and many rapid-fire correspondences evolve from formal to intimate in a few back-and-forths.

5   Although salutations that begin messages can be tricky—there is a world of difference, it seems, between a "Hi," a "Hello" and a "Dear"—the sign-off is the place where many writers attempt to express themselves, even when expressing personality, as in business correspondence, is not always welcome.

6   In other words, it is a land mine. Etiquette and communications experts agree that it is becoming increasingly difficult to say goodbye.

7   "So many people are not clear communicators," said Judith Kallos, creator of NetManners.com, a site dedicated to online etiquette, and author of *Because Netiquette Matters*. To be clear about what an e-mail message is trying to say, and about what is implied as well as what is stated, "the reader is left looking at everything from the greeting to the closing for clues," she said.

8   Mr. Troutwine is not alone in thinking that an e-mail sender who writes "Best," then a name, is offering something close to a brush-off. He said he chooses his own business sign-offs in a descending order of cordiality, from "Warmest regards" to "All the best" to a curt "Sincerely."

9   When Kim Bondy, a former CNN executive, e-mailed a suitor after a dinner date, she used one of her preferred closings: "Chat soon." It was her way of saying, "The date went well, let's do it again," she said.

10   She may have been the only one who thought that. The return message closed with the dreaded "Best." It left her feeling as though she had misread the evening. "I felt like, 'Oh, that's kind of formal. I don't think he liked me,'" she said, laughing. "A chill came with the 'Best.'" They have not gone out since.

11   "Best" does have its fans, especially in the workplace, where it can be an all-purpose step up in warmth from messages that end with no sign-off at all, just the sender coolly appending his or her name.

12   "I use 'Best' for all of my professional e-mails," said Kelly Brady, a perky publicist in New York. "It's friendly, quick and to the point."

13   Because people read so much into a sign-off, said Richard Kirshenbaum, chief creative officer of the advertising firm Kirshenbaum Bond and Partners, he has thought deeply about his preferred closing to professional correspondence, "Warmly, RK." He did not want something too emotional, like "Love," or too formal, like "Sincerely." "'Warmly' fell comfortably in between," he said. "I want to convey a sense of warmth and passion, but also be appropriate."

14   Which is just what a professional e-mail message should be, many executives say. Surprisingly, the sign-off "xoxo," offering hugs and kisses, has become common even for those in decidedly nonamorous relationships. Ms. Bondy, who received from 300 to 500 e-mail messages a day while at CNN, was no fan of the "xoxo" farewell, especially when it came from a stranger pitching a story idea. "They're trying to be warm and familiar when they shouldn't be," she said. "It's inappropriate, and that's probably the e-mail I'm not going to return."

15   Robert Verdi, a fashion stylist and a host of *Surprise by Design*, a makeover reality show on the Discovery Channel, is a self-described "xoxo offender." "Never in the first or second communication," he clarified. But after a few friendly phone conversations or e-mail exchanges, he feels comfortable with the affectionate and casual sign-off, though he generally waits for the other party to make the first move. "The other person gives you the cues," he said. "They send a 'You're the best! Love, Alison,' and you send a 'Hugs and kisses' and all of a sudden you're over that awkward hump and you're best friends."

16   Ms. Kallos said Mr. Verdi's approach is the correct one. "In business you want to maintain the highest level of formality until the other person indicates otherwise," she said. "Mirroring isn't a bad thing to do. You're letting the other side set the level of familiarity."

17   It is also important that the closing is in keeping with the spirit of the message or it may create some sort of cognitive dissonance, said Mary Mitchell, the author of *The Complete Idiot's Guide to Etiquette*. "If you're complaining to a company about a product and you sign off with 'Warmly,' you are miscommunicating," she said.

18   Many e-mail users don't bother with a sign-off, and Letitia Baldrige, the manners expert, finds that annoying. "It's so abrupt," she said, "and it's very unfriendly. We need grace in our lives, and I'm not talking about heavenly grace. I'm talking about human grace. We should try and be warm and friendly."

19   But it is important not to have too much fun with sign-offs, Ms. Baldrige cautioned, before recalling a closing from a man in his early 20s that read, "Don't let the bedbugs bite." It was "so pedestrian and boring and

such an unattractive image to leave with people," she said. "You want to leave an attractive warm image. Bedbugs are disgusting."

20   Not to mention they prove a point Ms. Mitchell makes about e-mail correspondence. "While on the one hand e-mail encourages people to write," she said, "on the other hand it discourages people to write thoughtfully."

COMPREHENSION QUESTIONS

1. According to Ogunnaike, what is in an e-mail sign-off?
2. Do you agree that how one signs off on an e-mail has significance? Explain your answer.
3. Why do you think Ogunnaike does not give the same amount of significance to the greeting in an e-mail? Are greetings important to consider as well? Why or why not?
4. How do you usually begin and end an e-mail? Or, if you do not e-mail, how might you begin and end a letter?
5. Why would some people not use any greetings or sign-offs in their e-mails?

QUESTIONS ON WRITING TECHNIQUE

1. Identify the thesis statement in this article. Does the author uphold the thesis statement? What kinds of evidence does she use?
2. Ogunnaike quotes the chief creative officer of an advertising firm. Why did she think he would be a good person to offer advice about e-mail communication? What others types of professionals did she consult? Did this make her case stronger? Explain your answer.
3. If you were asked to revise this article, what changes would you make? What information or evidence would you add from your own experiences or thoughts on the topic of e-mail etiquette?
4. How does Ogunnaike begin her article? Is this an effective way to draw in the reader? What are some other ways she might have begun her article?
5. This article ends very abruptly. Is this a good conclusion? How might it be improved, or does it work well the way it is? Explain your response.

PRE-READING QUESTIONS

1. Are tanning salons safer than prolonged exposure to natural sunlight?
2. Do you know many people who think it is important to always look
   as though they have a suntan?
3. Should teenagers be allowed to use tanning salons?

Young, Carefree and Hooked on Sunlamps

Deborah Netburn

Deborah Netburn is a writer and reporter living in Southern California. After graduating from Wesleyan University and interning at New York *magazine, she began her career at the* New York Observer, *where she covered a variety of subjects in and around Manhattan. Since moving to Los Angeles in 2003, she has written for the* Los Angeles Times, *the* New York Times, Los Ange- les *magazine, the* Telegraph Sunday Magazine, *and other publications. She currently works as an entertainment reporter for the* Los Angeles Times *web- site and writes style and culture stories about her beloved city of LA.*

1   She calls herself Miss Mary Sunshine. Not because she is a popular teenager, which she is, or because she can make a boy's day just by saying hello, which she can, but because of the maple-syrup hue of her skin. Whether she has just been to the Caribbean on a family vacation or has spent the last couple of months cooped up in her Upper East Side apartment with SAT tutors, Miss Mary Sunshine is never without a deep, dark tan.

2   "I don't like looking at myself when I'm not tan," she said. A student at the private Horace Mann School in the Bronx, she spoke on the condition that her name not be used because her mother believes her coppery skin tone comes from a bottle.

3   "My mother would kill me if she knew I went to a tanning salon. I know it's stupid," she said, alluding to the health dangers, "but I have become so accustomed to looking at myself when I'm tan. And it's not just me. When you walk into my school even in the dead of winter, it looks like it is St.-Tropez. Everybody is so tan. Even the guys are going tanning."

4   During the last few years, as dermatologists have sounded alarms about the spike in skin cancer rates, as women's magazines have hammered home the idea that the sun is little more than an aging-machine, and as cosmetic companies have packed sunscreen into everything from lip gloss to hair conditioner, increasing numbers of teenagers across America have been dedicating themselves to the pursuit of the perfect tan, sometimes obsessively.

5   "When you think of getting ready for a party, you think, 'I'll get my hair done, get a manicure and go tanning,'" the Horace Mann student said. "My friends and I call each other tanorexic. It's like you can't get tan enough."

6   According to surveys by the American Academy of Dermatology, 84.5 percent of people under 25 polled at the start of this year's peak tanning season said they look better with a tan, up from 61 percent in 1996. "Oh yeah, teenage tanning is back," said Atoosa Rubenstein, the editor in chief of *Cosmo Girl* magazine. "We're seeing the beginning of the trend now, and it's only going to get bigger."

7   Her explanation for the trend, which is echoed by dermatologists with adolescent patients, is this: the influence of bronzed pop stars like Britney Spears and Christina Aguilera, combined with a current wave of nut-brown fashion models who have supplanted pallid beauties of the 90's like Kate Moss and pop stars like Courtney Love.

8   "I'm definitely seeing more teenagers interested in a tan and being tan than I used to," said Dr. Darrell Rigel, a professor of dermatology at New York University, who warns them and everyone else of skin cancer dangers. "If you look at fashion magazines, from the mid-80's to the mid-90's, less tan people were fashionable. In the last few years, you see the tan look coming back. That's what's made the difference."

9   Dermatologists are alarmed that melanoma has become the most common cancer among people 25 to 29, according to American Cancer Society data. For young women 15 to 29, rates of melanoma, the most deadly form of skin cancer, have increased more than 60 percent since the mid-70's.

10   Although the tanning salon industry maintains that it offers a safe alternative to sun exposure, new research suggests that ultraviolet rays from sunlamps are just as harmful. One study published in April in the *Journal of the National Cancer Institute* suggested that users of tanning lamps were 2.5 times

more likely to develop squamous cell carcinoma and 1.5 times more likely to develop basal cell carcinoma—two less deadly forms of skin cancer—than people who did not use the lamps.

11   The study also indicated that the younger people were at the time of exposure, the greater the risk later on.

12   Such findings might be fodder for an after-school special about tanning risks, but they regularly fall on deaf ears at this moment when a tan abdomen—like hip-huggers and perfectly straight Jennifer Aniston hair— has become a staple of the teenage beauty regime.

13   Meghan Joss, an 11th grader from Agoura, Calif., a Los Angeles suburb, said she visits a tanning salon about once a week for half an hour, and especially before school dances and parties. "Tanning is really big out here because the whole blond tan look is really in," she said. "I'm not blond, but whatever. Maybe being a California girl it makes me feel healthier to have color."

14   Asked if she worried about skin cancer, Ms. Joss said: "I probably should be worried, but I'm not. I'm careful and I check any marks and go to a doctor if I need to, but tanning makes me happy."

15   A decade ago, dermatologists' warnings of the risks of skin cancer and premature aging seemed to have an effect, dampening interest in tanned skin among girls and young women. But now the old obsession is back with a vengeance.

16   Molly Nover, the beauty director of *Cosmo Girl*, which is aimed at teenagers, traced the obsession to a shift in fashion a few seasons ago. "It started in 2000," she said. "The models in the Channel and Valentino and Guess? ads that year were that savage tan. At the spring shows this year, they were putting shimmer creams on the models and mixing baby oil and bronzer."

17   Ms. Rubenstein emphasized the influences of pop stars as role models. "Britney and Christina are 90 percent responsible for this trend," she said. "Britney is really tan, and she dresses to accentuate that tan. She is No. 1 on every guy's list, and even if girls can't dance like her or don't have a body like hers, at least they can be as tan as she is."

18   When Ms. Aguilera was being shot for the cover of *Cosmo Girl*, Ms. Rubenstein said, her first mandate to the makeup artists was "Make me four shades darker."

19   Therapists who work with teenage girls see tanning as part of a larger trend of a growing adolescent obsession with looks.

20   "I work with a lot of adolescent girls and what I see is troubling," said Ann Kearney-Cook, the director of the Helping Girls Become Strong Women Project at Columbia University. "I feel like, 'Who am I?' has been

replaced by 'What image should I project?' and part of that image involves for many girls engaging in unhealthy behaviors: dieting, tanning, smoking to keep your weight down."

21   That many teenagers are aware that tanning can be harmful does not prevent them from doing it. Nor are they lured away from tanning beds or outdoor basking by the array of self-tanners now available. Many say the creams can't match the look of a salon or outdoor tan.

22   "We can never underestimate the importance that girls and women place on their looks and their appearance to the opposite sex," said Dr. Debbie Then, a psychologist who works with teenagers in Los Angeles and Northern California. "It is not that they are vain or conceited; they are realistic in the way they are reacting to societal pressures."

23   Dr. Mark Naylor, associate professor of dermatology at the University of Oklahoma Health Sciences Center, said: "This is a battle of attitudes. Pick up any fashion magazine and you'll see beautiful people with dark tans. Young girls look at them and try to emulate them because this is what is attractive to the opposite sex."

24   A sophomore at Briarcliff High School in Westchester County continues to visit a tanning salon at least twice a week despite the fact that her mother has had several operations for skin cancer.

25   "I know it will probably happen to me too," she said, giggling nervously. "But I feel like I look so bad unless I'm really tan."

26   Because there is virtually no way to ensure that America's adolescents are covered head to toe in S.P.F. 45 and wearing broad-rimmed hats outdoors, efforts to protect them from skin cancer have been directed primarily at the artificial tanning industry. The Food and Drug Administration requires that tanning beds carry a sticker describing a recommended schedule, based on skin type and tanning history. Twenty-seven states have regulations limiting teenagers' access to salons, including Ohio, Louisiana and California.

27   Texas passed a law last year requiring adolescents 13 to 15 to be escorted by a parent and those 16 to 17 to have a parent's written permission. But the $5 billion tanning salon industry often opposes the regulations. In April, Missouri legislators rejected a bill that would have required teenagers to have written parental consent to use tanning beds.

28   Joe Levy, a spokesman for the Indoor Tanning Association, a trade group in Jackson, Mich., that represents 11 percent of the 45,000 salons and other businesses with tanning beds nationwide, said it is standard procedure for salons to get parental consent for minors. (He said he did not lobby against the Missouri bill.)

29   Mr. Levy said that about 30 percent of salon customers were women 20 to 30, and about 5 percent were girls 16 to 20, based on a 1997 survey by his group. He maintained that the recent study published in the *Journal of the National Cancer Institute* linking tanning lamps to skin cancers was misleading. Many of the subjects, he said, "were people who were tanning before 1975, back when they were using home units which were dangerously high in UVB radiation."

30   But Dr. Shelley Sekula-Rodriguez, a dermatology professor at the Baylor College of Medicine in Houston, said a series of studies have concluded that indoor tanning may be just as harmful as outdoor exposure.

31   "Most salon bulbs provide a significant amount of UVB and UVA radiation," she said at a news conference in April. "Both types are also found in the outdoor sun and cause various types of damage to the skin that may lead to skin cancer and should be avoided."

32   In an interview, Dr. Sekula-Rodriguez said that peer pressure to be tan, for boys as well as girls, rises around prom time and weddings. "I see the young girls coming in dark, dark, dark whenever there's a big event," she said. "Girls feel that they look prettier tan. When more models were pale, it was wonderful."

33   Not all teenagers are convinced of the beauty of a coppery tan or deaf to doctors' warnings. Just as with smoking and drinking, peer pressure often wrestles in their psyches with an awareness of the dangers.

34   "I like tans; I know they are not great for you, but I think that most people look better tan," said Rachel Jay, 14, a freshman at Scarsdale High School in Scarsdale, N.Y. "But I'm in a weird position," she added, "because my dad's a dermatologist."

35   Kendall Swett, a sophomore at the Hawken School in Gates Mills, Ohio, said she visited a tanning salon four times, but then stopped. "It was horrible," she said. "All I could think about was how I was going to get covered in cancer."

36   Elizabeth Wolff, a senior at the Brearley School in New York, sometimes visits tanning salons with friends because she thinks it makes her look better. But she said it always makes her a little nervous. "I have never been able to last one session," she said. "I keep thinking that the timer has stopped, it is bright in there and then I always get out early. So it tends to be $17 for me to just be sitting there, freaking out."

COMPREHENSION QUESTIONS

1. Describe three of the characters in the essay.
2. What is the author's purpose?
3. Who goes to tanning salons?
4. What were the results of tanning studies in the article?
5. What are some of the costs of tanning?

QUESTIONS ON WRITING TECHNIQUE

1. What is the author's purpose?
2. How does the author make her point?
3. What is the most effective example in the essay?
4. How does the author conclude the essay?

PRE-READING QUESTIONS

1. How many hours of television do you watch each day?
2. Do you ever feel you should really be doing something else, but you continue to watch television anyway?
3. In your house, is watching television a family activity?

Family Life

Marie Winn Miller

Marie Winn Miller was born in Czechoslovakia and was brought by her family to New York as a child. She attended New York public schools and graduated from Radcliffe College and Columbia University. She has written for the New York Times Magazine *and the* New York Times Book Review, Parade, *the* Village Voice, *and other publications. The best known of her eleven books is* The Plug-in Drug: Television, Children, and the Family *(1977, revised and updated in 2002), which discusses the problems of child rearing occasioned by the constant presence of the television. In this chapter from that book, note that she has strong convictions, as the title indicates, and read critically, asking yourself questions about logic and evidence.*

1 Not much more than fifty years after the introduction of television into American society, the medium has become so deeply ingrained in daily life that in many states the TV set has attained the rank of a legal necessity, safe from repossession in case of debt along with clothes and cooking utensils. Only in the early years after television's introduction did writers and commentators have sufficient perspective to separate the activity of watching television from the actual content it offers the viewer. In those days writers frequently discussed the effects of television on family life. However, a curious myopia afflicted those first observers: almost without exception they regarded television as a favorable, beneficial, indeed, wondrous influence upon the family.

2   "Television is going to be a real asset in every home where there are children," predicted a writer in 1949.

3   "Television will take over your way of living and change your children's habits, but this change can be a wonderful improvement," claimed another commentator.

4   "No survey's needed, of course, to establish that television has brought the family together in one room," wrote the *New York Times*'s television critic in 1949.

5   The early articles about television were almost invariably accompanied by a photograph or illustration showing a family cozily sitting together before the television set, Sis on Mom's lap, Buddy perched on the arm of Dad's chair, Dad with his arm around Mom's shoulder. Who could have guessed that twenty or so years later Mom would be watching a drama in the kitchen, the kids would be looking at cartoons in their room, while Dad would be taking in the ball game in the living room?

6   Of course television sets were enormously expensive when they first came on the market. The idea that by the year 2000 more than three quarters of all American families would own two or more sets would have seemed preposterous. The splintering of the multiple-set family was something the early writers did not foresee. Nor did anyone imagine the number of hours children would eventually devote to television, the changes television would effect upon child-rearing methods, the increasing domination of family schedules by children's viewing requirements—in short, the power of television to dominate family life.

7   As children's consumption of the new medium increased together with parental concern about the possible effects of so much television viewing, a steady refrain helped soothe and reassure anxious parents. "Television always enters a pattern of influences that already exist: the home, the peer group, the school, the church and culture generally," wrote the authors of an early and influential study of television's effects on children. In other words, if the child's home life is all right, parents need not worry about the effects of too much television watching.

8   But television did not merely influence the child; it deeply influenced that "pattern of influences" everyone hoped would ameliorate the new medium's effects. Home and family life have changed in important ways since the advent of television. The peer group has become television-oriented, and much of the time children spend together is occupied by television viewing. Culture generally has been transformed by television. Participation in church and community activities has diminished, with

television a primary cause of this change. Therefore it is improper to assign to television the subsidiary role its many apologists insist it plays. Television is not merely one of a number of important influences upon today's child. Through the changes it has made in family life, television emerges as *the* important influence in children's lives today.

The Quality of Life

9   Television's contribution to family life has been an equivocal one. For while it has, indeed, kept the members of the family from dispersing, it has not served to bring them together. By its domination of the time families spend together, it destroys the special quality that distinguishes one family from another, a quality that depends to a great extent on what a family does, what special rituals, games, recurrent jokes, familiar songs, and shared activities it accumulates.

10   Yet parents have accepted a television-dominated family life so completely that they cannot see how the medium is involved in whatever problems they might be having. A first-grade teacher reports:

> I have one child in the group who's an only child. I wanted to find out more about her family life because this little girl was quite isolated from the group, didn't make friends, so I talked to her mother. Well, they don't have time to do anything in the evening, the mother said. The parents come home after picking up the child at the baby-sitter's. Then the mother fixes dinner while the child watches TV. Then they have dinner and the child goes to bed. I said to this mother, "Well, couldn't she help you fix dinner? That would be a nice time for the two of you to talk," and the mother said, "Oh, but I'd hate to have her miss *Zoom*. It's such a good program!"

11   Several decades ago a writer and mother of two boys aged three and seven described her family's television schedule in a newspaper article. Though some of the programs her kids watched then have changed, the situation she describes remains the same for great numbers of families today:

> We were in the midst of a full-scale War. Every day was a new battle and every program was a major skirmish. We agreed it was a bad scene all around and were ready to enter diplomatic negotiations. . . . In principle we have agreed on 2½ hours of TV a day; *Sesame Street*, *Electric Company* (with dinner gobbled up in between) and two half-hour shows between 7 and 8:30, which enables the grown-ups to eat

in peace and prevents the two boys from destroying one another. Their pre-bedtime choice is dreadful, because, as Josh recently admitted, "There's nothing much on I really like," So . . . it's *What's My Line* or *To Tell the Truth*. . . . Clearly there is a need for first-rate children's shows at this time . . .

12 Consider the "family life" described here: Presumably the father comes home from work during the *Sesame Street–Electric Company* stint. The children are either watching television, gobbling their dinner, or both. While the parents eat their dinner in peaceful privacy, the children watch another hour of television. Then there is only a half-hour left before bedtime, just enough time for baths, getting pajamas on, brushing teeth, and so on. The children's evening is regimented with an almost military precision. They watch their favorite programs, and when there is "nothing much on I really like," they watch whatever else is on—because *watching* is the important thing. Their mother does not see anything amiss with watching programs just for the sake of watching; she only wishes there were some first-rate children's shows on at those times.

13 Without conjuring up fantasies of bygone eras with family games and long, leisurely meals, the question arises: isn't there a better family life available than this dismal, mechanized arrangement of children watching television for however long is allowed them, evening after evening?

14 Of course, families today still do things together at times: go camping in the summer, go to the zoo on a nice Sunday, take various trips and expeditions. But their ordinary daily life together is diminished—those hours of sitting around at the dinner table, the spontaneous taking up of an activity, the little games invented by children on the spur of the moment when there is nothing else to do, the scribbling, the chatting, and even the quarreling, all the things that form the fabric of a family, that define a childhood. Instead, the children have their regular schedule of television programs and bedtime, and the parents have their peaceful dinner together.

15 The author of the quoted newspaper article notes that "keeping a family sane means mediating between the needs of both children and adults." But surely the needs of the adults in that family were being better met than the needs of the children. The kids were effectively shunted away and rendered untroublesome, while their parents enjoyed a life as undemanding as that of any childless couple. In reality, it is those very demands that young children make upon a family that lead to growth, and it is the way parents respond to those demands that builds the relationships upon which the

future of the family depends. If the family does not accumulate its backlog of shared experiences, shared everyday experiences that occur and recur and change and develop, then it is not likely to survive as anything other than a caretaking institution.

Family Rituals

16 Ritual is defined by sociologists as "that part of family life that the family likes about itself, is proud of and wants formally to continue." Another text notes that "the development of a ritual by a family is an index of the common interest of its members in the family as a group."

17   What has happened to family rituals, those regular, dependable, recurrent happenings that give members of a family a feeling of belonging to a home rather than living in it merely for the sake of convenience, those experiences that act as the adhesive of family unity far more than any material advantages?

18   Mealtime rituals, going-to-bed rituals, illness rituals, holiday rituals—how many of these have survived the inroads of the television set?

19   A young woman who grew up near Chicago reminisces about her childhood and gives an idea of the effects of television upon family rituals:

As a child I had millions of relatives around—my parents both come from relatively large families. My father had nine brothers and sisters. And so every holiday there was this great swoop-down of aunts, uncles, and millions of cousins. I just remember how wonderful it used to be. The cousins would come and everyone would play and ultimately, after dinner, all the women would be in the front of the house, drinking coffee and talking, all the men would be in the back of the house, drinking and smoking, and all the kids would be all over the place, playing hide and seek. Christmas time was particularly nice because everyone always brought all their toys and games. Our house had a couple of rooms with go-through closets, so there were always kids running in a great circle route. I remember it was just wonderful.

And then all of a sudden one year I remember becoming suddenly aware of how different everything had become. The kids were no longer playing Monopoly or Clue or the other games we used to play together. It was because we had a television set which had been turned on for a football game. All of that socializing that had gone on previously had ended. Now everyone was sitting in front of the television set, on a holiday, at a family party! I remember being stunned by how awful that was. Somehow the television had become more attractive.

20   As families have come to spend more and more of their time together engaged in the single activity of television watching, those rituals and pastimes that once gave family life its special quality have become more and more uncommon. Not since prehistoric times, when cave families hunted, gathered, ate, and slept, with little time remaining to accumulate a culture of any significance, have families been reduced to such a sameness.

Real People

21   The relationships of family members to each other are affected by television's powerful competition in both obvious and subtle ways. For surely the hours that children spend in a one-way relationship with television people, an involvement that allows for no communication or interaction, must have some effect on their relationships with real-life people.

22   Studies show the importance of eye-to-eye contact, for instance, in real-life relationships, and indicate that the nature of one's eye-contact patterns, whether one looks another squarely in the eye or looks to the side or shifts one's gaze from side to side, may play a significant role in one's success or failure in human relationships. But no eye contact is possible in the child-television relationship, although in certain children's programs people purport to speak directly to the child and the camera fosters this illusion by focusing directly upon the person being filmed. How might such a distortion affect a child's development of trust, of openness, of an ability to relate well to *real* people?

23   Bruno Bettelheim suggested an answer:
        Children who have been taught, or conditioned, to listen passively most of the day to the warm verbal communications coming from the TV screen, to the deep emotional appeal of the so-called TV personality, are often unable to respond to real persons because they arouse so much less feeling than the skilled actor. Worse, they lose the ability to learn from reality because life experiences are much more complicated than the ones they see on the screen.

24   A teacher makes a similar observation about her personal viewing experiences:
        I have trouble mobilizing myself and dealing with real people after watching a few hours of television. It's just hard to make that transition from watching television to a real relationship.

I suppose it's because there was no effort necessary while I was watching, and dealing with real people always requires a bit of effort. Imagine, then, how much harder it might be to do the same thing for a small child, particularly one who watches a lot of television every day.

25   But more obviously damaging to family relationships is the elimination of opportunities to talk and converse, or to argue, to air grievances between parents and children and brothers and sisters. Families frequently use television to avoid confronting their problems, problems that will not go away if they are ignored but will only fester and become less easily resolvable as time goes on.

26   A mother reports:

I find myself, with three children, wanting to turn on the TV set when they're fighting. I really have to struggle not to do it because I feel that's telling them this is the solution to the quarrel—but it's so tempting that I often do it.

27   A family therapist discusses the use of television as an avoidance mechanism:

In a family I know the father comes home from work and turns on the television set. The children come and watch with him and the wife serves them their meal in front of the set. He then goes and takes a shower, or works on the car or something. She then goes and has her own dinner in front of the television set. It's a symptom of a deeper-rooted problem, sure. But it would help them all to get rid of the set. It would be far easier to work on what the symptom really means without the television. The television simply encourages a double avoidance of each other. They'd find out more quickly what was going on if they weren't able to hide behind the TV. Things wouldn't necessarily be better, of course, but they wouldn't be anesthetized.

28   A number of research studies done when television was a relatively new medium demonstrated that television interfered with family activities and the formation of family relationships. One survey showed that 78 percent of the respondents indicated no conversation taking place during viewing except at specified times such as commercials. The study noted: "The television atmosphere in most households is one of quiet absorption on the part of family members who are present. The nature of the family social life during a program could be described as 'parallel' rather than interactive, and the set does seem to dominate family life when it is on." Thirty-six percent of

the respondents in another study indicated that television viewing was the only family activity participated in during the week.

29   The situation has only worsened during the intervening decades. When the studies were made, the great majority of American families had only one television set. Though the family may have spent more time watching TV in those early days, at least they were all together while they watched. Today the vast majority of all families have two or more sets, and nearly a third of all children live in homes with four or more TVs. The most telling statistic: almost 60 percent of all families watch television during meals, and not necessarily at the same TV set. When do they talk about what they did that day? When do they make plans, exchange views, share jokes, tell about their triumphs or little disasters? When do they get to be a real family?

Undermining the Family

30 Of course television has not been the only factor in the decline of family life in America. The steadily rising divorce rate, the increase in the number of working mothers, the trends towards people moving far away from home, the breakdown of neighborhoods and communities—all these have seriously affected the family.

31   Obviously the sources of family breakdown do not necessarily come from the family itself, but from the circumstances in which the family finds itself and the way of life imposed upon it by those circumstances. As Urie Bronfenbrenner has suggested:

> When those circumstances and the way of life they generate undermine relationships of trust and emotional security between family members, when they make it difficult for parents to care for, educate and enjoy their children, when there is no support or recognition from the outside world for one's role as a parent and when time spent with one's family means frustration of career, personal fulfillment and peace of mind, then the development of the child is adversely affected.

32   Certainly television is not the single destroyer of American family life. But the medium's dominant role in the family serves to anesthetize parents into accepting their family's diminished state and prevents them from struggling to regain some of the richness the family once possessed.

33   One research study alone seems to contradict the idea that television has a negative impact on family life. In their important book *Television and the Quality of Life*, sociologists Robert Kubey and Mihaly Csikszentmihalyi

observe that the heaviest viewers of TV among their subjects were "no less likely to spend time with their families" than the lightest viewers. Moreover, those heavy viewers reported feeling happier, more relaxed, and satisfied when watching TV with their families than light viewers did. Based on these reports, the researchers reached the conclusion that "television viewing harmonizes with family life."

34   Using the same data, however, the researchers made another observation about the heavy and light viewers: "families that spend substantial portions of their time together watching television are likely to experience greater percentages of their family time feeling relatively passive and unchallenged compared with families who spend small proportions of their time watching TV."

35   At first glance the two observations seem at odds: the heavier viewers feel happy and satisfied, yet their family time is more passive and unchallenging—less satisfying in reality. But when one considers the nature of the television experience, the contradiction vanishes. Surely it stands to reason that the television experience is instrumental in preventing viewers from recognizing its dulling effects, much as a mind-altering drug might do.

36   In spite of everything, the American family muddles on, dimly aware that something is amiss but distracted from an understanding of its plight by an endless stream of television images. As family ties grow weaker and vaguer, as children's lives become more separate from their parents', as parents' educational role in their children's lives is taken over by the media, the school, and the peer group, family life becomes increasingly more unsatisfying for both parents and children. All that seems to be left is love, an abstraction that family members know is necessary but find great difficulty giving to each other since the traditional opportunities for expressing it within the family have been reduced or eliminated.

COMPREHENSION QUESTIONS

1. In what ways could television be described as a "plug-in drug"?
2. In addiction situations, experts categorize a substance or activity as a problem when it affects work, home life, or relationships. Do you know anyone for whom television adversely affects those areas of that person's life?
3. What negative effects does Winn Miller believe television has on the typical American family?

4. According to the author how did early predictions about the effects of television on the American family differ from the reality of modern times?

5. List three specific examples that the author uses to make her thesis clear.

QUESTIONS ON WRITING TECHNIQUE

1. Who is the intended audience, and what is Winn Miller's purpose in writing this essay?

2. Is the thesis obvious, or is it implied? Find the thesis, or create one that would work well.

3. The author has made a possibly unpopular statement in saying that television is bad for families. How does she uphold that claim?

4. What flaws, if any, do you see in the author's argument?

5. Is the author's argument dated? Why or why not?

PRE-READING QUESTIONS

1. Do you know any little boys who play with dolls? How do you feel about little boys playing with dolls?
2. In today's society, many fathers equally share in child care with their wives, and many are even stay-at-home dads. Could a little boy who plays with a baby doll simply be imitating his caring father?
3. What comes to mind when you hear the word "feminism"? Does it hold positive or negative connotations for you? How does that connect with children's playthings?

Why Boys Don't Play with Dolls

Katha Pollitt

Katha Pollitt, a graduate of Radcliffe College, won the Mademoiselle *undergraduate poetry contest in 1971. She has taught in the graduate writing program at New York University and the graduate program in liberal studies at the New School for Social Research, and she has published hundreds of book reviews and essays, as well as poetry, in a variety of periodicals, including the* Atlantic Monthly, *the* New Yorker, Harper's, Mother Jones, *and* Dissent. *A popular lecturer on feminist issues, she has also written the books* Reasonable Creatures: Essays on Women and Feminism *(1994) and* Subject to Debate: Sense and Dissents on Women, Politics, and Culture *(2001).*

1 It's 28 years since the founding of NOW,* and boys still like trucks and girls still like dolls. Increasingly, we are told that the source of these robust preferences must lie outside society—in prenatal hormonal influences, brain chemistry, genes—and that feminism has reached its natural limits. What else could possibly explain the love of preschool girls for party dresses or the desire of toddler boys to own more guns than Mark from Michigan.

---

*EDS. NOTE—The National Organization for Women (NOW) was founded in 1966. Katha Pollitt, "Why Boys Don't Play with Dolls," *The New York Times Magazine,* October 8, 1995. Copyright © 1995, Katha Pollitt. Reprinted by permission.

2   True, recent studies claim to show small cognitive differences between the sexes: he gets around by orienting himself in space, she does it by remembering landmarks. Time will tell if any deserve the hoopla with which each is invariably greeted, over the protests of the researchers themselves. But even if the results hold up (and the history of such research is not encouraging), we don't need studies of sex-differentiated brain activity in reading, say, to understand why boys and girls still seem so unalike.

3   The feminist movement has done much for some women, and something for every woman, but it has hardly turned America into a playground free of sex roles. It hasn't even got women to stop dieting or men to stop interrupting them.

4   Instead of looking at kids to "prove" that differences in behavior by sex are innate, we can look at the ways we raise kids as an index to how unfinished the feminist revolution really is, and how tentatively it is embraced even by adults who fully expect their daughters to enter previously male-dominated professions and their sons to change diapers.

5   I'm at a children's birthday party. "I'm sorry," one mom silently mouths to the mother of the birthday girl, who has just torn open her present—Tropical Splash Barbie. Now, you can love Barbie or you can hate Barbie, and there are feminists in both camps. But *apologize* for Barbie? Inflict Barbie, against your own convictions, on the child of a friend you know will be none too pleased?

6   Every mother in that room had spent years becoming a person who had to be taken seriously, not least by herself. Even the most attractive, I'm willing to bet, had suffered over her body's failure to fit the impossible American ideal. Given all that, it seems crazy to transmit Barbie to the next generation. Yet to reject her is to say that what Barbie represents—being sexy, thin, stylish—is unimportant, which is obviously not true, and children know it's not true.

7   Women's looks matter terribly in this society, and so Barbie, however ambivalently, must be passed along. After all, there are worse toys. The Cut and Style Barbie styling head, for example, a grotesque object intended to encourage "hair play." The grown-ups who give that probably apologize, too.

8   How happy would most parents be to have a child who flouted sex conventions? I know a lot of women, feminists, who complain in a comical, eyeball-rolling way about their sons' passion for sports: the ruined weekends, obnoxious coaches, macho values. But they would not think of discouraging their sons from participating in this activity they find so foolish. Or do they? Their husbands are sports fans, too, and they like their husbands a lot.

9   Could it be that even sports-resistant moms see athletics as part of manliness? That if their sons wanted to spend the weekend writing up their diaries, or reading, or baking, they'd find it disturbing? Too antisocial? Too lonely? Too gay?

10   Theories of innate differences in behavior are appealing. They let parents off the hook—no small recommendation in a culture that holds moms, and sometimes even dads, responsible for their children's every misstep on the road to bliss and success.

11   They allow grown-ups to take the path of least resistance to the dominant culture, which always requires less psychic effort, even if it means more actual work: just ask the working mother who comes home exhausted and nonetheless finds it easier to pick up her son's socks than make him do it himself. They let families buy for their children, without too much guilt, the unbelievably sexist junk that the kids, who have been watching commercials since birth, understandably crave.

12   But the thing the theories do most of all is tell adults that the *adult* world—in which moms and dads still play by many of the old rules even as they question and fidget and chafe against them—is the way it's supposed to be. A girl with a doll and a boy with a truck "explain" why men are from Mars and women are from Venus, why wives do housework and husbands just don't understand.

13   The paradox is that the world of rigid and hierarchical sex roles evoked by determinist theories is already passing away. Three-year-olds may indeed insist that doctors are male and nurses female, even if their own mother is a physician. Six-year-olds know better. These days, something like half of all medical students are female, and male applications to nursing school are inching upward. When tomorrow's three-year-olds play doctor, who's to say how they'll assign the roles?

14   With sex roles, as in every area of life, people aspire to what is possible and conform to what is necessary. But these are not fixed, especially today. Biological determinism may reassure some adults about their present, but it is feminism, the ideology of flexible and converging sex roles, that fits our children's future. And the kids, somehow, know this.

15   That's why, if you look carefully, you'll find that for every kid who fits a stereotype, there's another who's breaking one down. Sometimes it's the same kid—the boy who skateboards *and* takes cooking in his after-school program; the girl who collects stuffed animals *and* A-pluses in science.

16   Feminists are often accused of imposing their "agenda" on children. Isn't that what adults always do, consciously or unconsciously? Kids aren't born

religious, or polite, or kind, or able to remember where they put their sneakers. Inculcating these behaviors, and the values behind them, is a tremendous amount of work, involving many adults. We don't have a choice, really, about *whether* we should give our children messages about what it means to be male and female—they're bombarded with them from morning till night.

17   The question, as always, is what do we want those messages to be?

COMPREHENSION QUESTIONS

1. In the United States, are there still roles that are set aside just for men and just for women? If so, what are they?
2. How are the differences in girls' and boys' toys a reflection of how girls and boys may be valued in society as adults?
3. What is the connection that Pollitt is trying to make between toys and feminism?
4. What is the connection that Pollitt makes between toys, attitudes toward child rearing, and the dominant culture?
5. Give three specific examples that Pollitt uses to make her point.

QUESTIONS ON WRITING TECHNIQUE

1. Examine Pollitt's introduction. Where does the introduction end and the body begin? What kind of information does Pollitt include in her introduction?
2. Pollitt seems to examine a lot of theories versus observational facts. What effect does this have on upholding Pollitt's thesis?
3. What effect does ending the essay with a question have? How might some people answer that question on a personal level?
4. Does Pollitt title her essay effectively?
5. What is Pollitt's most effective example and why?

The Ways We Lie

Stephanie Ericsson

Stephanie Ericsson grew up in San Francisco and began writing as a teenager. She has been a screenwriter and an advertising copywriter and has published several books based on her own life. Shamefaced: The Road to Recovery *and* Women of AA: Recovering Together *(both 1985) focus on her experiences with addiction;* Companion through the Darkness: Inner Dialogues on Grief *(1993) deals with the sudden death of her husband; and* Companion into the Dawn: Inner Dialogues on Loving *(1994) is a collection of essays.*

1   The bank called today and I told them my deposit was in the mail, even though I hadn't written a check yet. It'd been a rough day. The baby I'm pregnant with decided to do aerobics on my lungs for two hours, our three-year-old daughter painted the living-room couch with lipstick, the IRS put me on hold for an hour, and I was late to a business meeting because I was tired.

2   I told my client the traffic had been bad. When my partner came home, his haggard face told me his day hadn't gone any better than mine, so when he asked, "How was your day?" I said, "Oh, fine," knowing that one more straw might break his back. A friend called and wanted to take me to lunch. I said I was busy. Four lies in the course of a day, none of which I felt the least bit guilty about.

3   We lie. We all do. We exaggerate, we minimize, we avoid confrontation, we spare people's feelings, we conveniently forget, we keep secrets, we justify lying to the big-guy institutions. Like most people, I indulge in small

falsehoods and still think of myself as an honest person. Sure I lie, but it doesn't hurt anything. Or does it?

4   I once tried going a whole week without telling a lie, and it was paralyzing. I discovered that telling the truth all the time is nearly impossible. It means living with some serious consequences: the bank charges me $60 in overdraft fees, my partner keels over when I tell him about my travails, my client fires me for telling her I didn't feel like being on time, and my friend takes it personally when I say I'm not hungry. There must be some merit to lying.

5   But if I justify lying, what makes me any different from slick politicians or the corporate robbers who raided the S&L industry? Saying it's okay to lie one way and not another is hedging. I cannot seem to escape the voice deep inside that tells me: when someone lies, someone loses.

6   What far-reaching consequences will I, or others, pay as a result of my lie? Will someone's trust be destroyed? Will someone else pay *my* penance because I ducked out? We must consider the *meaning of our actions*. Deception, lies, capital crimes, and misdemeanors all carry meanings. *Webster's* definition of *lie* is specific:

> a false statement or action especially made with the intent to deceive; anything that gives or is meant to give a false impression.

7   A definition like this implies that there are many, many ways to tell a lie. Here are just a few.

The White Lie

> A man who won't lie to a woman has very little consideration for her feelings.
> —*BERGEN EVANS*

8   The white lie assumes that the truth will cause more damage than a simple, harmless untruth. Telling a friend he looks great when he looks like hell can be based on a decision that the friend needs a compliment more than a frank opinion. But, in effect, it is the liar deciding what is best for the lied to. Ultimately, it is a vote of no confidence. It is an act of subtle arrogance for anyone to decide what is best for someone else.

9   Yet not all circumstances are quite so cut-and-dried. Take, for instance, the sergeant in Vietnam who knew one of his men was killed in action but listed him as missing so that the man's family would receive indefinite

compensation instead of the lump-sum pittance the military gives widows and children. His intent was honorable. Yet for twenty years this family kept their hopes alive, unable to move on to a new life.

Facades

> Et tu, Brute?
> —CAESAR*

10 We all put up facades to one degree or another. When I put on a suit to go to see a client, I feel as though I am putting on another face, obeying the expectation that serious businesspeople wear suits rather than sweatpants. But I'm a writer. Normally, I get up, get the kid off to school, and sit at my computer in my pajamas until four in the afternoon. When I answer the phone, the caller thinks I'm wearing a suit (though the UPS man knows better).

11   But facades can be destructive because they are used to seduce others into an illusion. For instance, I recently realized that a former friend was a liar. He presented himself with all the right looks and the right words and offered lots of new consciousness theories, fabulous books to read, and fascinating insights. Then I did some business with him, and the time came for him to pay me. He turned out to be all talk and no walk. I heard a plethora of reasonable excuses, including in-depth descriptions of the big break around the corner. In six months of work, I saw less than a hundred bucks. When I confronted him, he raised both eyebrows and tried to convince me that I'd heard him wrong, that he'd made no commitment to me. A simple investigation into his past revealed a crowded graveyard of disenchanted former friends.

Ignoring the Plain Facts

> Well, you must understand that Father Porter is only human.
> —A MASSACHUSETTS PRIEST

12 In the '60s, the Catholic Church in Massachusetts began hearing complaints that Father James Porter was sexually molesting children. Rather than

---

*EDS. NOTE—"And you, Brutus?" (Latin). In Shakespeare's play *Julius Caesar*, Caesar asks this question when he sees Brutus, whom he has believed to be his friend, among the conspirators who are stabbing him.

relieving him of his duties, the ecclesiastical authorities simply moved him from one parish to another between 1960 and 1967, actually providing him with a fresh supply of unsuspecting families and innocent children to abuse. After treatment in 1967 for pedophilia, he went back to work, this time in Minnesota. The new diocese was aware of Father Porter's obsession with children, but they needed priests and recklessly believed treatment had cured him. More children were abused until he was relieved of his duties a year later. By his own admission, Porter may have abused as many as a hundred children.

13   Ignoring the facts may not in and of itself be a form of lying, but consider the context of this situation. If a lie is *a false action done with the intent to deceive*, then the Catholic Church's conscious covering for Porter created irreparable consequences. The church became a co-perpetrator with Porter.

Deflecting

> When you have no basis for an argument, abuse the plaintiff.
> —*CICERO*

14 I've discovered that I can keep anyone from seeing the true me by being selectively blatant. I set a precedent of being up-front about intimate issues, but I never bring up the things I truly want to hide; I just let people assume I'm revealing everything. It's an effective way of hiding.

15   Any good liar knows that the way to perpetuate an untruth is to deflect attention from it. When Clarence Thomas exploded with accusations that the Senate hearings were a "high-tech lynching," he simply switched the focus from a highly charged subject to a radioactive subject. Rather than defending himself, he took the offensive and accused the country of racism. It was a brilliant maneuver. Racism is now politically incorrect in official circles—unlike sexual harassment, which still rewards those who can get away with it.

16   Some of the most skillful deflectors are passive-aggressive people who, when accused of inappropriate behavior, refuse to respond to the accusations. This you-don't-exist stance infuriates the accuser, who, understandably, screams something obscene out of frustration. The trap is sprung and the act of deflection successful, because now the passive-aggressive person can indignantly say, "Who can talk to someone as unreasonable as you?" The real issue is forgotten and the sins of the original victim become the focus. Feeling guilty of name-calling, the victim is fully tamed and crawls into a hole, ashamed. I have watched this fighting technique work thousands of

times in disputes between men and women, and what I've learned is that the real culprit is not necessarily the one who swears the loudest.

OMISSION

The cruelest lies are often told in silence.
—*R. L. STEVENSON*

17 Omission involves telling most of the truth minus one or two key facts whose absence changes the story completely. You break a pair of glasses that are guaranteed under normal use and get a new pair, without mentioning that the first pair broke during a rowdy game of basketball. Who hasn't tried something like that? But what about omission of information that could make a difference in how a person lives his or her life?

18   For instance, one day I found out that rabbinical legends tell of another woman in the Garden of Eden before Eve. I was stunned. The omission of the Sumerian goddess Lilith from Genesis—as well as her demonization by ancient misogynists as an embodiment of female evil—felt like spiritual robbery. I felt like I'd just found out my mother was really my stepmother. To take seriously the tradition that Adam was created out of the same mud as his equal counterpart, Lilith, redefines all of Judeo-Christian history.

19   Some renegade Catholic feminists introduced me to a view of Lilith that had been suppressed during the many centuries when this strong goddess was seen only as a spirit of evil. Lilith was a proud goddess who defied Adam's need to control her, attempted negotiations, and when this failed, said adios and left the Garden of Eden.

20   This omission of Lilith from the Bible was a patriarchal strategy to keep women weak. Omitting the strong-woman archetype of Lilith from Western religions and starting the story with Eve the Rib has helped keep Christian and Jewish women believing they were the lesser sex for thousands of years.

Stereotypes and Clichés

Where opinion does not exist, the status quo becomes stereotyped and all originality is discouraged.
—*BERTRAND RUSSELL*

21   Stereotype and cliché serve a purpose as a form of shorthand. Our need for vast amounts of information in nanoseconds has made the stereotype

vital to modern communication. Unfortunately, it often shuts down original thinking, giving those hungry for the truth a candy bar of misinformation instead of a balanced meal. The stereotype explains a situation with just enough truth to seem unquestionable.

22   All the "isms"—racism, sexism, ageism, et al.—are founded on and fueled by the stereotype and the cliché, which are lies of exaggeration, omission, and ignorance. They are always dangerous. They take a single tree and make it a landscape. They destroy curiosity. They close minds and separate people. The single mother on welfare is assumed to be cheating. Any black male could tell you how much of his identity is obliterated daily by stereotypes. Fat people, ugly people, beautiful people, old people, large-breasted women, short men, the mentally ill, and the homeless all could tell you how much more they are like us than we want to think. I once admitted to a group of people that I had a mouth like a truck driver. Much to my surprise, a man stood up and said, "I'm a truck driver, and I never cuss." Needless to say, I was humbled.

Groupthink

Who is more foolish, the child afraid of the dark, or the man afraid of the light?
—*MAURICE FREEHILL*

23   Irving Janis, in *Victims of Group Think*, defines this sort of lie as a psychological phenomenon within decision-making groups in which loyalty to the group has become more important than any other value, with the result that dissent and the appraisal of alternatives are suppressed. If you've ever worked on a committee or in a corporation, you've encountered groupthink. It requires a combination of other forms of lying—ignoring facts, selective memory, omission, and denial, to name a few.

24   The textbook example of groupthink came on December 7, 1941. From as early as the fall of 1941, the warnings came in, one after another, that Japan was preparing for a massive military operation. The Navy command in Hawaii assumed Pearl Harbor was invulnerable—the Japanese weren't stupid enough to attack the United States' most important base. On the other hand, racist stereotypes said the Japanese weren't smart enough to invent a torpedo effective in less than 60 feet of water (the fleet was docked in 30 feet); after all, U.S. technology hadn't been able to do it.

25   On Friday, December 5, normal weekend leave was granted to all the commanders at Pearl Harbor, even though the Japanese consulate in Hawaii

was busy burning papers. Within the tight, good-ole-boy cohesiveness of the U.S. command in Hawaii, the myth of invulnerability stayed well entrenched. No one in the group considered the alternatives. The rest is history.

Out-and-Out Lies

> The only form of lying that is beyond reproach is lying for its own sake.
> —OSCAR WILDE

26 Of all the ways to lie, I like this one the best, probably because I get tired of trying to figure out the real meanings behind things. At least I can trust the bald-faced lie. I once asked my five-year-old nephew, "Who broke the fence?" (I had seen him do it.) He answered, "The murderers." Who could argue?

27   At least when this sort of lie is told it can be easily confronted. As the person who is lied to, I know where I stand. The bald-faced lie doesn't toy with my perceptions—it argues with them. It doesn't try to refashion reality, it tries to refute it. *Read my lips.* . . . No sleight of hand. No guessing. If this were the only form of lying, there would be no such thing as floating anxiety or the adult-children of alcoholics movement.

Dismissal

> Pay no attention to that man behind the curtain! I am the Great Oz!
> —THE WIZARD OF OZ

28 Dismissal is perhaps the slipperiest of all lies. Dismissing feelings, perceptions, or even the raw facts of a situation ranks as a kind of lie that can do as much damage to a person as any other kind of lie.

29   The roots of many mental disorders can be traced back to the dismissal of reality. Imagine that a person is told from the time she is a tot that her perceptions are inaccurate. "*Mommy, I'm scared.*" "No, you're not, darling." "*I don't like that man next door, he makes me feel icky.*" "Johnny, that's a terrible thing to say, of course you like him. You go over there right now and be nice to him."

30   I've often mused over the idea that madness is actually a sane reaction to an insane world. Psychologist R. D. Laing supports this hypothesis in *Sanity, Madness and the Family*, an account of his investigations into families of schizophrenics. The common thread that ran through all of the

families he studied was a deliberate, staunch dismissal of the patient's perceptions from a very early age. Each of the patients started out with an accurate grasp of reality, which, through meticulous and methodical dismissal, was demolished until the only reality the patient could trust was catatonia.

31   Dismissal runs the gamut. Mild dismissal can be quite handy for forgiving the foibles of others in our day-to-day lives. Toddlers who have just learned to manipulate their parents' attention sometimes are dismissed out of necessity. Absolute attention from the parents would require so much energy that no one would get to eat dinner. But we must be careful and attentive about how far we take our "necessary" dismissals. Dismissal is a dangerous tool, because it's nothing less than a lie.

Delusion

> We lie loudest when we lie to ourselves.
> —*ERIC HOFFER*

32 I could write the book on this one. Delusion, a cousin of dismissal, is the tendency to see excuses as facts. It's a powerful lying tool because it filters out information that contradicts what we want to believe. Alcoholics who believe that the problems in their lives are legitimate reasons for drinking rather than results of the drinking offer the classic example of deluded thinking. Delusion uses the mind's ability to see things in myriad ways to support what it wants to be the truth.

33   But delusion is also a survival mechanism we all use. If we were to fully contemplate the consequences of our stockpiles of nuclear weapons or global warming, we could hardly function on a day-to-day level. We don't want to incorporate that much reality into our lives because to do so would be paralyzing.

34   Delusion acts as an adhesive to keep the status quo intact. It shamelessly employs dismissal, omission, and amnesia, among other sorts of lies. Its most cunning defense is that it cannot see itself.

> The liar's punishment . . . is that he cannot believe anyone else.
> —*GEORGE BERNARD SHAW*

35   These are only a few of the ways we lie. Or are lied to. As I said earlier, it's not easy to entirely eliminate lies from our lives. No matter how pious we may try to be, we will still embellish, hedge, and omit to lubricate the daily machinery of living. But there is a world of difference between telling

functional lies and living a lie. Martin Buber* once said, "The lie is the spirit committing treason against itself." Our acceptance of lies becomes a cultural cancer that eventually shrouds and reorders reality until moral garbage becomes as invisible to us as water is to a fish.

36   How much do we tolerate before we become sick and tired of being sick and tired? When will we stand up and declare our *right* to trust? When do we stop accepting that the real truth is in the fine print? Whose lips do we read this year when we vote for president? When will we stop being so reticent about making judgments? When do we stop turning over our personal power and responsibility to liars?

37   Maybe if I don't tell the bank the check's in the mail I'll be less tolerant of the lies told me every day. A country song I once heard said it all for me: "You've got to stand for something or you'll fall for anything."

COMPREHENSION QUESTIONS

1. Is Ericsson saying that we cannot effectively survive in today's society unless we lie? Do you agree or disagree with that theory?
2. What are the pros and cons of the different types of lies Ericsson describes?
3. Which kinds of lies seem dangerous as opposed to some that may be seen as kind?
4. Do you agree or disagree with all of the definitions Ericsson gives for each kind of lie? Which definition (find at least one) do you disagree with the most? Why? How would you change it?
5. Do you think that Ericsson is justifying lying?

QUESTIONS ON WRITING TECHNIQUE

1. What is Ericsson's claim or thesis?
2. Ericsson mentions religion in many of her examples. What effect might this have on the reader?
3. What is a rhetorical question? Ericsson uses this technique a lot in her essay. What effect does this have on the reader?
4. How does the author conclude the essay?
5. Is the conclusion effective? Why or why not?

---

*EDS. NOTE—Austrian-born Judaic philosopher (1878–1965).

WRITING SUGGESTIONS

1. Write an essay that agrees or disagrees with Marie Winn Miller's argument in "Family Life."

2. Watch a favorite television sitcom or drama and pay attention to the number of lies the characters tell in the course of the show. Write a short synopsis of the episode and describe each of the lies that you noticed.

3. In your opinion, and according to your own personal definition of feminism, how has feminism helped or hurt our society over the past thirty years.

4 Define popular culture and the ways in which U.S. citizens are affected by it. Does popular culture dictate attitudes and behavior, or do attitudes and behavior dictate popular culture?

5. Choose a topic related to popular culture. Make a claim and support it in an essay with an introduction that includes a thesis, a body that supports the thesis, and a conclusion that sums up the essay and shows how you upheld your thesis.

6. Write an extended obituary that projects how you think your life will have been lived.

PRE-READING QUESTIONS

1. What part does social networking play in your life
2. Is it a good idea for children to participate in social networking?
3. What changes do you predict in the future for social networking?

Social Networking Benefits Validated

Karen Goldberg Goff

Karen Goldberg Goff lives and works in the Washington D.C. area as an editor and writer for The Washington Times. *She graduated from Ohio State University and also does freelance writing. Her other areas of expertise include social media for marketing and business, public relations, and media relations.*

1   Texting, blogs, Facebook, gaming and instant messages might seem, to some, to be just more reasons to stare at a computer screen.

2   Thinking like that is so 2008, any middle schooler will tell you. Now a study that looked at the online habits of 800 teenagers backs them up.

3   Researchers in the study, titled the Digital Youth Project and conducted primarily at the University of Southern California and the University of California at Berkeley, found that in our increasingly technological world, the constant communication that social networking provides is encouraging useful skills. The study looked at more than 5,000 hours of online observation and found that the digital world is creating new opportunities for young people to grapple with social norms, explore interests, develop technical skills and work on new forms of self-expression.

4   "There are myths about kids spending time online—that it is dangerous or making them lazy," says Mizuko Ito, lead author of the study, which will be the basis of a forthcoming book, *Hanging Out, Messing Around, Geeking Out: Living and Learning with New Media.* "But we found that spend-

ing time online is essential for young people to pick up the social and technical skills they need to be competent citizens in the digital age."

5   Co-author Lisa Tripp, now an assistant professor at Florida State University, says technology, including YouTube, iPods and podcasting, creates avenues for extending one's circle of friends, boosts self-directed learning and fosters independence.

6   "Certain technical skills in the coming years are not going to be just about consuming media," she says. "It is also going to be about producing media. It is not just about writing a blog, but also how to leave comments that say something. Learning to communicate like this is contributing to the general circulation of culture."

7   That means anything from a video clip to a profile page is going to reflect the self-expression skills one has, so teens might as well practice what will say who they are.

8   Social networking also contributes greatly to teens' extended friendships and interests, Ms. Tripp says. While the majority of teens use sites such as MySpace and Facebook to "hang out" with people they already know in real life, a smaller portion uses them to find like-minded people. Before social networking, the one kid in school who was, say, a fan of Godzilla or progressive politics might find himself isolated. These days, that youngster has peers everywhere.

9   "This kind of communication has let teens expand their social circle by common interests," Ms. Tripp says. "They can publicize and distribute their work to online audiences and become sort of a microexpert in that area." The study found that young people's learning with digital media often is more self-directed, with a freedom and autonomy that is less apparent than in a classroom. The researchers said youths usually respect one another's authority online, and they often are more motivated to learn from one another than from adults.

10   Parents, however, still have an important role to play when it comes to tweens, teens and social networking, the researchers say. They need to accept that technology is a necessary and important part of the culture for young people and, other experts say, be aware of with whom the teens are communicating.

11   Monica Vila, founder of theonlinemom.com, an online resource for digital-age parenting, says parents need to set parameters just as they would "at any other playground." This kind of study puts a lot of facts behind the value of social networking," Ms. Vila says.

12   It is up to parents to monitor what is being expressed, she says. She recommends that parents "have a presence" in their child's online social network. That doesn't necessarily mean "friending," communicating and

commenting, but it does mean having a password or knowing who your child's online friends are. One Fairfax County mother of a middle schooler, who asked that her name not be used to protect her daughter's privacy, says she was skeptical at first when her daughter wanted a Facebook page.

13   "I was hesitant for all the reasons we hear about, such as how it could bring in unwelcome visitors," the woman says, "but eventually I realized that this is the main medium for kids keeping in touch. It has gone from e-mail to IM to texting to Facebook in such a quick progression. [Social networking] is like the modern-day equivalent of the lunch table. If you are not on Facebook, then you are not in the loop."

14   The woman says she stays in the loop because she knows her daughter's password, and her daughter knows her mom can access her page whenever she wants—and can see who is there and what they are posting.

15   A few rules: no putting your exact whereabouts on your status update, and be aware of who is tagging you in a photo because if that photo contains unflattering behavior, it could come back to haunt you. Also, the mom has a Facebook page of her own, although she is not yet among her daughter's 100-plus friends.

16   "I have become accepting that there are more positives than negatives from social networking," the woman says, noting that she is pleased to see the connection of her daughter's network through various circles such as school and sports. "It is allowing a lot of dialogue among people who may not otherwise have a chance for a lot of dialogue." Those are all good rules and observations, Ms. Vila says.

17   "I like to catch parents before this whole process starts," she says. "That way you can set the ground rules early and [not] be trying to catch up. If your kids know that you have a presence in their online community, you are acting like a chaperone. If they won't friend you, you should at least have their password."

18   "It is not that kids are untrustworthy," Ms. Vila says. "It is that they often lack processing skills. Parents need to explain that images may be damaging. They may not be able to think past the next day, let alone what will happen when they are looking for a job six years later." Studies such as the Digital Youth Project and the report "Enhancing Child Safety and Online Technologies," issued recently by Harvard University's Berkman Center for Internet and Society, show that social networking has earned a place in American culture from which there is no turning back, Ms. Vila says.

19   "A few years ago, parents were saying, 'I don't want any of that stuff coming into my house,' even about video games," she says. "Then they realized, 'I have no choice, it is all around me.' Now studies are saying technology is going to encourage skills for jobs we didn't know existed. At the very least, social networking is encouraging technology skills, and that is going to be essential to the digital economy." *To read the full report from the Digital Youth Project, visit http://digitalyouth.ischool.berkeley.edu/report.*

COMPREHENSION QUESTIONS

1. What is social networking as it is defined in this essay?
2. Identify the data used to back up the results of the university study examined in this essay.
3. Describe two ways that the author claims that social networking is beneficial for young people.
4. Explain the rules that Goff claims will safeguard children.
5. In what ways do benefits outweigh the dangers in social networking according to Goff?

QUESTIONS ON WRITING TECHNIQUE

1. What kind of background information does the author provide before making her argument?
2. Does this background information create a stronger argument than it would have been without its use?
3. Is Goff's use of personal examples effective? If so, how? If not, why not?
4. How would you describe the audience and purpose for this essay? Who was she writing it to and why?
5. If you were to propose a counter-argument to the benefits of social networking, what would it be?

IN-SIGHT

Ewing Galloway/Jupiter.

Television was very popular in the 1950s in America. It remains popular today. In the early years of television, families were presented as nearly perfect groups of individuals. Americans tried to mirror these television images but often fell short.

1. How has television changed in your lifetime?

2. Are families in television series still presented as nearly perfect units? Give examples to support your statement.

3. Do you believe that television has a responsibility to be more than just entertainment? Why or why not?

GROUP ACTIVITY

In a small group, discuss television programs of the last forty years. Remember that many older television shows are now available on cable stations. Starting with the 1970s, each group member should list his or her favorite television shows for each decade. Once all of the lists are finished, cross reference them and look for similarities and patterns among your group's members. Come up with reasons why certain television shows appealed to many types of individuals.

PEER CRITIQUE

Your Name _____

The Author's Name _____

1. Read your partner's essay.

2. What is your immediate reaction to the essay? Was it clear? Passionate? Organized?

3. Who did you think the author's audience is?

4. Is there an explicit thesis statement? If so, write it here. If it is not explicit, was it clear? If so, put it in your own words here.

5. What was the purpose for the essay—to inform, to entertain, or to persuade? Give reasons for your answers.

6. Did the author use consistent subject–verb agreement? If not, list faulty examples here.

7. Whether you agree with the author's viewpoint, was this an effective essay? Why or why not?

8. How did the author conclude the essay? Was the conclusion effective? Why or why not?

9. What other suggestions do you have for this author?

MECHANICS AND GRAMMAR
Spelling

English is a language in which many irregular spellings of words occur. We have borrowed words from other languages and occasionally do not change them to sound or even appear as if they belong in our language. The burden falls on us, as writers, to become excellent spellers. The best way to learn spelling is through reading and recognition. The more we read, the more comfortable we are with words in English both in their meanings and in their spelling.

If you are not a good speller, you will need to proofread your essays several times before turning them in as a final draft. You will need a good dictionary and thesaurus to assist you in this process. Also, it would be helpful if you kept a list of words that you constantly misspell and make an effort to learn the correct spelling. Remember that the spell-check software on your computer will only tell you if you have misspelled a word, not if a word is unwisely or erroneously used.

The first step in improving your spelling is to take an inventory of your own spelling errors. Keep a record of the words that you misspell in your writing. Even the poorest speller can correct 90 percent of his or her spelling errors by concentrating on a carefully selected list of words that were misspelled.

It is nearly impossible for someone to learn all of the rules of spelling in the English language. The time would be wisely spent reading. However, it may be helpful to learn a few of the common rules, then proceed from there.

Rule Number 1: The Silent Final *e*

If a word ends in a silent *e* (as in give), drop the *e* before adding any ending that begins with a vowel. Keep the final *e* before endings that begin with a consonant.

> Example: rate + ing = rating
>
> rate + ed = rated

Rule Number 2: The Use of *ei* and *ie*

When *ie* and *ei* have the long *e* sound (as in greet), use *i* before *e* except after *c*. Otherwise use *ei*.

> Example: believe, cashier, ceiling, conceit, freight, sleigh

Rule Number 3: Doubling the Final Consonant

If a word of one syllable ends with a single consonant preceded by a single vowel (as in bit), double the final consonant before adding a suffix beginning with a vowel. If the word has more than one syllable, the emphasis should be on the final syllable.

Single syllable	Multisyllable
fit + ing = fitting	permit + ing = permitting
jam + ed = jammed	begin + er = beginner

Rule Number 4: The Final *y*

When a word ends with *y* preceded by a consonant, change the *y* to *i* when adding a suffix or plural ending, except those beginning with an *i*. When a word ends with *y* preceded by a vowel, do not change the *y*.

Consonant + y	Vowel + y
thirty + eth = thirtieth	key + s = keys
baby + es = babies	attorney + s = attorneys

Rule Number 5: The Plural *es*

Most singular nouns ending in -s, -ss, -sh, -ch, -x, or –z form their plurals by adding *es*.

> Examples: ash–ashes; match–matches; fox–foxes; buzz–buzzes

Exercise

The following paragraph contains common spelling errors. Find and correct the misspellings.

Last Feburary, we tried to acommodate the kindergarden class's teacher, Mrs. Kimbal, with a new play area. Uhfortunatly, the budget did not allow for such an expantion. The secretery for the school was mischievious and decided to funnel some funds to the class, however, and the play area came to fruition. The new play area was noticable to the outside and eventuelly the mistake was discovered. Despite the secretery's couragous action, she was fired and transfered to another district of the communitie. The fourteen children in the class were overjoyed by there new play area and are now surounded by plants and trees when they play.

7

THE CALL
OF THE WILD

In some parts of the United States, going outdoors means walking down busy sidewalks, sitting in traffic on the freeway, or finding a tree to ponder in a nearby park. For a great many Americans, the Great Outdoors is a mystical place that can only be enjoyed during vacation time, and even then, only after a great deal of planning. Some people don't really like the idea of being out in the wilds of nature at all and prefer to remain encased within the concrete and glass of the city.

Fortunately, there are still some wide-open spaces that as yet have not been zoned for a planned community or a mini-mall. And whether you are a couch potato who prefers to view nature boxed up on the living-room television set, or whether you prefer to experience nature firsthand from time to time or throughout each and every day, the Great Outdoors is a treasure that deserves our protection, understanding, and reverence.

This chapter looks at nature from several points of view. Blake takes the reader into the jungle to ponder the wonders of wildlife, predators, and prey. In quite a different twist, Frost's "The Road Not Taken" uses nature as a metaphor for life's journey. Martin describes the adventure of a little bird that takes on a big job. Adler looks at animal self-awareness and how we see ourselves. French examines how the seasons may affect us. Frazier explains the danger in believing everything you hear about spending time in the Great Outdoors, except things one might hear about a guy named Killer.

PRE-READING QUESTIONS

1. The poem "The Tyger" by William Blake was written in 1794. What do you think of when you think of a tiger?
2. Have you ever seen a tiger in a zoo or some other controlled environment? How did you feel looking at it?
3. How have tigers been depicted in movies or on television?

The Tyger

William Blake

William Blake (1757–1827) was born in London and from childhood claimed he saw visions: angels in a tree and the prophet Ezekiel in a field. When his brother Robert fell ill and died in 1787, Blake said that he had seen Robert's soul rising through the ceiling and that Robert had revealed to him a new method of engraving books. Blake used the technique given him in his vision to engrave his own poems and illustrations together on copper plates from which his books were printed. Considered one of the greatest poets ever to write in English, Blake produced a number of works in which religious feeling, sensuality, imagination, and technical brilliance were expressed in words and pictures. Two of his most famous works are Songs of Innocence, *produced in 1789, and* Songs of Experience, *printed in a double collection with* Songs of Innocence *in 1794. Blake wanted the collection to show "the two contrary states of the human soul." Blake depicted the innocent child's soul, which simply grows, in contrast with the experienced adult's soul, which is repressed by law and morality. In the following poem, written in 1794, innocence is represented by the lamb while experience is represented by the strong, cruel tyger.*

Tyger, Tyger, burning bright
In the forests of the night,
What immortal hand or eye
Could frame thy fearful symmetry?

In what distant deeps or skies
Burnt the fire of thine eyes?
On what wings dare he aspire?
What the hand dare seize the fire?

And what shoulder and what art
Could twist the sinews of thy heart?
And, when thy heart began to beat,
What dread hand and what dread feet?

What the hammer? What the chain?
In what furnace was thy brain?
What the anvil? What dread grasp
Dare its deadly terror clasp?

When the stars threw down their spears,
And watered heaven with their tears,
Did he smile his work to see?
Did he who made the Lamb make thee?

Tyger, Tyger, burning bright
In the forests of the night,
What immortal hand or eye
Dare frame thy fearful symmetry?

COMPREHENSION QUESTIONS

1. There are a lot of questions in this poem. What is the author trying to find out?
2. Poems are often open to the interpretation of the reader. What did you "see" while reading this poem? Why might your inner vision be different from that of others?
3. What do you think Blake meant by the phrase "Tyger, Tyger, burning bright"? How is the tiger burning?
4. What do you think Blake meant by the phrase "frame thy fearful symmetry"? What does symmetry mean?
5. If a tiger eats a lamb, is the tiger evil? Why or why not? What if a tiger eats a person?

QUESTIONS ON WRITING TECHNIQUE

1. Blake describes the creator of the tiger as some sort of blacksmith. Why do you think he did that?
2. What comparison is made in the poem? Why do you think Blake chose that particular comparison?
3. Many of the lines in Blake's poem are in the form of questions. Why do you think he chose to ask questions instead of make statements?
4. If Blake had written statements instead of questions, what might some of those statements be?
5. What is the thesis statement of this essay?

PRE-READING QUESTIONS

1 Do you think one person can really make a difference?
2 What are some examples of people who made a difference?
3 What other titles does "The Brave Little Parrot" remind you of? Based on the title, what do you think "The Brave Little Parrot" will be about?

The Brave Little Parrot

Rafe Martin

Rafe Martin is an award-winning author and story-teller. He has been featured at many of the most prestigious story-telling events around the country and has performed as far away as Japan. His work has received several Parents Choice Gold Awards, several ALA Noble Book Awards, the IRA Teachers Choice Awards, the Golden Sower Award, the Georgia State Picture Award, and many others. He is often featured in Time, Newsweek, *and* USA Today.

1 Once a little parrot lived happily in a beautiful forest. But one day without warning, lightning flashed, thunder crashed, and a dead tree burst into flames. Sparks, carried on the rising wind, began to leap from branch to branch and tree to tree.

2 The little parrot smelled the smoke. "Fire!" she cried. "Run to the river!" Flapping her wings, rising higher and higher, she flew toward the safety of the river's far shore. After all, she was a bird and could fly away.

3 But as she flew, she could see that many animals were already surrounded by the flames and could not escape. Suddenly a desperate idea, a way to save them, came to her.

4 Darting to the river, she dipped herself in the water. Then she flew back over the now-raging fire. Thick smoke coiled up, filling the sky. Walls of flame shot up, now on one side, now on the other. Pillars of fire leapt before her. Twisting and turning through a mad maze of flame, the little parrot flew bravely on.

5   Having reached the heart of the burning forest, the little parrot shook her wings. And the few tiny drops of water that still clung to her feathers tumbled like jewels down into the flames and vanished with a hiss.

6   Then the little parrot flew back through the flames and smoke to the river. Once more she dipped herself in the cool water and flew back over the burning forest. Once more she shook her wings, and a few drops of water tumbled like jewels into the flames. *Hisssss.*

7   Back and forth she flew, time and time again from the river to the forest, from the forest to the river. Her feathers became charred. Her feet and claws were scorched. Her lungs ached. Her eyes burned. Her mind spun as dizzily as a spinning spark. Still the little parrot flew on.

8   At that moment some of the blissful gods floating overhead in their cloud palaces of ivory and gold happened to look down and see the little parrot flying among the flames. They pointed at her with their perfect hands. Between mouthfuls of honied foods, they exclaimed, "Look at that foolish bird! She's trying to put out a raging forest fire with a few sprinkles of water! How absurd!" They laughed.

9   But one of those gods, strangely moved, changed himself into a golden eagle and flew down, down toward the little parrot's fiery path.

10   The little parrot was just nearing the flames again, when a great eagle with eyes like molten gold appeared at her side. "Go back, little bird!" said the eagle in a solemn and majestic voice. "Your task is hopeless. A few drops of water can't put out a forest fire. Cease now, and save yourself before it is too late."

11   But the little parrot continued to fly on through the smoke and flames. She could hear the great eagle flying above her as the heat grew fiercer. He called out, "Stop, foolish little parrot! Stop! Save yourself!"

12   "I didn't need some great, shining eagle," coughed the little parrot, "to tell me that. My own mother, the dear bird, could have told me the same thing long ago. Advice! I don't need advice. I just"—cough, cough—"need someone to help!"

13   Rising higher, the eagle, who was a god, watched the little parrot flying through the flames. High above he could see his own kind, those carefree gods, still laughing and talking even as many animals cried out in pain and fear far below. He grew ashamed of the gods' carefree life, and a single desire was kindled in his heart.

14   "God though I am," he exclaimed, "how I wish I could be just like that little parrot. Flying on, brave and alone, risking all to help—what a rare and marvelous thing! What a wonderful little bird!"

15   Moved by these new feelings, the great eagle began to weep. Stream after stream of sparkling tears began pouring from his eyes. Wave upon wave they

fell, washing down like a torrent of rain upon the fire, upon the forest, upon the animals and the little parrot herself.

16   Where those cooling tears fell, the flames shrank down and died. Smoke still curled up from the scorched earth, yet new life was already boldly pushing forth—shoots, stems, blossoms, and leaves. Green grass sprang up from among the still-glowing cinders.

17   Where the eagle's teardrops sparkled on the little parrot's wings, new feathers now grew: red feathers, green feathers, yellow feathers too. Such bright colors! Such a pretty bird!

18   The animals looked at one another in amazement. They were whole and well. Not one had been harmed. Up above in the clear blue sky they could see their brave friend, the little parrot, looping and soaring in delight. When all hope was gone, somehow she had saved them.

19   "Hurray!" they cried. "Hurray for the brave little parrot and for this sudden, miraculous rain!"

COMPREHENSION QUESTIONS

1. What was the little parrot trying to accomplish? Why do you think the parrot continued to try to put out the fire even though she could only bring drops at a time?
2. Why did the god turn into an eagle? What do you think the outcome to the story would have been if the eagle/god had not started to cry?
3. In the end, the little parrot got most of the credit for saving the forest. Was she being given false praise?
4. If this story had a moral or message, what would it be?
5. Can you think of any true-life situations that might in some ways be similar to this story?

QUESTIONS ON WRITING TECHNIQUE

1. What is the tone of the story—happy, sad, sarcastic, hopeful?
2. What is the purpose of the story? What message is the author trying to generate?
3. The tears of the eagle ultimately put out the fire. What might the tears of the eagle represent?
4. What might the thunder, lightning, and fire represent in the real world?
5. Do you think the parrot is used as a symbol? If so, of what?

PRE-READING QUESTIONS

1. Can you pass a mirror without looking at yourself?
2. Are we a vain society? How?
3. Can an animal be vain?

Vanity, Thy Name Is...

Jerry Adler

Jerry Adler was promoted to senior editor of Newsweek *in January 1993 after serving as general editor and senior writer. In his career at* Newsweek, *he has covered a wide range of subjects, including stress, political correctness, America's infatuation with self-esteem, the heroes of September 11, and the blackout of 2003.*

1   What does an animal see in a mirror? Until 1970, the accepted answer was "another animal": a stranger to be greeted, threatened, courted—or ignored. In that year, psychologist Gordon Gallup Jr. came up with the idea of giving a chimpanzee a mirror and painting a mark on his face while he slept. With one small gesture—reaching to touch the mark on his own face when he awakened—the chimp touched off a revolution not only in psychology, but philosophy as well. He saw himself.

2   It was a minor revolution at first, because only chimps and other closely related primates passed the "mirror test." Then, in 2001, Diana Reiss of the New York Aquarium showed that bottlenose dolphins marked with dye recognized their reflections. Last week, Reiss, Joshua Plotkin and Frans de Waal of Emory University announced that Happy, a 34-year-old Asian elephant at the Bronx Zoo, had shown the same ability. (Two other elephants who live there also took the mirror test; they flunked.) "The mirror test asks something quite hard," says Patricia Churchland, a professor of philosophy at the University of California at San Diego. "The animal has to say, 'I'm here, that is a perfect replica of me, but it isn't me'." The experiment appears to measure something more, or different, than what we usually mean by

"animal intelligence," which we tend to define in practical terms. Animals are "smart" if they can communicate or use tools to get food. But recognizing one's reflection has no obvious survival value; it's a kind of intellectual luxury that until recently only human beings were believed to enjoy.

3   In fact, this ability might not even be confined to mammals. Many researchers think the next breakthrough in animal intelligence will be among smart, social birds such as crows, ravens and parrots. African gray parrots may be among the smartest animals on earth. Irene Pepperberg of Brandeis University has been training one for nearly three decades and reporting her results in peer-reviewed journals. According to Pepperberg, Alex has a vocabulary of 50 to 100 words that he combines spontaneously to answer questions or make requests; he names colors and shapes, counts objects up to at least five and can do simple addition. Confronted with a tray of scattered blocks and balls of different colors, he can answer a question like "How many green blocks?" After that he usually asks for a nut, but often lets the nut drop; he seems to perform to please his trainers. Or perhaps to annoy them. When he wants to go back to his cage, Pepperberg says, he will sometimes give every possible answer to a question except the right one.

4   Intuitively, Alex seems to possess self-awareness, but he's never had the mirror test. He can't, because a student once took him with her to the restroom, and when Alex saw himself in the mirror, he squawked "What's that?" "It's you," the student replied, fatally contaminating any possible future results from the test. Pepperberg did try the mirror test on another of her parrots, but the results were "equivocal," she says; he scratched at a red mark for nine seconds, couldn't get it to go away, and then ignored it. In the wild, she notes, parrots are frequently covered with glop from their meals, so it's possible they're just not programmed to care about a spot on their faces.

5   That speaks to the practical difficulties in animal research, but also a conceptual one, says Colin Allen, a professor of philosophy at Indiana University. He sees a danger that the mirror experiment could become a kind of pass/fail exam for species. Self-awareness, he says, "is not a simple trait; animals will have it in various degrees and different kinds, not all lined up in a single continuum."

6   So the simple answer is, we don't know what an animal sees in the mirror. Not even Alex, wonderful as he is, has words for "think" and "feel." But dolphins, elephants and human beings all have large brains, a complex social structure and a capacity for altruism toward members of the same social group. Is it just a coincidence that they pass the mirror test? Or does empathy, which implies an awareness of the state of other individuals, depend on

a measure of self-consciousness? "This research," says Reiss, "links us to the rest of the natural world. It shows there are other minds around us." Think about that the next time you look in the mirror.

COMPREHENSION QUESTIONS

1. How have scientific perceptions changed of what animals see in a mirror?
2. What proof has backed up these findings?
3. How has the mirror test affected scientific research?
4. What are some practical difficulties in animal research?
5. What is the answer to the author's question: what does an animal see in a mirror?

QUESTIONS ON WRITING TECHNIQUE

1. What is the author's purpose?
2. How does the author use the introduction to draw the reader in and create interest in the essay? Is this effective?
3. Why does the author go from discussing elephants to discussing parrots?
4. How does the story of Alex add to the effectiveness of the essay?
5. Ultimately, the author answers his initial question with more questions. Why?

PRE-READING QUESTIONS

1. How do you view choices you make in your life—with excitement or confusion?
2. Do you enjoy poetry? Do you have a favorite poet?
3. Have you ever had to make an important decision that would affect the rest of your life?

The Road Not Taken

Robert Frost

Robert Frost is often considered the greatest American poet. Although born in San Francisco, he frequently drew inspiration from rural life in New England, using the setting to explore complex social and philosophical themes. A popular and often-quoted poet, Frost was highly honored during his lifetime, receiving four Pulitzer Prizes. Upon his death in Boston in 1963, Frost was buried in the Old Bennington Cemetery in Bennington, Vermont. During his lifetime, the Robert Frost Middle School in Fairfax, Virginia, as well as the main library of Amherst College were named after him. Frost's choice of familiar topics, his use of natural settings, and his use of common language appeal to a wide audience. In this poem he effectively expresses a dilemma felt by most of us at some point in our lives.

Two roads diverged in a yellow wood,
And sorry I could not travel both
And be one traveler, long I stood
And looked down one as far as I could
To where it bent in the undergrowth;

Then took the other, as just as fair,
And having perhaps the better claim,
Because it was grassy and wanted wear;
Though as for that the passing there
Had worn them really about the same,

And both that morning equally lay
In leaves no step had trodden black.
Oh, I kept the first for another day!
Yet knowing how way leads on to way,
I doubted if I should ever come back.

I shall be telling this with a sigh
Somewhere ages and ages hence:
Two roads diverged in a wood, and I—
I took the one less traveled by,
And that has made all the difference.

COMPREHENSION QUESTIONS

1. Describe both of the roads the author finds.
2. Which road does the author choose?
3. Which road would you choose? Why?
4. What is the decision that the speaker must make? Is he happy about it?
5. What does the speaker mean when he says "the road less traveled by"?

QUESTIONS ON WRITING TECHNIQUE

1. What is a symbol in literature?
2. How is the image of a fork in the road symbolic? What is it symbolic of?
3. What mood is established in the first few lines of the poem?
4. How does the first line of the last stanza change the mood?
5. Why has this poem endured?

PRE-READING QUESTIONS

1. Do you feel different in the winter and summer due to the climate?
2. Are you happy in your current climate? What would you change?
3. What is your favorite month of the year? Why?

To Everything There Is a Season

Jeanie French

Jeanie French teaches writing, literature, and creative writing at the College of Southern Nevada in Las Vegas, and she is the poetry editor for the Red Rock Review. *She has also taught creative writing to inmates in the California prison system. Her essays, fiction, and poetry have appeared in books, regional newspapers, and in online and print literary journals. Her current collection of poems, Paean, is published by Finishing Line Press.*

Nature's first green is gold
Her hardest hue to hold.
Her early leaf's a flower;
But only so an hour.

Then leaf subsides to leaf.
So Eden sank to grief,
So dawn goes down to day.
Nothing gold can stay.

—*Robert Frost*

1 As summer's golden sunshine gives way to autumn hues, soon to be followed by winter's monochromatic shades, I'm reminded of Frost's poem. The oaks and aspens near my home have darkened from shades of gold and orange to a sere brown. Leaves have begun to fall, lying in drifts on the forest floor. Many

Jeanie French, "To Everything There Is a Season." This essay was first published in *Red Rock Reader*, 3rd edition. Pearson Education, 2005. Reprinted by permission of the author. "Nothing Gold Can Stay" from *The Poetry of Robert Frost* edited by Edward Connery Lathem. Copyright 1923, 1969 by Henry Holt and Company. Copyright 1951 by Robert Frost. Reprinted by permission of Henry Holt and Company, LLC.

of the songbirds which inhabit the high desert country east of California's northern Sierra Nevada have migrated out before the coming of winter. These are the times when I wish I too could sprout wings and fly south to brighter and warmer climes.

2   In the summer, when the sun comes up at four-thirty in the morning and the sky is completely light by five, I wake at first light to birdsong— loud and vivid calls of jays and flycatchers, robins and chickadees. I am filled with energy, ready to leap up and start my day with writing, gardening, or whatever household chore is on the agenda for the day. I have energy to burn, and it propels me through a sixteen-hour, activity-filled day with ease. It is a different story in the fall.

3   In September, the sun rises later in the morning—at about 6:30. My abundance of energy begins to wane. As the days shorten, I find it difficult to rise in the dark at six a.m. and prepare to teach my eight o'clock class. I am slow to wake—the alarm jerks me from sleep with pounding heart and a rush of startle-induced adrenaline, but my eyes are heavy and my body drags; my mind is less alert than it should be when facing a class full of college freshmen resistant to learning anything about writing. By twelve o'clock, my body insists on a nap so that I can face my evening classes, which begin at six o'clock— after dark has fallen—and end at nine. By eight, nap or no, I am dragging once more struggling to make it through to the end of class. And this sluggishness only becomes more pronounced as autumn wears into winter. What has happened to the body which breezed through a sixteen-hour summer day?

4   The problem, when severe, is called Seasonal Affective Disorder (SAD). The symptoms are depression, loss of energy, increased need for sleep and difficulty getting up in the morning, difficulty doing tasks that are normally easy, increased appetite and carbohydrate cravings often accompanied by weight gain, a desire to avoid people, irritability and crying spells, decreased sex drive, suicidal thoughts or feelings.

5   This disorder has been around a long time—people used to call it "winter blues." Researchers believe that the areas in our brains which control our moods and biological rhythms are affected by the amount of light that enters our eyes. One theory is that the reduced light levels of winter cause the brain to produce lower levels of serotonin, a neurotransmitter which carries signals from nerve ending to nerve ending inside the brain. Reduced serotonin levels can result in depression, and depression can cause folks to have difficulty performing accustomed tasks. It seems clear that there is a connection between lower natural light levels and the symptoms of Seasonal Affective Disorder. The longer, darker, and colder the winter, the more severe the

symptoms may become. Like every other problem in life, stress aggravates the condition. SAD may affect as many as 11 million people in the U.S., and more than twice as many others may suffer from a milder form of the "winter blues." Four times more women than men are affected by SAD.

6   It was this last fact that made me begin to question the label. It occurred to me that the "disorder" is not actually a disorder at all, but a kind of order that makes perfect sense when looked at from a natural perspective. Many mammals experience a reduction in metabolism in the wintertime called "hibernation" or "winter sleep." During the darkest, coldest months of the year, these mammals—bears come immediately to mind—drowse away periods of severe weather, living on their fat layers. Food would be impossible to find during these periods, and animals would waste energy looking for it. Winter sleep is a natural, healthy, protective reaction of the animal body to a reduction of stimuli, primarily light and warmth. I began to think about how we have created a "disorder" out of a natural, biological process.

7   The "disordering" of SAD occurs because modern life requires us to punch a time clock at eight o'clock in the morning, regardless of when *daytime* actually begins. We force our bodies into artificial patterns in wintertime, using artificial lights to extend our "days" on both ends, when the natural pattern for many mammals is a reduction of activity in extended periods of colder, shorter days. Our modern lifestyles have us working contrary to our internal, biological clocks.

8   Our present custom of switching back and forth from Standard to Daylight Savings Time exacerbates the problem. Some relief occurs in October when Daylight Standard Time allows us to rise an hour later. But while Daylight Standard Time gives us daylight an hour "earlier" in the winter, midday occurs at about 10:30 a.m., with full dark falling at five o'clock in the afternoon. Rather than ending our day at dark, as the natural pattern would indicate, most of us are still up at eleven o'clock at night, watching the evening news, even though we will be rising in the dark for work the next "day"—and most likely this will be before *day* actually begins. In the spring, when we switch to Savings Time, 6 a.m. is actually 5 a.m., and once again we are rising in the dark for several months until the sun moves farther north of the equator and daylight hours begin to increase.

9   Why do more women than men suffer from Seasonal Affective Disorder? The answer is actually very simple, I think. Because of their reproductive systems, women are often more aware of their bodies than men are. They have to be. Women must track and understand their cycles of menstruation, fertility, pregnancy, lactation, and menopause. It is vital for

a woman's health that she be in tune with her body's cycles. Because of this, women are more prone to SAD than are men, because they are more aware of their bodies' responses to natural cycles and stimuli, or, in this case, the lack of light stimuli.

10   What are those of us to do who suffer from the symptoms of SAD? Obviously, those who experience severe depression or suicidal thoughts should seek the help of a professional therapist. But for those of us who simply find it difficult to function in the wintertime and don't have the luxury of hibernating the season away, there are some self-help solutions. Some of these tips were gleaned from *The Medical Advisor: The Complete Guide to Alternative and Conventional Treatments* published by TimeLife Books; others were compiled from various Internet sources.

- Exercise to keep your body's metabolism high and reduce winter slow-down.

- Get out into natural light at midday once a day, if possible. Take a walk on your lunch break when the sun is highest in the sky and natural light is strongest. One study of SAD showed that walking for an hour outside, even in winter sunlight, was as effective as more than twice as much time spent under strong, artificial lights.

- Install stronger lights in your home; at least 2500 lux (five times brighter than the average office) is needed according to some sources, and brighter is supposed to be better. Some people have reported good results with plant lights which simulate full spectrum daylight. One sufferer recommends putting plant lights in the bathroom, where you can get the benefit of light that mimics natural daylight while you're getting ready for work in the morning. (Remember, however, that plant lights do emit ultraviolet light rays.)

- Consider installing a lamp in your bedroom with a dimmer switch on a timer, so that the light comes on automatically and gradually brightens with the "dawn effect." Dawn simulation has been reported to be effective even at low light levels. (An added benefit might be that you'll be able to get rid of your noisy, heart-stopping alarm because you will wake up naturally and gradually as the light increases.)

- Increase natural light in your home by pruning trees and bushes away from your windows. When you're home, open the drapes to natural light. You can install sheers if you have nosy neighbors.

- Do whatever is possible to reflect the light that enters your home. Paint the walls light colors in glossy or semi-gloss paint, which reflects rather than absorbs light. Decorate with mirrors and other reflective materials to magnify the effects of natural light.

- Stay warm. Warmth gives the illusion of light.
- Concentrate on pleasurable activities and avoid stress as much as possible. Learn to say "no" when necessary to reduce stress.
- Balance carbohydrates and proteins in your diet if you want to avoid putting on that extra layer of winter fat.
- Take winter vacations in warm, sunny climates, and if you are suffering severe symptoms, consider moving south!

11   One other piece of advice from a fellow sufferer. Stop looking at the problem as a disorder, and start seeing it as part of a natural process that has gone just a bit awry. There is no need to compound the problem with the guilt and shame that so many of us feel when faced with something that has been labeled as a disorder. Being aware of our bodies is a good thing, and, ultimately, it is the thing that will allow us to cope with the "winter blues."

COMPREHENSION QUESTIONS

1. What is SAD?
2. Why are women more often affected with SAD than men?
3. What treatments are available for SAD? Name three.
4. According to French, is SAD actually a disorder?
5. What is another term for SAD?

QUESTIONS ON WRITING TECHNIQUE

1. Why does French include Frost's poem at the beginning?
2. Where does French get her information?
3. What is French's thesis?
4. French uses personal experience to begin her essay. What effect does this have on her audience?
5. How does French conclude her essay? Is the conclusion effective?

PRE-READING QUESTIONS

1. From the title, what do you think this essay will be about?
2. Have you ever been given advice that turned out to be completely wrong?
3. Have you ever given out advice or information that you were not really sure about?

Trust Me. In These Parts, Hot Dogs Actually Repel Bears

Ian Frazier

Ian Frazier, born in 1951 in Cleveland, Ohio, is an American writer and humorist. In his nonfiction books such as Great Plains, Family, *and* On the Rez, *Frazier combines first-person narrative with in-depth research on topics, including American history, Native Americans, fishing, and the outdoors. He attended Western Reserve Academy and later Harvard University, where he worked on the staff of the* Harvard Lampoon. *In 1982, he moved to Montana and began collecting material that he would later use in* Great Plains.

Let us now celebrate one of our most bountiful outdoor resources: bad advice. And if you listen carefully and act right away, it's absolutely free!

1 Some years ago, on a camping trip in the pine woods of northern Michigan, my friend Don brought along a copy of an outdoor cookbook that appeared on the best-seller lists at the time. This book contained many ingenious and easy-sounding recipes; one that Don especially wanted to try was called "Breakfast in a Paper Bag." According to this recipe, you could take a small paper lunch sack, put strips of bacon in the bottom, break an egg into the sack on top of the bacon, fold down the top of the sack, push a stick through the fold, hold the sack over hot coals, and cook the bacon and egg in the sack in about ten minutes.

Ian Frazier, "Trust Me. In These Parts, Hot Dogs Actually Repel Bears," *Outside*, December 1999. Reprinted by permission of the author.

2   I watched as Don followed the directions exactly. Both he and I remarked that we would naturally have thought the sack would burn; the recipe, however, declared, "grease will coat the bottom of the bag as it cooks." Somehow we both took this to mean that the grease, counterintuitively, actually made the bag less likely to burn. Marveling at the "who would have guessed" magic of it, we picked a good spot in the hot coals of our campfire, and Don held the sack above them. We watched. In a second and a half, the bag burst into leaping flames. Don was yelling for help, waving the bag around trying to extinguish it, scattering egg yolk and smoldering strips of bacon and flaming paper into the combustible pines while people at adjoining campfires stared in horror and wondered what they should do.

3   The wild figures that the burning breakfast described in midair as Don waved the stick, the look of outraged, imbecile shock reflected on our faces— those are images that stay with me. I replay the incident often in my mind. It is like a parable. Because a book told us to, we attempted to use greased paper as a frying pan on an open fire. For all I know, the trick is possible if you do it just so; we never repeated the experiment. But to me the incident illustrates a larger truth about our species when it ventures out of doors. We go forth in abundant ignorance, near-blind with fantasy, witlessly trusting words on a page or a tip a guy we'd never met before gave us at a sporting-goods counter in a giant discount store. About half of the time, the faith that leads us into the outdoors is based on advice that is half-baked, made-up, hypothetical, uninformed, spurious, or deliberately, heedlessly bad.

4   Greenland, for example, did not turn out to be very green, Viking hype to the contrary. Despite what a Pawnee or Wichita Indian told the Spanish explorer Francisco Vásquez de Coronado, there were no cities of gold in western Kansas, no canoes with oarlocks made of gold, no tree branches hung with little gold bells that soothed the king (also nonexistent) during his afternoon nap; a summer's march on the Great Plains in piping-hot armor presumably bore these truths upon the would-be conquistador in an unforgettable way. Lewis and Clark found no elephants on their journey, though President Jefferson, believing reports from the frontier, had said they should be on the lookout for them. And then there was Lansford W. Hastings, the adventurer and promoter of Sacramento, purveyor of some of the worst advice of all time. He told the prospective wagon-train emigrants to California that he had discovered a shortcut (modestly named the Hastings Cutoff) that reduced travel time by many days. Yes, it did cross a few extra deserts and some unusually high mountain ranges; the unfortunate Donner Party read Hastings's book, followed his route, and famously came to its

grisly end below the narrow Sierra pass that now bears its name. According to local legend, the air in the Utah foothills is still blue from the curses that emigrants heaped on Lansford W. Hastings along the way.

5   People will tell you just any damn thing. I have found this to be especially so in establishments called Pappy's, Cappy's, Pop's, or Dad's. The wizened, senior quality of the names seems to give the people who work in such places a license to browbeat customers and pass on whatever opinionated misinformation they please. When I go through the door of a Pappy's or Cappy's—usually it's a fishing tackle shop, a general store, or a bar—usually there's a fat older guy sitting behind the counter with his T-shirt up over his stomach and his navel peeking out. That will be Pappy, or Cappy. Sometimes it's both. Pappy looks at me without looking at me and remarks to Cappy that the gear I've got on is too light for the country at this time of year, and Cappy agrees, crustily; then I ask a touristy, greenhorn question, and we're off. Cappy, backed by Pappy, says the rig I'm driving won't make it up that forest service road, and I'm headed in the wrong direction anyhow, and the best place to camp isn't where I'm going but far in the other direction, up top of Corkscrew Butte, which is closed now, as is well known.

6   The saddest part is that I crumble in this situation, every time. I have taken more wrong advice, have bought more unnecessary maps, trout flies, water filtration devices, and assorted paraphernalia from Pappys and Cappys with their navels showing than I like to think about. Some essential element left out of my psychic immune system causes me always to defer to these guys and believe what they say. And while the Lansford W. Hastings type of bad advice tells people they can do things they really can't, the Cappy-Pappy type of advice is generally the opposite. Cappy and Pappy have been sitting around their failing store for so long that they are now convinced you're a fool for trying to do anything at all.

7   Complicating matters still further is Happy. She used to be married to Cappy but is now married to Pappy, or vice-versa. Happy has missing teeth and a freestyle hairdo, and she hangs out in the back of the store listening in and irritatedly yelling statements that contradict most of what Pappy and Cappy say. The effect is to send you out the door as confused as it is possible to be. What's different about Happy, however, is that eventually she will tell you the truth. When you return your rented bicycle or rowboat in the evening, Pappy and Cappy are packed away in glycolene somewhere and Happy is waiting for you in the twilight, swatting mosquitoes and snapping the elastic band of her trousers against her side. You have found no berries, seen no birds, caught no fish; and Happy will tell you that the birds were

right in front of the house all afternoon, the best berry bushes are behind the snow-machine shed, and she herself just caught 50 fish right off the dock. She will even show you her full stringer, cackling, "You gotta know the right place to go!"

8   Of course, people usually keep their best advice to themselves. They'd be crazy not to, what with all the crowds tramping around outdoors nowadays. I can understand such caution, in principle; but I consider it stingy and mean when it is applied to me. There's a certain facial expression people often have when they are withholding the one key piece of information I really need. They smile broadly with lips shut tight as a mason jar, and a cheery blankness fills their eyes. This expression irks me to no end. Misleading blather I can put up with, and even enjoy if it's preposterous enough; but smug, determined silence is a posted sign, a locked gate, an unlisted phone. Also, I think it's the real message behind today's deluge of information-age outdoor advice, most of which seems to be about crampons, rebreathers, and synthetic sleeping bag fill. What you wanted to know does not appear. Somehow, especially in the more desirable destinations outdoors, withheld advice is the most common kind.

9   I craved good advice one summer when I fished a little-known midwestern river full of brown trout. Every few days I went to the local fly-fishing store and asked the guys who worked there where in the river the really big fish I had heard about might be. The guys were friendly, and more than willing to sell me stuff, but when I asked that question I met the mason-jar expression I've described. I tried being winsome; I portrayed myself as fishless and pitiable, told jokes, drank coffee, hung around. On the subject of vital interest, nobody offered word one.

10   I halfway gave up and began driving the back roads aimlessly. Then just at sunset one evening I suddenly came upon a dozen or more cars and pickups parked in the high grass along a road I'd never been on before. I pulled over, got out, and crashed through the brush to investigate. There in a marshy lowland was a section of river I had never tried, with insects popping on its surface and monster brown trout slurping them down and fly rods swishing like scythes in the summer air. Among the intent anglers along the bank I recognized the fishing-store owner's son, one of the mason-jar-smiling regulars. The experience taught me an important outdoor fact: regardless of what the people who know tell you or don't tell you, an off-road gathering of parked cars doesn't lie.

11   In case you're wondering, this particular good fishing spot was on the Pigeon River near the town of Vanderbilt, Michigan, upstream from the

dam. It's been years since I fished there, so I can't vouch for the up-to-dateness of my information. But unlike smarter outdoorsmen, I am happy to pass along whatever I can because I myself am now gabby and free with advice to an embarrassing degree. I noticed the change as I got older; I hit my midforties, and from nowhere endless, windy sentences of questionable advice began coming out of me. An old-guy voice takes on its own momentum, and I seem unable to stop it even when I have no idea what I'm talking about. Sometimes when strangers ask me for directions on a hiking trail or just around town, I give detailed wrong answers off the top of my head rather than admit I don't know. When my hearers are out of sight my reason returns and I realize what I've done. Then I make myself scarce, for fear that they will discover my ridiculousness and come back in a rage looking for me.

12   Outdoor magazines I read as a child featured authoritative fellows in plaid shirts and fedoras who offered sensible tips about how to find water in the desert by cutting open cacti, how to make bread from cattail roots, or how to predict the weather by the thickness of the walls of muskrat dens. I wish I had down-to-earth wisdom like that to impart, but when I search my knowledge all that comes to mind is advice that would cause me to run and hide after I gave it. The one piece of real advice that I do have is not outdoor advice, strictly speaking; I think, however, that its soundness makes up for that drawback. It is true virtually every time, in all lands and cultures. I offer it as the one completely trustworthy piece of advice I know, and it is this: never marry a man whose nickname is "The Killer."

13   Other than that, you're on your own.

COMPREHENSION QUESTIONS

1. What is this essay actually about?
2. What is the purpose in telling the story of the eggs and bacon in a bag at the beginning of the essay?
3. Why do the store owners always seem to disappear when the author returns to confront them on their bad advice?
4. How is "Happy" different from "Pappy" or "Cappy?"
5. How does the author relate to people who gave him bad advice in the past now that he is older?

QUESTIONS ON WRITING TECHNIQUE

1. There was nothing in the essay about hotdogs and bears, so why the title?
2. Find the thesis statement in this essay, or write one that would work if the thesis is implied.
3. How does the author support his thesis? Give examples.
4. Why does the author end his essay the way he does? In your opinion, what message is he trying to leave the reader with?
5. Is this essay effective overall? Why or why not?

WRITING SUGGESTIONS

1. Write an essay that describes a particularly beautiful or unsightly place that you have visited. You will need to use a lot of rich descriptive language so the reader can "see" with words what you yourself have seen with your eyes.

2. Write an essay that shows how two places you have lived in or visited are environmentally the same, and how those two places are different. It is possible that they are more different than alike, or more alike than different.

3. Does the size of the world's population along with the consumption of material goods have a direct effect on the environment? Explain your position in an essay that supports your claim.

4. Write a narrative about something local that holds special meaning to you.

5. Have you ever seen or been involved in a natural disaster? Flood? Hurricane? Describe the experience.

6. How do the seasons affect you? Are you happier or bluer during certain times of the year? Describe your experiences.

IN-SIGHT

Sandra Barker/Photographer's Choice/Getty.

Although crude oil is a product that comes from the natural environment, what ill effects does it have on our environment when refined into fuel and used in automobiles?

1. How has our increased use of gas affected the people of the United States?
2. How has it affected the global community?
3. How does the fluctuation in gas prices affect you personally?

GROUP ACTIVITY

In small groups, consider the following questions and come up with suggestions your group can offer the rest of the class.

How might more effective public transportation systems improve the environment, international affairs, and the U.S. economy?

What kinds of public transportation systems would work best in your area?

PEER CRITIQUE

Your name _____

The author's name_____

1. Read your partner's essay.

2. What is your immediate reaction to the essay? Is the essay clear? Passionate? Organized?

3. What method of introduction does the author use (anecdote, quotation, general statement, question)?

4. Is there an explicit thesis statement? If so, write it here. If it is not explicit, is it clear? If so, put it in your own words here.

5. Who do you think is the author's audience?

6. List at least two statements the author makes that support his thesis. How do they support the thesis, and do you agree with those statements?

7. How does the author conclude the essay? What is the method (prediction, call for action, summary, question)? Is it effective? Why or why not?

8. What other suggestions do you have for this writer?

MECHANICS AND GRAMMAR

The Mysterious Comma and Semicolon

Here are five basic ways to use a comma.

With Beginning Elements

Use a comma after an introductory phrase at the start of a sentence.

Example: In conclusion, there are many ways to use a comma correctly.

With Coordinating Conjunctions

A comma should separate two independent clauses (complete sentences) that are joined by a coordinating conjunction.

Example: There was a fork in the road, and I could choose only one path.

No comma is used if the conjunction just joins two nouns or phrases.

Example: There were two ways to go and arrows with directions.

Incorrect: There was a fork in the road, I could choose only one path.

With Subordinating Conjunctions

When a subordinating conjunction such as *because* or *although* appears at the beginning of a sentence, a comma will be needed. When it appears in the middle of a sentence, a comma is not needed.

Examples:

Because of my bad ankle, I was unable to go ice-skating.
I was unable to go ice-skating because of my bad ankle.

With Lists

Use commas to separate items in a list.

Example: We went to the bank, the bookstore, and the supermarket.

With Dates and States

Commas are needed with dates and between cities and states.

Examples:

I lived in Las Vegas, Nevada, for three years.
On April 1, 2002, he was promoted.

Using a Semicolon

A semicolon may be used between two independent clauses (complete sentences) when no coordinating conjunction (and, but, or) is used.

Examples:

Reading is fun; it is also good for you.

I like to read; my husband likes to write; my sister watches television.

Use a semicolon when a conjunctive adverb comes between independent clauses.

Examples:

I think; therefore, I am.

Writing can be difficult for some people; however, guided practice is helpful.

I seldom have time to read for enjoyment; consequently, I spend most vacations with my nose in a book.

Teacher in Training

Proofread, edit, and revise the following paragraph. Pay special attention to pronouns and commas. There might even be a couple of places where a semicolon would be useful.

I remember the first time I ever taught a class on my own. I had signed up to be a substitute teacher in my junior year of college but they never called me for three months. Finally, one morning I got a call from the elementary school principal and she asked if I was free that afternoon. They wanted me to teach the afternoon session of a kindergarten class. I was scared to death because I knew it would be a lot of work to manage little tiny kids like that. It might seem like five and six year olds would be really easy to work with but you will find that they are quite a challenge when it comes to classroom management. Anyway, I said I would be there and it was actually a lot of fun. Most of the day was a blur however I do remember that the children were supposed to make these little necklaces out of pasta and they were pretty confused as to how to go about it. You had to put the pasta on the string in a certain order and the little kids kept messing up and starting over. Because it took those little kids hours to do his or her projects I barely got them cleaned up and on the bus on time. Although it was extremely exhausting the kids were really good and really cute however I was not looking forward to teaching kindergarten again. Fortunately I seldom did.

8

ISSUES AND CONTROVERSIES

Controversy has been a part of the United States since its inception with the Declaration of Independence. Many would argue that it is what makes America great. We tolerate different cultures, religions, and lifestyles. Since we consider America the "Land of the Free," we believe Americans have the right to express themselves. This often generates debatable issues that are not easily resolved. Some of these issues have been a topic of debate for decades. Some of these issues will never be resolved for all Americans.

Americans continuously examine the topic of abortion, for example. Most Americans fall somewhere in the gray area on this topic, as many aspects must be considered when pondering this issue as a whole. Some of these considerations include religion, mental health, and culture.

Controversial topics seldom have only two sides but are often multifaceted with several gray areas. Some of these issues are considered in the following essays. Mujica examines bilingual education. Dalton asks whether schools have failed male students. Hasselstrom looks at gun ownership. Atwood responds to unrealistic media images of the female body in an interesting and unique way. The chapter also includes the Declaration of Independence, with its statement of basic rights.

PRE-READING QUESTIONS

1. What are some reasons that people might have for choosing to eat fast food?
2. Why does fast food have such a bad reputation? Or does it?
3. Would you be surprised to see your doctor eating fast food?

Burgers for the Health Professional

Marc Santora

Marc Santora, a reporter for the New York Times, *was a Pulitzer Prize finalist for his coverage of the national epidemic of diabetes. His work as a journalist has taken him from Blacksburg, Virginia, to cover the Virginia Tech massacre, to Baghdad, Iraq, where he has reported as a journalist not embedded with a U.S. Army or Marine unit. Instead, he and a driver/ translator traveled on their own.*

1 Under the smiling clown-face of Ronald McDonald, a woman and her 5-year-old daughter had spread before them a burger, Chicken McNuggets and fries. Nearby, a young couple were enjoying two Quarter Pounders with cheese. A neurologist was downing some hot cakes.

2   Just a few of the billions served, as the company proudly proclaims beneath its golden arches.

3   What made the scene unusual was where these arches were located—at Elmhurst Hospital Center in Queens, one of the city's busiest places of healing.

4   As obesity and its consequences are increasingly taxing the health care system, the fact that a fast food place serves as a hospital's cafeteria strikes some as jarring. But Elmhurst Hospital is not alone. There are two other city-run hospitals with fast food outlets, Jacobi Medical Center and Coney Island Hospital. And in public and private hospitals across the country, fast food is not an uncommon sight, even at some of the nation's premier institutions, like the Children's Hospital of Philadelphia.

5   It's hard to find a doctor who says that a steady diet of burgers and fries is healthy. But hospitals with fast food outlets say that these franchises were a good option—in some cases the only one—for their food services.

6   Saint Barnabas Medical Center in Livingston, N.J., opened its doors to McDonald's a decade ago. Robin Lally, a spokeswoman for Saint Barnabas, said the hospital still has a McDonald's, as well as another cafeteria offering a wider variety of healthier food selections. McDonald's filled a need for round-the-clock meals, she said.

7   While financial considerations were part of the equation (though hospitals would not say how much they earned from franchise contracts), Miriam Pappo, a registered dietitian and the clinical nutrition manager at Montefiore Medical Center in the Bronx, said a 10-year-old study in a New Jersey hospital found that children in pediatric units who ate a McDonald's meal once a week ate better the rest of the time than children who did not eat at McDonald's.

8   "When you are scared in the hospital you want something that brings back fun memories," she said. "This is where this started."

9   Ken Barun, a senior vice president of McDonald's, cited the company's experience at Texas Children's Hospital in Houston, where McDonald's has had a restaurant for 17 years.

10   "The doctors liked McDonald's because they could get something fast, and they said, 'Our sick kids will eat this food,' " Mr. Barun said. "Happy Meals provide kids with the nutrients they need," he said. "From the emotional side, it really does help them get better."

11   Menus at McDonald's include healthy items like salads, Mr. Barun says, and the company is always willing to make adjustments at hospitals, like offering soup on the side instead of fries. He also said the company gives generously to charities that benefit hospitals and, through the Ronald McDonald House program, provides 6,000 beds around the world every night for families with members staying in hospitals.

12   Kate McGrath, spokeswoman for the New York City Health and Hospital Corporation, which oversees Elmhurst, said that McDonald's was

one of the few companies that bid for the right to run food service at the hospital, and that McDonald's has a "Made for You" option that enables customers to reduce the calories, fat or sodium of menu items. For example, omitting the mayonnaise on the Chicken McGrill sandwich eliminates 100 calories and reduces the fat content to 6 grams.

13   Nonetheless, Ms. McGrath said, when the McDonald's contract at Elmhurst is up in 2007, it will not be renewed. (She said that Jacobi and Coney Island hospitals, which are also run by the Health and Hospital Corporation, have not yet decided what they will do when their McDonald's contracts expire.)

14   Dietary concerns have changed in the years since fast food restaurants first appeared in hospitals in the metropolitan area.

15   From movies like "Super Size Me" to books like "Fast Food Nation" to a flood of studies showing the impact of obesity on countless things, from sperm counts to the cost of health care, the questions and issues surrounding fat are unavoidable.

16   The obesity rate among adults in New York State doubled between 1990 and 2002, according to the Centers for Disease Control and Prevention, whose data showed that about 57 percent of New Yorkers are overweight or obese.

17   As obesity has reached epidemic proportions in recent years, Ms. Pappo of Montefiore said, hospitals have begun to rethink the food they serve. Montefiore decided years ago to stay away from fast food establishments in favor of providing its own healthier choices.

18   "It's probably very similar to how schools would get revenue from Coca-Cola and they are now saying we are going to have to do without this because we have to send a good message," Ms. Pappo said.

19   For its part, McDonald's consistently says that its food is not unhealthy and that a host of other factors contribute to the widening of the American waistline—not the least of which is a lack of exercise.

20   "Fast food is not necessarily bad food," said Dr. Cathy Kapica, the global director of nutrition for McDonald's.

21   McDonald's restaurants make up only 2 percent of all the eating establishments in the United States, she said, so other dietary choices must be fueling America's weight problem. Most of the people grabbing a bite at the Elmhurst McDonald's said they thought the food they were eating was not very healthy.

22   "I know it is not good, but I like it," said Sandra Campbell, 26. She came to the hospital with her mother, who had an appointment. Ms. Campbell said she eats fast food nearly every day.

23   "I have my baby, and I work five days a week, and I have no money to make food," she said. "After I had the baby, I got fat. This doesn't help at all."

24   Bienviendo Medreno, 38, a social worker at the hospital, sat with his aunt and cousin as they ate. He abstained, saying he was not happy that McDonald's was the only food available where he works.

25   "I'm very against it, to be honest with you," he said.

26   A neurologist, who was sitting nearby disagreed.

27   "I am a surgeon, and the food we have here is the food I like," he said, while acknowledging that obesity is a significant health problem.

28   "It's not the fault of McDonald's," he said. "It's the fault of the people eating too much."

29   When asked his name, however, he would not give it, saying it would be embarrassing to be the brain surgeon in favor of fast food.

COMPREHENSION QUESTIONS

1. Why did the hospitals in the article agree to have a fast food franchise on their property? Did you find their rationale reasonable? Why or why not?
2. Why does Santora seem concerned about fast food being available in a hospital? In your opinion, why is there such an obesity problem in the United States? Is fast food to blame?
3. The book *Fast Food Nation* and the film *Super Size Me* are both mentioned in the article. What do you know from the article about this book and film? What do you know from your own experience?
4. Is it possible to eat healthy at McDonald's? How about at other fast food restaurants? What are some healthier choices?
5. What are some positives about having fast food available at a hospital?

QUESTIONS ON WRITING TECHNIQUE

1. For what audience is Santora writing this article?
2. How does Santora support his ideas? Give some examples.
3. How does McDonald's charity work with Ronald McDonald House influence the reader regarding the issue of fast food in hospitals?
4. Does Santora give a balanced argument? Does he look closely at both sides of the issue?
5. What might be added or left out of this article?

PRE-READING QUESTIONS

1. How often do you run into people who live here in the United States but speak and understand little or no English?
2. What resources are currently available for people who come to the United States and need to learn English?
3. What does bilingual education mean?

No Comprendo

Barbara Mujica

Barbara Mujica is a novelist, short story writer, and critic. Her novel Frida, *an international bestseller, has appeared in fourteen languages. She is president of the Association for Hispanic Classical Theater and editor of* Comedia Performance, *a journal devoted to early modern Spanish theater. A professor of Spanish at Georgetown University, she writes extensively on Spanish literature, in particular, Teresa de Avila, and her articles have appeared in many academic journals.*

1 Last spring, my niece phoned me in tears. She was graduating from high school and had to make a decision. An outstanding soccer player, she was offered athletic scholarships by several colleges. So why was she crying?

2 My niece came to the United States from South America as a child. Although she had received good grades in her schools in Miami, she spoke English with a heavy accent and her comprehension and writing skills were deficient. She was afraid that once she left the Miami environment she would feel uncomfortable and, worse still, have difficulty keeping up with class work.

3 Programs that keep foreign-born children in Spanish-language classrooms for years are only part of the problem. During a visit to my niece's former school, I observed that all business, not just teaching, was conducted in Spanish. In the office, secretaries spoke to the administrators and the children in Spanish. Announcements over the public-address system were made in an English so fractured that it was almost incomprehensible.

4   I asked my niece's mother why, after years in public schools, her daughter had poor English skills. "It's the whole environment," she replied. "All kinds of services are available in Spanish or Spanglish. Sports and after-school activities are conducted in Spanglish. That's what the kids hear on the radio and in the street."

5   Until recently, immigrants made learning English a priority. But even when they didn't learn English themselves, their children grew up speaking it. Thousands of first-generation Americans still strive to learn English, but others face reduced educational and career opportunities because they have not mastered this basic skill they need to get ahead.

6   According to the 1990 census, 40 percent of the Hispanics born in the U.S. do not graduate from high school, and the Department of Education says that a lack of proficiency in English is an important factor in the dropout rate.

7   People and agencies that favor providing services only in foreign languages want to help people who do not speak English, but they may be doing them a disservice by condemning them to a linguistic ghetto from which they can not easily escape.

8   And my niece? She turned down all of her scholarship opportunities, deciding instead to attend a small college in Miami, where she will never have to put her English to the test.

COMPREHENSION QUESTIONS

1. Since a large percentage of non-English speakers in the United States are fluent in Spanish, does Mujica think that Americans should try to offer more materials in both languages, or should more opportunities for English language learning be made available? What are the pros and cons of both of these options?
2. According to Mujica, what are some of the negative outcomes when American schools support other first languages but do not adequately teach students the English language?
3. What do you think of Mujica's concerns? Are they valid? Do you know of people who have found themselves in similar situations as Mujica's niece?
4. What advice would you give to a fellow student or a friend who is not fluent in English but wants to learn?
5. Are Americans good at learning foreign languages? Why or why not?

QUESTIONS ON WRITING TECHNIQUE

1. What is the author's claim in this essay? Where is it stated or implied?
2. In what ways does the author uphold her claim (stories, examples, statistics)?
3. Does the author offer any solutions? Does this help or hurt the effectiveness of the essay?
4. How does the author conclude the essay? Is the conclusion effective?
5. Do you think this essay could apply to all immigrants? Why or why not?

PRE-READING QUESTIONS

1. What is the Declaration of Independence? Why is it valued over 200 years after it was written?
2. In what year was the Declaration of Independence written?
3. What do you know about Thomas Jefferson?

The Declaration of Independence

Thomas Jefferson

Thomas Jefferson (1743–1826) was born in Virginia in a well-to-do land-owning family. He graduated from the College of William and Mary and then studied law. When he was elected at age twenty-six to the Virginia legislature, he had already begun forming his revolutionary views. As a delegate to the Second Continental Congress in 1775, he was the principal writer of the Declaration of Independence, which was adopted on July 4, 1776. After the Revolution, Jefferson served in various federal positions, including secretary of state and ambassador to France. In 1801, he became the third president of the United States. Jefferson was influential as an advocate of democracy in the early years of the United States, although his ideas were more typical of the eighteenth-century "enlightened man" than original. The Declaration of Independence shows his ideas and style as well as those of the times and remains not merely an important historical document but also an eloquent statement of the founding principles of this country.

1 When in the course of human events, it becomes necessary for one people to dissolve the political bands which have connected them with another, and to assume among the powers of the earth, the separate and equal station to which the Laws of Nature and of Nature's God entitle them, a decent respect to the opinions of mankind requires that they should declare the causes which impel them to the separation.

2   We hold these truths to be self-evident, that all men are created equal, that they are endowed by their Creator with certain inalienable rights, that among these are life, liberty, and the pursuit of happiness. That to secure these rights, governments are instituted among men, deriving their just powers from the consent of the governed. That whenever any form of government becomes destructive of these ends, it is the right of the people to alter or to abolish it, and to institute new government, laying its foundation on such principles and organizing its powers in such form, as to them shall seem most likely to effect their safety and happiness. Prudence, indeed, will dictate that governments long established should not be changed for light and transient causes; and accordingly all experience hath shown, that mankind are more disposed to suffer, while evils are sufferable, than to right themselves by abolishing the forms to which they are accustomed. But when a long train of abuses and usurpations, pursuing invariably the same object, evinces a design to reduce them under absolute despotism, it is their right, it is their duty, to throw off such government, and to provide new guards for their future security. Such has been the patient sufferance of these Colonies; and such is now the necessity which constrains them to alter their former systems of government. The history of the present King of Great Britain is a history of repeated injuries and usurpations, all having in direct object the establishment of an absolute tyranny over these States. To prove this, let facts be submitted to a candid world.

3   He has refused his assent to laws, the most wholesome and necessary for the public good.

4   He has forbidden his Governors to pass laws of immediate and pressing importance, unless suspended in their operation till his assent should be obtained; and when so suspended, he has utterly neglected to attend to them.

5   He has refused to pass other laws for the accommodation of large districts of people, unless those people would relinquish the right of representation in the legislature, a right inestimable to them and formidable to tyrants only.

6   He has called together legislative bodies at places unusual, uncomfortable, and distant from the depository of their public records, for the sole purpose of fatiguing them into compliance with his measures.

7   He has dissolved representative houses repeatedly, for opposing with manly firmness his invasions on the rights of the people.

8   He has refused for a long time, after such dissolutions, to cause others to be elected; whereby the legislative powers, incapable of annihilation, have

returned to the people at large for their exercise; the State remaining in the meantime exposed to all the dangers of invasion from without and convulsions within.

9   He has endeavoured to prevent the population of these states; for that purpose obstructing the laws for naturalization of foreigners; refusing to pass others to encourage their migration hither, and raising the conditions of new appropriations of lands.

10   He has obstructed the administration of justice, by refusing his assent to laws for establishing judiciary powers.

11   He has made judges dependent on his will alone, for the tenure of their offices, and the amount and payment of their salaries.

12   He has erected a multitude of new offices, and sent hither swarms of officers to harass our people, and eat out their substance.

13   He has kept among us, in times of peace, standing armies without the consent of our legislatures.

14   He has affected to render the military independent of and superior to the civil power.

15   He has combined with others to subject us to a jurisdiction foreign of our constitution, and unacknowledged by our laws; giving his assent to their acts of pretended legislation:

16   For quartering large bodies of armed troops among us:

17   For protecting them, by a mock trial, from punishment for any murders which they should commit on the inhabitants of these States:

18   For cutting off our trade with all parts of the world:

19   For imposing taxes on us without our consent:

20   For depriving us in many cases of the benefits of trial by jury:

21   For transporting us beyond seas to be tried for pretended offences:

22   For abolishing the free system of English laws in a neighbouring Province, establishing therein an arbitrary government, and enlarging its boundaries so as to render it at once an example and fit instrument for introducing the same absolute rule into these Colonies:

23   For taking away our Charters, abolishing our most valuable laws, and altering fundamentally the forms of our governments:

24   For suspending our own legislatures, and declaring themselves invested with power to legislate for us in all cases whatsoever.

25   He has abdicated government here, by declaring us out of his protection and waging war against us.

26   He has plundered our seas, ravaged our coasts, burnt our towns, and destroyed the lives of our people.

27   He is at this time transporting large armies of foreign mercenaries to complete the works of death, desolation, and tyranny, already begun with circumstances of cruelty and perfidy scarcely paralleled in the most barbarous ages, and totally unworthy the head of a civilized nation.

28   He has constrained our fellow citizens taken captive on the high seas to bear arms against their country, to become the executioners of their friends and brethren, or to fall themselves by their hands.

29   He has excited domestic insurrections amongst us, and has endeavoured to bring on the inhabitants of our frontiers, the merciless Indian savages, whose known rule of warfare, is an undistinguished destruction of all ages, sexes, and conditions.

30   In every stage of these oppressions we have petitioned for redress in the most humble terms: our repeated petitions have been answered only by repeated injury. A prince whose character is thus marked by every act which may define a tyrant is unfit to be the ruler of a free people.

31   Nor have we been wanting in attention to our British brethren. We have warned them from time to time of attempts by their legislature to extend an unwarrantable jurisdiction over us. We have reminded them of the circumstances of our emigration and settlement here. We have appealed to their native justice and magnanimity, and we have conjured them by the ties of our common kindred to disavow these usurpations, which would inevitably interrupt our connections and correspondence. They too have been deaf to the voice of justice and of consanguinity. We must, therefore, acquiesce in the necessity, which denounces our separation, and hold them, as we hold the rest of mankind, enemies in war, in peace friends.

32   We, therefore, the Representatives of the United States of America, in General Congress assembled, appealing to the Supreme Judge of the world for the rectitude of our intentions, do, in the name, and by authority of the good people of these Colonies, solemnly publish and declare, That these United Colonies are, and of right ought to be, Free and Independent States; that they are absolved from all allegiance to the British Crown, and that all political connection between them and the state of Great Britain, is and ought to be totally dissolved; and that as Free and Independent States, they have full power to levy war, conclude peace, contract alliances, establish commerce, and to do all other acts and things which Independent States may of right do. And for the support of this declaration, with a firm reliance on the protection of Divine Providence, we mutually pledge to each other our lives, our fortunes, and our sacred honor.

COMPREHENSION QUESTIONS

1. Jefferson begins the second paragraph with the very famous phrase "We hold these truths to be self-evident." What does that phrase mean?
2. What does Jefferson mean by "unalienable rights"?
3. Who is the "He" referred to in paragraphs 3 through 29?
4. What is "Divine Providence"?
5. What did Jefferson mean specifically when he said "all men are created equal"?

QUESTIONS ON WRITING TECHNIQUE

1. Why is this considered an example of an argument essay? What is Jefferson's claim? How does he support it?
2. Who do you think is Jefferson's audience? What was his purpose?
3. Where in the essay is Jefferson's thesis? Why do you think Jefferson did not put his thesis in the introduction?
4. What writing techniques does Jefferson use?
5. If you could change one phrase, what would it be?

PRE-READING QUESTIONS

1. Do you think that boys learn differently than girls? If so, in what ways?
2. Do you think that educators treat students of both sexes equally?
3. Have you ever felt that you were educationally stereotyped in some way because of your gender?

Have Today's Schools Failed Male Students?

Patricia Dalton

Patricia Dalton is a Washington, D.C., clinical psychologist. In this selection, she suggests that in our attempt to overcome the disadvantages of female students, we may have shortchanged male students.

1 For all the unfathomable horror of the shootings . . . at Columbine High School, there was one thing that came as no surprise to me.

2 It was boys who fired the guns in Littleton, Colo. Just as it was boys who fired the guns in the school shootings in Pearl, Miss., in West Paducah, Ky., in Jonesboro, Ark., in Springfield, Ore., and . . . in Conyers, Ga.

3 It seems clear to me, both as a psychologist and as the mother of two daughters and a son, that we should be concerned about how we are failing our boys.

4 I'm not suggesting that every boy is a potential killer. Far from it. But from observing my patients and my son's friends, I think we are missing cues.

5 I can recall a teenage boy I saw some time ago in therapy. He had changed schools after his parents divorced. His dad was concerned that he was not interested in sports and was not hanging around with the other guys. I knew that the boy was unhappy, but the underlying problem was that his behavior simply didn't fit his father's picture of being a man. His dad seemed surprised—even embarrassed—that his son was going through a hard time, as if real guys shouldn't have doubts and worries. What his son needed, I realized, was for his father to understand that real guys do have doubts and worries.

Patricia Dalton, "Have Today's Schools Failed Male Students?", *Orlando Sentinel*, May 23, 1999. Reprinted by permission of the author.

6   To really help boys, we need to think not only about issues such as the violence they are exposed to and the availability of weapons; we also need to widen the lens and look at their daily lives, both in and out of school, and examine the expectations and messages they get from us.

7   Because of legitimate concerns about gender discrimination, for years we tended to play down differences between boys and girls, even though research and common sense tell us to ask a parent who has raised children of both sexes. The differences show up at a young age, they persist, and they are probably there for good evolutionary reasons: they bring the sexes together and promote procreation.

8   More recently, as we've begun to acknowledge gender differences, we've focused our attention on girls. Think of Mary Pipher's bestseller, *Reviving Ophelia*, which catalogued problems such as anorexia nervosa, bulimia and self-mutilation that girls are likely to exhibit. Think of Harvard professor of education Carol Gilligan and her research team as they described girls who are confident at 11 but confused by 16. And think of all the recent studies of single-sex education that have addressed almost exclusively the special needs of girls.

9   Where does all this leave boys?

10   The statistics that cross my desk are not encouraging. They suggest that boys may be the more fragile sex. Approximately three out of every four children identified as learning disabled are boys. Boys are much more likely than girls to have drug and alcohol problems. Four of every five juvenile-court cases involve crimes committed by boys. Ninety-five percent of juvenile homicides are committed by boys. And while girls attempt suicide four times more often, boys are seven times as likely to succeed as girls—usually because they choose more lethal methods, such as guns.

11   While girls tend to internalize problems, taking their unhappiness out on themselves, boys externalize them, taking their unhappiness out on others. Boys have more problems than girls in virtually every category you can think of with the exception of eating disorders.

12   The signs of depression my colleagues and I are likely to see in girls are typically straightforward—sadness, tearfulness and self-doubt. In boys, depression is generally hidden behind symptoms such as irritability, agitation and explosiveness.

13   Since our kids spend the majority of their day in the structured setting of school, that's where problems are most likely to come to light. Many boys think that their grade schools are boy-unfriendly. I well remember my son bursting into the kitchen one day after school, yelling "They want us to be girls, Mom, they want us to be girls!" A seventh-grader once told me he was

planning that night to write a book report that was due the next day—"not like the perfect girls who did theirs three weeks ago."

14   We all know that boys mature more slowly than girls, and that they reach the cognitive milestones essential for doing well at school later than girls do. Take reading, for example. Girls are usually ready to read earlier than boys. This means that average boys wind up feeling less successful, and learning-disabled boys can feel easily defeated.

15   What have schools done to accommodate these well-documented differences in rates of maturity? Very little. Schools, like researchers, have been concentrating on girls. In recent years, some parents have been holding their boys back voluntarily, because they don't seem ready for first grade. Maturity differences persist through adolescence, although adults sometimes seem to ignore them. Teenagers seem to have an implicit understanding of them, though; boys are often a year or two older than the girls they date.

16   So here's a radical proposal: have boys start school a year later than girls so that the two sexes are more evenly matched.

17   Besides their different maturity rates, boys are more active than girls and slower to develop control of their impulses. I'm not the first one to suggest this; even Plato observed that of all the animal young, the hardest to tame is the boy. A young boy put the matter to me succinctly: "I figured it out. I'm bad before recess."

18   But many schools have not accommodated boys' need to work off excess energy. Instead, many have shortened lunch and recess periods in order to cram more class time into the day, as the pressure to become more competitive and test-oriented has increased.

19   A fifth-grade boy once told me, "School just sucks the fun out of everything." And my high-school-age son, who enjoyed preschool and kindergarten so much that he left for first grade one day saying, "Ready to rock and roll," had changed his tune by middle school. "Mom," he said, "It's like going to prison."

20   While parents and schools have often failed to respond to these signals, popular culture has picked up on them. Matt Groening once said that he created *The Simpsons* because of all the teachers who, when he was enjoying himself, would shoot him a look that said, "Take that stupid grin off your face right now."

21   Groening has it right. I hear a lot about *The Simpsons* from the kids I see in therapy. Girls like *The Simpsons*; boys love the show.

22   One of the ways boys can blow off steam is sports. Yet even this outlet is tainted by the student and adult adulation of athletes that pervades many

of the big high schools. That's a problem for several reasons: it gives athletes an inflated idea of themselves and nonathletes feelings of inferiority and resentment. The boys I see in my office often tell me how sports provide an arena in which they can test themselves, and many feel like failures when they get cut from a team—something that is increasingly likely to happen in our highly competitive mega-schools. All kids need to exercise and play sports, and not just for the short time they have physical education. It would be good to see all schools offering intramural after-school sports to all students.

23   There's no question in my mind that, in our haste to make up for the disadvantages that girls have historically suffered, we've tended to overlook the needs of ordinary boys.

24   Like everyone else, boys of all ages need adults to love them, appreciate them and enjoy them, so that they can come to value and have faith in themselves. We need to help them find outlets for their natural exuberance, vitality and even devilishness. One of my favorite sights is the look on boys' faces on the baseball field as they steal bases—when it's good to be bad.

COMPREHENSION QUESTIONS

1. What answer does Dalton offer to the question, "Have today's schools failed male students?"
2. What reasons does Dalton give for the ways that boys behave in school?
3. What does Dalton mean by the term "cognitive milestones"?
4. Give some examples of the ways Dalton compares and contrasts the behavior of male and female children and adolescents.
5. Why do you think young boys "love" *The Simpsons?*

QUESTIONS ON WRITING TECHNIQUE

1. Why does Dalton begin her essay with her observations on the Columbine High School shootings?
2. What is Dalton's thesis?
3. What techniques does Dalton use to uphold her claim?
4. How does Dalton conclude her essay? What suggestions does she make?
5. What are two examples that Dalton uses to make her point?

PRE-READING QUESTIONS

1. What kinds of advertising might include an attractive woman?
2. Could those same advertisements have the same effect if an attractive man were used instead of a woman?
3. Can women and men be commodified? What is commodification?

The Female Body

Margaret Atwood

Margaret Atwood, born in Ottawa, Canada, attended the University of Toronto, Radcliffe, and Harvard. At a young age she decided to become a writer, and she has published a remarkable list of novels, poetry, and essays, along with forays into other genres such as children's stories and television scripts. She is best known, however, for her novels, including The Edible Woman *(1969),* Life Before Man *(1979),* Bodily Harm *(1982),* The Handmaid's Tale *(1985),* Cat's Eye *(1989),* The Robber Bride *(1994), and* Alias Grace *(1996). In the following selection, published in 1992, she uses an innovative approach to explore images of the female body in our culture.*

> . . .entirely devoted to the subject of "The Female Body." Knowing how well you have written on this topic . . . this capacious topic . . .
> LETTER FROM *MICHIGAN QUARTERLY REVIEW*

1

1 I agree, it's a hot topic. But only one? Look around, there's a wide range. Take my own, for instance.

2 I get up in the morning. My topic feels like hell. I sprinkle it with water, brush parts of it, rub it with towels, powder it, add lubricant. I dump in the fuel and away goes my topic, my topical topic, my controversial topic, my capacious topic, my limping topic, my nearsighted topic, my topic with back problems, my badly behaved topic, my vulgar topic, my outrageous topic, my aging topic, my topic that is out of the question and anyway still can't spell,

in its oversized coat and worn winter boots, scuttling along the sidewalk as if it were flesh and blood, hunting for what's out there, an avocado, an alderman, an adjective, hungry as ever.

2

3   The basic Female Body comes with the following accessories: garter belt, pantigirdle, crinoline, camisole, bustle, brassiere, stomacher, chemise, virgin zone, spike heels, nose ring, veil, kid gloves, fishnet stockings, fichu, bandeau, Merry Widow, weepers, chokers, barrettes, bangles, beads, lorgnette, feather boa, basic black, compact, Lycra stretch one-piece with modesty panel, designer peignoir, flannel nightie, lace teddy, bed, head.

3

4   The Female Body is made of transparent plastic and lights up when you plug it in. You press a button to illuminate the different systems. The circulatory system is red, for the heart and arteries, purple for the veins; the respiratory system is blue; the lymphatic system is yellow; the digestive system is green, with liver and kidneys in aqua. The nerves are done in orange and the brain is pink. The skeleton, as you might expect, is white.

5   The reproductive system is optional, and can be removed. It comes with or without a miniature embryo. Parental judgment can thereby be exercised. We do not wish to frighten or offend.

4

6   He said, I won't have one of those things in the house. It gives a young girl a false notion of beauty, not to mention anatomy. If a real woman was built like that she'd fall on her face.

7   She said, If we don't let her have one like all the other girls she'll feel singled out. It'll become an issue. She'll long for one and she'll long to turn into one. Repression breeds sublimation. You know that.

8   He said, It's not just the pointy plastic tits, it's the wardrobes. The wardrobes and that stupid male doll, what's his name, the one with the underwear glued on.

9   She said, Better to get it over with when she's young. He said, All right, but don't let me see it.

10   She came whizzing down the stairs, thrown like a dart. She was stark naked. Her hair had been chopped off, her head was turned back to front,

she was missing some toes and she'd been tattooed all over her body with purple ink in a scrollwork design. She hit the potted azalea, trembled there for a moment like a botched angel, and fell.

11   He said, I guess we're safe.

5

12   The Female Body has many uses. It's been used as a door knocker, a bottle opener, as a clock with a ticking belly, as something to hold up lampshades, as a nutcracker, just squeeze the brass legs together and out comes your nut. It bears torches, lifts victorious wreaths, grows copper wings and raises aloft a ring of neon stars; whole buildings rest on its marble heads.

13   It sells cars, beer, shaving lotion, cigarettes, hard liquor; it sells diet plans and diamonds, and desire in tiny crystal bottles. Is this the face that launched a thousand products? You bet it is, but don't get any funny big ideas, honey, that smile is a dime a dozen.

14   It does not merely sell, it is sold. Money flows into this country or that country, flies in, practically crawls in, suitful after suitful, lured by all those hairless pre-teen legs. Listen, you want to reduce the national debt, don't you? Aren't you patriotic? That's the spirit. That's my girl.

15   She's a natural resource, a renewable one luckily, because those things wear out so quickly. They don't make 'em like they used to. Shoddy goods.

6

16   One and one equals another one. Pleasure in the female is not a requirement. Pair-bonding is stronger in geese. We're not talking about love, we're talking about biology. That's how we all got here, daughter.

17   Snails do it differently. They're hermaphrodites, and work in threes.

7

18   Each Female Body contains a female brain. Handy. Makes things work. Stick pins in it and you get amazing results. Old popular songs. Short circuits. Bad dreams.

19   Anyway: each of these brains has two halves. They're joined together by a thick cord; neural pathways flow from one to the other, sparkles of electric information washing to and fro. Like light on waves. Like a conversation. How does a woman know? She listens. She listens in.

20   The male brain, now, that's a different matter. Only a thin connection. Space over here, time over there, music and arithmetic in their own sealed

compartments. The right brain doesn't know what the left brain is doing. Good for aiming through, for hitting the target when you pull the trigger. What's the target? Who's the target? Who cares? What matters is hitting it. That's the male brain for you. Objective.

21   This is why men are so sad, why they feel so cut off, why they think of themselves as orphans cast adrift, footloose and stringless in the deep void. What void? she asks. What are you talking about? The void of the universe, he says, and she says Oh and looks out the window and tries to get a handle on it, but it's no use, there's too much going on, too many rustlings in the leaves, too many voices, so she says, Would you like a cheese sandwich, a piece of cake, a cup of tea? And he grinds his teeth because she doesn't understand, and wanders off, not just alone but Alone, lost in the dark, lost in the skull, searching for the other half, the twin who could complete him.

22   Then it comes to him: he's lost the Female Body! Look, it shines in the gloom, far ahead, a vision of wholeness, ripeness, like a giant melon, like an apple, like a metaphor for "breast" in a bad sex novel; it shines like a balloon, like a foggy noon, a watery moon, shimmering in its egg of light.

23   Catch it. Put it in a pumpkin, in a high tower, in a compound, in a chamber, in a house, in a room. Quick, stick a leash on it, a lock, a chain, some pain, settle it down, so it can never get away from you again.

COMPREHENSION QUESTIONS

1. What is the "hot topic" Atwood refers to in section 1?
2. What do you think is being described in section 4?
3. How does Atwood describe the male attitude toward the female body?
4. What are the "shoddy goods" Atwood refers to at the end of section 5?
5. Who is the speaker in section 7? How is that speaker different from the author?

QUESTIONS ON WRITING TECHNIQUE

1. Does Atwood's essay have an introduction, body, and conclusion? How about a thesis? If you cannot find a thesis in the text, what might be the implied thesis?
2. Why do you think Atwood decided to construct her essay this way?
3. What is the tone of the essay? Happy? Sad? Funny? Sarcastic?
4. What seems to be Atwood's purpose in writing the essay?
5. Similes and metaphors compare. A simile uses "like" or "as" and a metaphor uses "is" or "was." Find some examples of similes and metaphors in each section.

PRE-READING QUESTIONS

1. What precautions, if any, do you take when in public or at home to feel safe?
2. Do you think gun ownership is a good idea? Why or why not?
3. What precautions should a responsible gun owner take if there are children in the house?

Why One Peaceful Woman Carries a Pistol

Linda M. Hasselstrom

Linda M. Hasselstrom grew up in rural South Dakota, the daughter of a cattle-ranching family. After receiving a master's degree in journalism from the University of Missouri, she returned to South Dakota to run her own ranch and now lives in Cheyenne, Wyoming. A highly respected poet, essayist, and writing teacher, she often focuses in her work on everyday life in the American West. Her publications include the poetry collections Caught by One Wing *(1984),* Roadkill *(1987), and* Dakota Bones *(1991); the essay collection* Land Circle *(1991); and two books about ranching,* Feels Like Far: A Rancher's Life on the Great Plains *(1999) and* Between Grass and Sky: Where I Live and Work *(2002). In this essay from* Land Circle, *Hasselstrom explains her reluctant decision to become licensed to carry a concealed handgun.*

I'm a peace-loving woman. I also carry a pistol. For years, I've written about my decision in an effort to help other women make intelligent choices about gun ownership, but editors rejected the articles. Between 1983 and 1986, however, when gun sales to men held steady, gun ownership among women rose fifty-three percent, to more than twelve million. We learned that any female over the age of twelve can expect to be criminally assaulted some time in her life, that women aged thirty have a fifty-fifty chance of being raped, robbed, or attacked, and that many police officials say flatly that they cannot protect citizens from crime. During the same period, the number of women considering gun ownership quadrupled to nearly two million. Manufacturers began showing lightweight weapons with small grips, and purses with built-in holsters. A new magazine is called *Guns and Women*, and more than eight thousand copies of the video *A Woman's Guide to Firearms* were sold by 1988. Experts say female gun buyers are not limited to any particular age group, profession, social class, or area of the country, and most are buying guns to protect themselves. Shooting instructors say women view guns with more caution than do men, and may make better shots.

2   I decided to buy a handgun for several reasons. During one four-year period, I drove more than a hundred thousand miles alone, giving speeches, readings, and workshops. A woman is advised, usually by men, to protect herself by avoiding bars, by approaching her car like an Indian scout, by locking doors and windows. But these precautions aren't always enough. And the logic angers me: *because* I am female, it is my responsibility to be extra careful.

3   As a responsible environmentalist, I choose to recycle, avoid chemicals on my land, minimize waste. As an informed woman alone, I choose to be as responsible for my own safety as possible: I keep my car running well, use caution in where I go and what I do. And I learned about self-protection—not an easy or quick decision. I developed a strategy of protection that includes handgun possession. The following incidents, chosen from a larger number because I think they could happen to anyone, helped make up my mind.

4   When I camped with another woman for several weeks, she didn't want to carry a pistol, and police told us Mace was illegal. We tucked spray deodorant into our sleeping bags, theorizing that any man crawling into our tent at night would be nervous anyway; anything sprayed in his face would slow him down until we could hit him with a frying pan, or escape. We never used our improvised weapon, because we were lucky enough to camp beside people who came to our aid when we needed them. I returned from that trip determined to reconsider.

5   At that time, I lived alone and taught night classes in town. Along a city street I often traveled, a woman had a flat tire, called for help on her CB, and got a rapist; he didn't fix the tire either. She was afraid to call for help again and stayed in her car until morning. Also, CBs work best along line-of-sight; I ruled them out.

6   As I drove home one night, a car followed me, lights bright. It passed on a narrow bridge, while a passenger flashed a spotlight in my face, blinding me. I braked sharply. The car stopped, angled across the bridge, and four men jumped out. I realized the locked doors were useless if they broke

my car windows. I started forward, hoping to knock their car aside so I could pass. Just then, another car appeared, and the men got back in their car, but continued to follow me, passing and repassing. I dared not go home. I passed no lighted houses. Finally, they pulled to the roadside, and I decided to use their tactic: fear. I roared past them inches away, horn blaring. It worked; they turned off the highway. But it was desperate and foolish, and I was frightened and angry. Even in my vehicle I was too vulnerable.

7   Other incidents followed. One day I saw a man in the field near my house, carrying a shotgun and heading for a pond full of ducks. I drove to meet him, and politely explained that the land was posted. He stared at me, and the muzzle of his shotgun rose. I realized that if he simply shot me and drove away, I would be a statistic. The moment passed; the man left.

8   One night, I returned home from class to find deep tire ruts on the lawn, a large gas tank empty, garbage in the driveway. A light shone in the house; I couldn't remember leaving it on. I was too embarrassed to wake the neighbors. An hour of cautious exploration convinced me the house was safe, but once inside, with the doors locked, I was still afraid. I put a .22 rifle by my bed, but I kept thinking of how naked I felt, prowling around my own house in the dark.

9   It was time to consider self-defense. I took a kung fu class and learned to define the distance to maintain between myself and a stranger. Once someone enters that space without permission, kung fu teaches appropriate evasive or protective action. I learned to move confidently, scanning for possible attack. I learned how to assess danger, and techniques for avoiding it without combat.

10   I also learned that one must practice several hours every day to be good at kung fu. By that time I had married George; when I practiced with him, I learned how *close* you must be to your attacker to use martial arts, and decided a 120-pound woman dare not let a six-foot, 220-pound attacker get that close unless she is very, very good at self-defense. Some women who are well trained in martial arts have been raped and beaten anyway.

11   Reluctantly I decided to carry a pistol. George helped me practice with his .357 and .22. I disliked the .357's recoil, though I later became comfortable with it. I bought a .22 at a pawn shop. A standard .22 bullet, fired at close range, can kill, but news reports tell of attackers advancing with five such bullets in them. I bought magnum shells, with more power, and practiced until I could hit someone close enough to endanger me. Then I bought a license making it legal for me to carry the gun concealed.

12 George taught me that the most important preparation was mental: convincing myself I could shoot someone. Few of us really wish to hurt or kill another human being. But there is no point in having a gun—in fact, gun possession might increase your danger—unless you know you can use it against another human being. A good training course includes mental preparation, as well as training in safety. As I drive or walk, I often rehearse the conditions which would cause me to shoot. Men grow up handling firearms, and learn controlled violence in contact sports, but women grow up learning to be subservient and vulnerable. To make ourselves comfortable with the idea that we are capable of protecting ourselves requires effort. But it need not turn us into macho, gun-fighting broads. We must simply learn to do as men do from an early age: believe in, and rely on, *ourselves* for protection. The pistol only adds an extra edge, an attention-getter; it is a weapon of last resort.

13 Because shooting at another person means shooting to kill. It's impossible even for seasoned police officers to be sure of only wounding an assailant. If I shot an attacking man, I would aim at the largest target, the chest. This is not an easy choice, but for me it would be better than rape.

14 In my car, my pistol is within instant reach. When I enter a deserted rest stop at night, it's in my purse, my hand on the grip. When I walk from a dark parking lot into a motel, it's in my hand, under a coat. When I walk my dog in the deserted lots around most motels, the pistol is in a shoulder holster, and I am always aware of my surroundings. In my motel room, it lies on the bedside table. At home, it's on the headboard.

15 Just carrying a pistol is not protection. Avoidance is still the best approach to trouble; watch for danger signs, and practice avoiding them. Develop your instinct for danger.

16 One day while driving to the highway mailbox, I saw a vehicle parked about halfway to the house. Several men were standing in the ditch, relieving themselves. I have no objection to emergency urination; we always need moisture. But they'd also dumped several dozen beer cans, which blow into pastures and can slash a cow's legs or stomach.

17 As I slowly drove closer, the men zipped their trousers ostentatiously while walking toward me. Four men gathered around my small foreign car, making remarks they wouldn't make to their mothers, and one of them demanded what the hell I wanted.

18 "This is private land; I'd like you to pick up the beer cans."

19 "What beer cans?" said the belligerent one, putting both hands on the car door, and leaning in my window. His face was inches from mine, the

beer fumes were strong, and he looked angry. The others laughed. One tried the passenger door, locked; another put his foot on the hood and rocked the car. They circled, lightly thumping the roof, discussing my good fortune in meeting them, and the benefits they were likely to bestow upon me. I felt small and trapped; they knew it.

20   "The ones you just threw out," I said politely.

21   "I don't see no beer cans. Why don't you get out here and show them to me, honey?" said the belligerent one, reaching for the handle inside my door.

22   "Right over there," I said, still being polite, "there and over there." I pointed with the pistol, which had been under my thigh. Within one minute the cans and the men were back in the car, and headed down the road.

23   I believe this small incident illustrates several principles. The men were trespassing and knew it; their judgment may have been impaired by alcohol. Their response to the polite request of a woman alone was to use their size and numbers to inspire fear. The pistol was a response in the same language. Politeness didn't work; I couldn't intimidate them. Out of the car, I'd have been more vulnerable. The pistol just changed the balance of power.

24   My husband, George, asked one question when I told him. "What would you have done if he'd grabbed for the pistol?"

25   "I had the car in reverse; I'd have hit the accelerator, and backed up; if he'd kept coming, I'd have fired straight at him." He nodded.

26   In fact, the sight of the pistol made the man straighten up; he cracked his head on the door frame. He and the two in front of the car stepped backward, catching the attention of the fourth, who joined them. They were all in front of me then, and as the car was still running and in reverse gear, my options had multiplied. If they'd advanced again, I'd have backed away, turning to keep the open window toward them. Given time, I'd have put the first shot into the ground in front of them, the second into the belligerent leader. It might have been better to wait until they were gone, pick up the beer cans, and avoid confrontation, but I believed it was reasonable and my right to make a polite request to strangers littering my property. Showing the pistol worked on another occasion when I was driving in a desolate part of Wyoming. A man played cat-and-mouse with me for thirty miles, ultimately trying to run my car off the road. When his car was only two inches from mine, I pointed my pistol at him, and he disappeared.

27   I believe that a handgun is like a car; both are tools for specific purposes; both can be lethal if used improperly. Both require a license, training, and alertness. Both require you to be aware of what is happening before and behind you. Driving becomes almost instinctive; so does handgun use.

When I've drawn my gun for protection, I simply found it in my hand. Instinct told me a situation was dangerous before my conscious mind reacted; I've felt the same while driving. Most good drivers react to emergencies by instinct.

28   Knives are another useful tool often misunderstood and misused; some people acquire knives mostly for display, either on a wall or on a belt, and such knives are often so large as to serve no useful purpose. My pocket knives are always razor sharp, because a small, sharp knife will do most jobs. Skinning blades serve for cutting meat and splitting small kindling in camp. A *sgian dubh*, a four-inch flat blade in a wooden sheath, was easily concealed inside a Scotsman's high socks, and slips into my dress or work boots as well. Some buckskinners keep what they call a "grace knife" on a thong around their necks; the name may derive from *coup de grâce*, the welcome throat-slash a wounded knight asked from his closest friend, to keep him from falling alive into the hands of his enemies. I also have a push dagger, with a blade only three inches long, attached to a handle that fits into the fist so well that the knife would be hard to lose even in hand-to-hand combat. When I first showed it, without explanation, to an older woman who would never consider carrying a knife, she took one look and said, "Why, you could push that right into someone's stomach," and demonstrated with a flourish. That's what it's for. I wear it for decoration, because it was handmade by Jerry and fits my hand perfectly, but I am intently aware of its purpose. I like my knives, not because they are weapons, but because they are well designed, and beautiful, and because each is a tool with a specific purpose.

29   Women didn't always have jobs, or drive cars or heavy equipment, though western women did many of those things almost as soon as they arrived here. Men in authority argued that their attempt to do so would unravel the fabric of society. Women, they said, would become less feminine; they hadn't the intelligence to cope with the of a car, or the judgment to cope with emergencies. Since these ideas were so wrong, perhaps it is time women brought a new dimension to the wise use of handguns as well.

30   We can and should educate ourselves in how to travel safely, take self-defense courses, reason, plead, or avoid trouble in other ways. But some men cannot be stopped by those methods; they understand only power. A man who is committing an attack already knows he's breaking laws; he has no concern for someone else's rights. A pistol is a woman's answer to his greater power. It makes her equally frightening. I have thought of revising the old Colt slogan: "God made man, but Sam Colt made them equal" to read "God made men *and women* but Sam Colt made them equal." Recently I have

seen an ad for a popular gunmaker with a similar sentiment; perhaps this is an idea whose time has come, though the pacifist inside me will be saddened if the only way women can achieve equality is by carrying a weapon.

31   As a society, we were shocked in early 1989 when a female jogger in New York's Central Park was beaten and raped savagely and left in a coma. I was even more shocked when reporters interviewed children who lived near the victim and quoted a twelve-year-old as saying, "She had nothing to guard herself; she didn't have no man with her; she didn't have no Mace." And another sixth-grader said, "It is like she committed suicide." Surely this is not a majority opinion, but I think it is not so unusual, either, even in this liberated age. Yet there is no city or county in the nation where law officers can relax because all the criminals are in jail. Some authorities say citizens armed with handguns stop almost as many crimes annually as armed criminals succeed in committing, and that people defending themselves kill three times more attackers and robbers than police do. I don't suggest all criminals should be killed, but some can be stopped only by death or permanent incarceration. Law enforcement officials can't prevent crimes; later punishment may be of little comfort to the victim. A society so controlled that no crime existed would probably be too confined for most of us, and is not likely to exist any time soon. Therefore, many of us should be ready and able to protect ourselves, and the intelligent use of firearms is one way.

32   We must treat a firearm's power with caution. "Power tends to corrupt, and absolute power corrupts absolutely," as a man (Lord Acton) once said. A pistol is not the only way to avoid being raped or murdered in today's world, but a firearm, intelligently wielded, can shift the balance and provide a measure of safety.

Comprehension Questions

1. Why does Hasselstrom carry a gun? Do you think her experiences are typical or are they unusual?
2. Where does the author live?
3. How would this essay be perceived differently if the title were "Why One Peaceful Man Carries a Pistol"?
4. What other methods had Hasselstrom tried in order to feel safe and protected from harm?
5. What does the author mean when she uses the quote, "Power tends to corrupt, and absolute power corrupts absolutely"?

QUESTIONS ON WRITING TECHNIQUE

1. Who is the intended audience for this essay, and what is Hasselstrom's purpose for writing it?
2. The author attempts to uphold her claim using only her own personal experiences. Does this strengthen or weaken her argument?
3. What other methods could Hasselstrom have used to uphold her claim, besides her own experiences?
4. In what ways does Hasselstrom refute people who disagree with her position?
5. Did Hasselstrom affect your opinion on gun control? Explain.

WRITING SUGGESTIONS

1. Write an essay about a societal problem that you do not believe will be corrected in your lifetime. Explain why you feel the way you do.
2. Watch several episodes of an animated family television sitcom such as *The Simpsons*. Pay close attention to the way boys and girls are portrayed as students in the public school system. With the understanding that television is in most cases an exaggeration of real life, use examples from the episodes that you watched to show ways in which girls and boys could be educationally stereotyped or stereotyped in any way.
3. What is right about America? People often complain about things that are wrong with our country. In essay form, explain why the United States is a great place to live, work, and go to school compared to other countries.
4. How does our culture shape gender identity? What are the twenty-first century's cultural expectations of men and women? How have expectations changed over the past fifty years? What further changes would you like to see in years to come?
5. Should states be required to educate children who are illegal immigrants? Why or why not? Write an argument essay on the topic.
6. Tattoos and body piercings have become very popular among young people. In what ways does this define our emerging culture?

PRE-READING QUESTIONS

1. What shows on television today would be considered reality television?
2. Do you watch any reality television? If so, which are your favorite shows?
3. Why do you think that reality television is such a big part of popular culture today?

Reality Television: Issues and Controversies

Facts on File

Facts on File *is a researchers' database that includes "Facts on File Issues and Controversies," an online resource that explores topics in today's politics, business, culture, education, and society. Each topic is presented with key facts, arguments, history, and the current context. The articles are written by Facts on File's expert authors and editors. The database includes over 900 in-depth articles providing pro and con thinking on controversial subjects. Find it at http://factsonfile.infobasepublishing.com.*

Terms to Recognize

purport (*para. 1*)	claim
spawned (*para. 2*)	gave birth to
adhering to (*para. 4*)	following
resonant (*para. 4*)	meaningful
voyeurism (*para. 5*)	obsessive observation of sensational events
formulaic (*para. 7*)	following an established pattern
counterparts (*para. 7*)	corresponding persons or things

1   "Reality television" is a broad term, covering various television programs that purport to be more "true to life" than purely fictional dramas and situation comedies. The typical reality show features ordinary people (i.e., non-actors) who are placed in apparently unscripted—and therefore unpredictable—

situations. The unique format of reality television lends it a spontaneous quality that has attracted huge audiences, and considerable controversy, around the world.

2   In the U.S., the popularity of reality television has surged dramatically since 2000, when the landmark show *Survivor* debuted on CBS. *Survivor*, which pits groups of contestants from different backgrounds against each other in seemingly hostile wilderness environments, popularized a competitive format for reality shows and spawned numerous imitators. Other influential reality shows soon followed, including *American Idol* (Fox, 2002–present), a hugely popular singing contest, and *The Apprentice* (NBC, 2004–present), a business-themed competition.

3   Not all popular reality shows have been based on the competitive format, however. Some have involved filming the everyday lives of regular people or celebrities, while others have focused on themes such as blind dating, makeovers, and "hidden camera" pranks. Although the different types of reality shows might appear distinct from each other on the surface, they often share common production techniques, and they can attract acclaim or criticism for very similar reasons.

4   Advocates of reality television shows argue they are generally more representative of "real life" than scripted television programs, which are often criticized for adhering to predictable dramatic formulas. In essence, fans maintain that reality television is more relevant and resonant to them than fictional television. They also praise competitive reality shows, such as *American Idol* and *The Amazing Race* (CBS, 2001–present), for showcasing the talents of previously "undiscovered" contestants and pushing them to perform at their best.

5   Critics of reality television, on the other hand, argue that it often treats its subjects cruelly. For instance, failed *American Idol* contestants are sometimes subjected to ridicule from the judges that damages their self-esteem, detractors assert, while competitors on *Survivor* are often placed in uncomfortable or potentially hazardous situations. Critics have also attacked other reality shows, such as MTV's *The Real World* (1992–present) and CBS's *Big Brother* (2000–present), for allegedly exposing their subjects to emotional strain and encouraging destructive behaviors such as binge drinking. At their very worst, reality shows exploit their subjects, encourage voyeurism, and amount to a "dumbing down" of television and American culture as a whole, critics assert.

6   In light of such concerns, a heated debate has arisen over the perceived merits, flaws, and cultural impact of reality television. Television experts,

sociologists, and other interested observers have raised a series of key questions on the issue: Does reality television too often exploit its subjects, or does it actually help them to achieve recognition and success? Is it a bold alternative to fictional entertainment, or is it actually less satisfying than scripted drama and comedy? And how "real," exactly, is reality television? Is it genuinely "true to life," or is it more artificial and engineered than it appears to be?

7   Advocates of reality television describe it as a refreshing change of pace from scripted (and often formulaic) entertainment. They describe the competitive format of many reality shows as energetic and exciting, and credit programs such as *American Idol* with allowing "everyday" people to demonstrate their talents and potentially find fame and success. There is nothing inherently cruel about reality television, supporters assert; reality shows simply reflect the highs and lows of "real" life more honestly than their fictional counterparts. In short, reality shows are stimulating, fun, and inoffensive, advocates say.

8   Critics of reality television, on the other hand, argue that it exploits "everyday" people who are typically unprepared for being thrust into the media spotlight. Reality show contestants are often mocked and exposed to mental or physical harm, and watching their suffering amounts to voyeurism, detractors contend. They further assert that reality shows are artificially engineered and therefore dishonest in their presentation of "real" events. Ultimately, scripted television programs are more socially relevant and intelligent—and far less manipulative—than reality shows, critics conclude.

COMPREHENSION QUESTIONS

1. What are the two most popular types of reality television in popular culture today?
2. Describe the viewpoints of advocates and critics of reality television.
3. Does reality television offer people a chance at their fifteen minutes of fame? Explain.
4. Is reality TV formulaic? Is there often a common pattern? If so, what is it?
5. What are some of the drawbacks in appearing on a reality television show?

QUESTIONS ON WRITING TECHNIQUE

1. How does the essay define reality television?
2. The essay uses the terms advocates and critics frequently. Explain those terms.
3. How does the essay outline the heated debate surrounding reality television?
4. What questions are left unanswered in this short essay?
5. Write a brief conclusion for the essay that wraps up the thoughts of advocates and critics.

IN-SIGHT

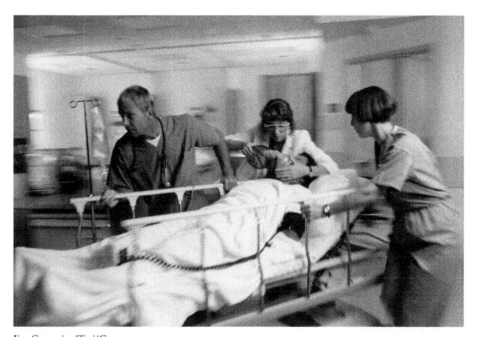

Jim Cummins/Taxi/Getty.

Millions of Americans do not have health insurance, and countless more have found themselves in serious debt due to the ever rising cost of medical care in America.

1. Do you believe that doctors are to blame for the high costs of medical care? If not, who is?

2. What do you believe can be done to stop the growth of rising health care costs?

3. Have you or anyone close to you ever been hospitalized and worried about covering the costs?

GROUP ACTIVITY

In small groups, consider how you would create a health system to serve the needs of all the people. Come up with a basic summarized plan to present to the class.

PEER CRITIQUE

Your Name _____

The Author's Name _____

1. Read your partner's essay.

2. What is your immediate reaction to the essay? Is the essay clear? Passionate? Organized?

3. What method of introduction does the author use (anecdote, quotation, general statement, question)?

4. Is there an explicit thesis statement? If so, write it here. If it is not explicit, is it clear? If so, put it in your own words here.

5. List at least two statements that the author makes that support his or her thesis. How do they support the thesis? Do you agree with the statements?

6. How does the author respond to people who might not agree with him or her? What statements in the essay seem to be a response to people who might not agree with the author's position?

7. Other than example, what methods of support are evident (questioning, counter-arguments, general statements, observations)?

8. Is the supporting material logical? How does it help support the author's argument?

9. How did the author conclude his or her essay? What was the method (prediction, call for action, summary, question)? Was it effective? Why or why not?

MECHANICS AND STYLE

Using and Acknowledging Sources

As you further develop your essays, you will find that you will need additional support to make critical points in your writing. These points can often be made with examples from your own life. However, usually more substantial information will be necessary in college writing. Therefore, you will need to use primary or secondary sources in your writing.

Primary sources are sources that you generate and investigate yourself. Examples include personal interviews, observations, and surveys that you conduct yourself to find out about certain issues or problems. One example would be to interview a Registered Nurse at your local hospital to find out about the job that he or she performs, then including that information in an expository essay about "Becoming a Registered Nurse in Nevada." You could also observe a high school class and write about the experience in your essay. These are primary sources because you did the investigation and write-up yourself.

Secondary sources are books, lectures, articles in scholarly journals, and similar materials that others have written on compiled. You can often use the words of others to help support your arguments and points. When you use the words of others, you need to give them credit for their writing and work. You do that through direct quotation, summarizing, and paraphrasing. Even if you do not use the exact words of an author, you must still give that person credit for his or her work. If you do not, you have committed plagiarism. Plagiarism is often punishable by a failing grade or even removal from college. It is a serious error that a writer should never commit.

Methods for Including Sources

Direct Quotation: Using the exact words of someone else in your writing.

Example: "The population of Nevada has grown for the past five years" (Solomon 6).

Paraphrase: Using information from someone else but putting it in your own words.

Example: For five years, the population has increased in Nevada (Solomon 6).

Summary: Using a brief statement of someone's main points.

Example: In a demographer's article on Nevada, the population increases for each of the counties and the state of Nevada is discussed at length. These increases are divided by ethnicity (Solomon).

Exercise

In the paragraph below, place an X after each sentence that would be better with evidence to support the claim.

A *National Lampoon* cartoon shows two electricians puzzling over chicken wings at "The Bureau of Unidentified Appetizers." Chicken wings—with all of their various sauces—are one of the most popular food items in America. In fact, John Friedburg reports that over 20,000 acres of chicken wings are consumed daily in the United States. From childhood, Americans eat chicken wings—at birthday parties, after school or sports events, on their first dates, or while at work on projects. In particular, chicken wings are a wise choice for a quick meal when there's a work deadline: they don't require utensils. They are low in calories compared to most other fast-food meals, and they are one of the first choices of nutritionists. Chicken wings are such standard fare during overtime that news reporters regularly monitor deliveries to the White House to see if a presidential announcement is forthcoming.

EXAMPLE OF A CITED ESSAY

The essay on the following page was written by a student. The student is explaining how cancer spreads and what treatments are available. Notice how the student skillfully uses quotations from others to help support her discussion. The student used MLA citation in her essay. Her work is a good example of the use of citation in writing.

Wayward Cells

Kerri Mertz

Imagine a room containing a large group of people all working hard toward the same goal. Each person knows his or her job, does it carefully, and cooperates with other group members. Together, they function efficiently and smoothly—like a well-oiled machine.

Then something goes wrong. One guy suddenly drops his task, steps into another person's workstation, grabs the material that she's working with, and begins something very different—he uses the material to make little reproductions of himself, thousands of them. These look-alikes imitate him—grabbing material and making reproductions of themselves. Soon the bunch gets so big that they spill into other people's workstations, getting in their way, and interrupting their work. As the number of look-alikes grows, the work group's activity slows, stutters, and finally stops.

A human body is like this room, and the body's cells are like these workers. If the body is healthy, each cell has a necessary job and does it correctly. For example, right now red blood cells are running throughout your body carrying oxygen to each body part. Other cells are digesting that steak sandwich that you had for lunch, and others are patching up that cut on your left hand. Each cell knows what to do because its genetic code—or DNA—tells it what to do. When a cell begins to function abnormally, it can initiate a process that results in cancer.

The problem starts when one cell "forgets" what it should do. Scientists call this "undifferentiating"—meaning that the cell loses its identity within the body (Pierce 75). Just like the guy in the group who decided to do his own thing, the cell forgets its job. Why this happens is somewhat unclear. The problem could be caused by a defect in the cell's DNA code or by something in the environment, such as cigarette smoke or asbestos (German 21). Causes from inside the body are called genetic, whereas causes from outside the body are called carcinogens, meaning "any substance that causes cancer" (Neufeldt and Sparks 90). In either case, an undifferentiated cell can disrupt the function of healthy cells in two ways: by not doing its job as specified in its DNA and by not reproducing at the rate noted in its DNA.

Most healthy cells reproduce rather quickly, but their reproduction rate is controlled. For example, your blood cells completely die off and replace themselves within a matter of weeks, but existing cells make only as many new cells as the body needs. The DNA codes in healthy cells tell them how many new cells to produce. However, cancer cells don't have this control, so they reproduce quickly with no stopping point, a characteristic called "autonomy" (Braun 3). What's more, all their "offspring" have the same qualities as their messed-up parents, and the resulting overpopulation produces growths called tumors.

Tumor cells can hurt the body in a number of ways. First, a tumor can grow so big that it takes up space needed by other organs. Second, some cells may detach from the original tumor and spread throughout the body, creating new tumors elsewhere. This happens with lymphatic cancer—a cancer that's hard to control because it spreads so quickly. A third way that tumor cells can hurt the body is by doing work not called for in their DNA. For example, a gland cell's DNA code may tell the cell to produce a necessary hormone in the endocrine system. However, if cancer damages or distorts that code, sick cells may produce more of the hormone than the body can use—or even tolerate (Braun 4). Cancer cells seem to have minds of their own, and this is why cancer is such a serious disease.

Fortunately, there is hope. Scientific research is already helping doctors do amazing things for people suffering with cancer. One treatment that has been used for some time is chemotherapy, or the use of chemicals to kill off all fast-growing cells, including cancer cells. (Unfortunately, chemotherapy can't distinguish between healthy and unhealthy cells, so it may cause negative side effects such as damaging fast-growing hair follicles, resulting in hair loss.) Another common treatment is radiation, or the use of light rays to kill cancer cells. One of the newest and most promising treatments is gene therapy—an effort to identify and treat chromosomes that carry a "wrong code" in their DNA. A treatment like gene therapy is promising because it treats the cause of cancer, not just the effect. Year by year, research is helping doctors better understand what cancer is and how to treat it.

Much of life involves dealing with problems like wayward workers, broken machines, or dysfunctional organizations. Dealing with wayward cells is just another problem. While the problem is painful and deadly, there is hope. Medical specialists and other scientists are making progress, and some day they will help us win our battle against wayward cells.

Works Cited

Braun, Armin C. *The Biology of Cancer*. Boston:
    Addison-Wesley, 1994.

German, James. *Chromosomes and Cancer*. New York: John
    Wiley and Sons, 1998.

Neufeldt, Victoria, and Andrew N. Sparks, eds.
    Webster's New World Dictionary. New York: Warner
    Books, 2001.

Pierce, G. Barry, *Cancer: A Problem of Development
    Biology*. Upper Saddle River: Prentice Hall, 1998.

QUESTIONS ON CITATION

1. List five times that the author uses citation in her essay. Write each sentence and explain how it helps the essay.
2. How did the author build her "road map" for the reader?
3. What is listed on the Works Cited page?
4. What is gained by the author's use of citation?

9

DOCUMENTATION IN THE HUMANITIES: MLA STYLE

Documentation is like a system of traffic signs and signals: everyone in a culture agrees to use the system so that nobody gets hurt. Communities of readers and writers do the same thing: they agree to identify their sources according to a given set of rules. There are several forms of documentation for particular areas of study and specific journals.

The Modern Language Association of America is an international organization of teachers and researchers dedicated to the study and teaching of language and literature. Many humanities departments in schools and colleges as well as a host of journals and magazines require that writers use the MLA style when presenting a manuscript. The details of MLA style are presented in two books: the *MLA Handbook for Writers of Research Papers*, used mostly by high school and undergraduate college students; and the *MLA Style Manual and Guide to Scholarly Publishing*, used by graduate students, scholars, and professional writers.

MLA MANUSCRIPT FORMAT

In addition to the many, many specifics of preparing a manuscript in MLA style, the following general rules apply.

Page Layout

- Use standard 8-1/2 by 11 paper and standard typeface. Avoid odd type-faces or other unusual variations available with word processing.
- Place name, date, and course information in the upper left-hand corner of the first page; double-space before the centered title.

- Double-space between lines.
- Leave at least one-inch margins.
- Place page numbers in the upper right-hand corner, one-half inch from the top of the paper; include your last name before the number for identification.

Body of the Paper

- Cite sources in the text, not in footnotes or endnotes.
- Don't use punctuation between the author's name and the page number in a citation.
- Cite the page number(s) of direct quotations in in-text citations.
- Indent the first line of each paragraph five spaces.
- Indent quotations of more than four typed lines ten spaces; omit the quotation marks.
- Leave one space after all punctuation; MLA allows either a single or a double space after periods or question and exclamation marks.
- Form a dash with two hyphens, using no spaces.

List of Sources

- Center the words "Works Cited" at the top of the page.
- List sources alphabetically by author's last name. If there is no author, alphabetize by book or selection title.
- Use hanging indentation (first line flush left against the margin, second and subsequent lines indented).
- Separate items in a citation (author, title, place and date of publication) with periods.
- If the city of publication is not easily recognizable, add the two-letter abbreviation for the state.

IN-TEXT CITATION

1. *Author named in text*
   If the author is named in the text, only page numbers are given.

   ```
   Stephen Jay Gould discusses the power of scientific
   drawings (18).
   ```

2. *Author not named in text*
   When the author is not named in the text, the name appears in the notation.

   ```
   Deep time appears as a new concept in Lavoisier
   (Gould 22).
   ```

3. *Two or three authors*
   Use only the last names of the authors.

   ```
   Scharton and Neuleib claim that professors change when
   they work with writing centers (65).
   ```

4. *Four or more authors*
   All four authors may be named, or author number one and "et al." (Latin for "et alia," which means "and others") may be referenced in the text or in parentheses.

   ```
   Duin, Lammers, Mason, and Graves suggest that mentors
   with much teaching experience will give more help than
   mentors who have taught little (143).
   ```

   ```
   Mentors with much teaching experience will give more help
   than mentors who have taught little (Duin et al. 143).
   ```

5. *Unknown author*
   The title substitutes for the author's name in the text or in parentheses.

   ```
   "The Twin Corbies" refers to crows (119).
   ```

6. *Corporate author*
   A corporate author can be named in either the text or in parentheses.

   ```
   Illinois State University notes that it employs 264
   professors (1).
   ```

7. *Two or more works by the same author*
   When two or more works by one author appear on the Works Cited page, either name the work in the text, or include a short form of the title in the parentheses.

   ```
   In "The Gift of Insight," Neuleib and Scharton explain
   the complexities of type preference (197).
   ```

   If author and shortened form both appear in parentheses, use this form:

   ```
   (Neuleib and Scharton, "Insight" 197)
   ```

8. *A source quoted in another source*
   To show that one author is quoting another, use the abbreviation "qtd. in."

   ```
   Flower notes that "research in composition shows an
   alternative picture of how knowledge can be developed"
   (qtd. in Neuleib and Scharton 54).
   ```

9. *Novel, play, or poem*
   Give the title if not mentioned in text when the work is first referred to, then follow with specific information as listed below.

   ```
   Novel: part or chapter
   Ged said, "I fear what follows behind me" (A Wizard of
   Earthsea 117: ch. 6).
   Play: act and scene and line numbers in arabic
   numerals
   "He waxes desperate with imagination," cries Horatio
   (Hamlet 1.4.87).
   Poem: refer to the part (if applicable) and line
   numbers
   "Surely some revelation is at hand," muses Yeats's
   "The Second Coming" (10).
   ```

10. *Work in an anthology*
Cite the author's name, not the editor's name.

In his essay "On Stories," Lewis observes that "No book
is really worth reading at the age of ten which is not
equally worth reading at the age of fifty" (100).

11. *Entire work*
Name the author in the text or note in parentheses.

Freire was introduced to North American scholars in
Freire for the Classroom (Shor).

WORKS CITED
Books

1. *One author*

    LeGuin, Ursula K. *A Wizard of Earthsea*. New York: Ace,
        1968. Print.

2. *Two or three authors*

    Scharton, Maurice, and Janice Neuleib. *Inside/Out: A
        Guide to Writing*. Needham Heights, MA: Allyn &
        Bacon, 1992. Print.

3. *More than three authors or editors*

    Lawson, Bruce, et al., eds. *Encountering Student
        Texts*. Urbana: NCTE, 1989. Print.

4. *Editor*

    Hooper, Walter, ed. *The Letters of C. S. Lewis*. New
        York: Macmillan, 1979. Print.

5. *Author with editor*

Tolkien, J. R. R. *The Tolkien Reader*. Ed. Christopher
    Tolkien. New York: Ballantine, 1966. Print.

6. *Unknown author*

Primary Colors. New York: Random House, 1996. Print.

7. *Corporate author*

Illinois State University. *Facts 1998-9*. Normal, IL:
    Illinois State UP, 1999. Print.

8. *Two or more works by the same author*

Lewis, C. S. *The Lion, the Witch, and the Wardrobe*.
    New York: Macmillan, 1950. Print.

—. *The Magician's Nephew*. New York: Macmillan, 1955.
    Print.

9. *Translation*

Tolstoy, L. N. *Anna Karenina*. Trans. Rosemary Edmunds.
    New York: Viking, 1954. Print.

10. *Work in an anthology*

Walsh, Chad. "The Reeducation of the Fearful Pilgrim."
    The Longing for a Form. Ed. Peter J. Schakel. Kent,
    OH: Kent State UP, 1977. 64-72. Print.

Periodicals

11. *Newspaper article*

(signed)

Flick, Bill. "This Year in History." *Daily Pantagraph*
31 Dec. 1998: A14. Print.

(unsigned)

"Honda Motor Recalls Several Models to Fix Ball-Joint
Assembly." *Wall Street Journal* 13 May 1999: B14.
Print.

12. *Magazine article*

(signed)

Gould, Stephen Jay. "Capturing the Center." *Natural
History* Dec. 1998: 14+. Print.

(unsigned)

"College Can Give You Grief." *Psychology Today* Oct.
1998: 20. Print.

13. *Journal article*

*(with continuous page numbering from issue to issue
within a year)*

Fleckenstein, Kristie. "Writing Bodies." *College
English* 61 (1999): 281–306. Print.

(with each issue paged separately)

Becker, Becky K. "Women Who Choose: The Theme of
Mothering in Selected Dramas." *American Drama* 6.2
(1997): 43+. Print.

Other Sources

14. *The Bible*

The New International Bible. Colorado Springs:
International Bible Society, 1972. Print.

```
[The King James Bible need not be named or
underlined. You need only note chapter and verse in
parentheses in the text (Matt 12:1—3). Translations
of the Bible other than King James should be
identified and underlined.]
```

15. *Letter to the editor*

```
White, Curt. Letter. The Vidette. 18 Feb. 1999: 6.
    Print.
```

16. *Personal or telephone interview*

```
Kay, Martha. Personal interview. 10 Mar. 1999. Print.
```

17. *Record, tape, or CD*

```
Kingston Trio. Greatest Hits. Curb Records, 1991.
    Print.
```

Electronic Sources

These sources include a variety of types of communication: personal e-mail between persons or among private group members, listservs among several individuals with common interests, or news groups that serve associations or subscribers. The World Wide Web connects the individual to a wider community, including businesses and other commercial groups. For all these sources, documentation should be used consistently. Note that the second date is always the date a website was accessed while the first date is the time of publication.

18. *Professional site*

```
NCTE Home Page. 6 January 2004. National Council of
    Teachers of English. Web. 4 March 2004.
```

19. *A personal site*

```
Neuleib, Janice Witherspoon. Home page. Illinois State
    University. Web. 26 February 2004.
```

20. *A book*

Crane, Stephen. *The Red Badge of Courage*. Guttenberg
     Project. University of California Berkeley Archives.
     4 September 1996. Sunsite Berkeley. Web. 4 March 2004.

21. *A poem*

Dickinson, Emily. "A Narrow Fellow in the Grass,"
     Poetry Archive. Web.

22. *An article in a reference database*

"On 'Behave.'" *Oxford English Dictionary Online*. Second
     Edition. 1989. Oxford English Dictionary. Web.
     5 March 2004.

23. *An article in a journal*

Applebee, Arthur N., and Judith A. Langer.
     "Discussion-Based Approaches to Student
     Understanding: Classroom Instruction in the Middle
     School Classroom." *American Education Research
     Journal* 40:3 (2003). Web. 2 March 2004.

24. *An article in a magazine*

Perkins, Sid. "Avalanche." *Science News On Line* 2 March
     2002. Web. 16 February 2004.

25. *A review*

Traister, Rebecca. "Is 'The Sopranos' a Chick Flick?" Rev.
     of *The Sopranos* TV Series. *Salon* 6 March 2004. Web.
     8 March 2004.

26. *A posting to a discussion group*

> Hesse, Doug. "What Makes a College Good." Online
>   posting. 5 Nov. 2003. ISU Teach. Web. 7 March 2004.

27. *A personal e-mail message*

> Neuleib, Janice. "Collaborative MR Chapter." E-mail to
>   Katherine Gretz. 19 Feb. 2004. E-mail.

28. *Graphic novels*

> Gibbons, Dave, illus. *Watchmen*. By Alan Moore. Ed.
>   Barry Marx. New York: DC Comics, 1995. Print.

29. *Online video clip*

> Jones, Maurice. "Cooking with Cilantro." *World of
>   Spices*. Youtube, 8 November 2010. Web. 14 February
>   2011.

APPENDIX:
A GUIDE TO
AVOIDING PLAGIARISM

WHAT IS PLAGIARISM?

Plagiarism is using someone else's work—words, ideas, or illustrations, published or unpublished—without giving the creator of that work sufficient credit. A serious breach of scholarly ethics, plagiarism can have severe consequences. Students risk a failing grade or disciplinary action ranging from suspension to expulsion. A record of such action can adversely affect professional opportunities in the future as well as graduate school admission. Scholars and teachers can face public disgrace and even be forced out of a position. In the business world, plagiarism leads to distrust and can damage careers.

Significance of Intellectual Honesty

Many would argue, in this age of the Internet and music downloads, that information should be "free." However, it's possible to preserve the free flow of information without plagiarizing. In fact, the careful documentation of information sources helps ensure that information remains not only available but reliable.

Others may ask, What's so terrible about copying someone else's work? The issues concerning plagiarism touch two significant points: preserving intellectual honesty and giving credit for work done. The academic community relies on the reciprocal exchange of ideas and information to further knowledge and research. Using material without acknowledging its source violates this expectation and consequently makes it hard for researchers to verify and build on others' results. It also cheats writers and researchers of the credit they deserve for their work and creativity.

Even with the writer's permission, presenting another's work as one's own is equivalent to lying: it's a form of dishonesty. Perhaps most important for students, plagiarizing damages a person's own self-respect and negates the very reasons he or she is in college. A student who hands in a plagiarized paper has missed an opportunity for growth and learning.

Intentional Plagiarism

Suppose you are pressed by a deadline for a paper in your history class and a friend offers you a paper he or she wrote for a similar class the previous year. Handing in that paper as your own is intentional plagiarism. In the same way, buying a paper from an Internet source—or taking one from a sorority or fraternity file—and handing it in, with or without making changes of your own, is plagiarism. Paying someone to write a paper that you then submit as yours is also plagiarism, as is handing in a paper of your own that someone else has rewritten or revised.

Ethical considerations aside, it's hard to get away with plagiarism. Experienced professors can easily tell when a paper is not written in a student's own style or is more professionally prepared than they would expect. In addition, online services now identify plagiarized papers for a fee, and academic institutions are subscribing to such services. The March 2, 2006, online edition of *The New York Sun* reported that in New York City, more and more schools were requiring students to hand in papers through Turnitin.com, "a service that compares students' papers against everything on the Internet and a database of more than 15 million student papers."

Students at these schools will have a hard time getting away with submitting unoriginal papers.

DOCUMENTATION: THE KEY TO AVOIDING UNINTENTIONAL PLAGIARISM

As a student, you may resolve never to be involved in plagiarism. But it can be difficult to tell when you have unintentionally plagiarized something. The legal doctrine of **fair use** allows writers to use a limited amount of another's work in their own papers and books. However, to make sure that they are not plagiarizing that work, writers need to take care that they accurately and clearly credit the source for *every* use.

In the academic and business worlds, documentation is the method writers employ to give credit to the creators of material they use. **Documentation** involves providing essential information about the source of the material—the information that would enable readers to find the material for themselves if they so choose. It tells the reader (1) what ideas are the writer's, (2) what ideas are someone else's, (3) where the writer got the facts and other information, and (4) how reliable the sources are.

Documentation requires two elements: (1) a list of sources used in the paper and (2) citations within the text that refer to items in that list. To use documentation and avoid unintentionally plagiarizing from a source, you need to know

- How to identify sources and information that must be documented.
- How to document sources in a Works Cited list.
- How to use material gathered from sources—in summary, paraphrase, and quotation.
- How to create in-text references.
- How to use correct grammar and punctuation to blend quotations into a paper.

IDENTIFYING SOURCES AND INFORMATION THAT NEED TO BE DOCUMENTED

Whenever you use information, facts, statistics, opinions, hypotheses, graphics, or ideas from **outside sources**—whenever you use any words or ideas that you have not thought up yourself—you need to identify the source of that material.

Virtually all the information you find in outside sources will require documentation. The one major exception is that you do not have to document common knowledge. **Common knowledge** is widely known information about current events, famous people, geographical facts, and familiar history. Asking these questions can help you determine whether a fact is common knowledge:

- Is this information that you know, or that you would expect others to know, without having to look it up?
- Is the information readily available in many sources without documentation?
- Is the information in a general dictionary?
- Is it a common saying or expression?
- Is this widely known information about authorship or creation?

If you have considered these questions and are still in doubt, the safest strategy is to provide documentation.

DOCUMENTING SOURCES IN A WORKS CITED LIST

You need to choose the documentation style that is dominant in your field or required by your instructor. Take care to use only one documentation style in any one paper and to follow its documentation formats consistently. Your documentation needs to be correctly placed within the body of your paper as well as in the list of sources that follows your paper, according to the documentation style you are using.

Documentation Styles and Their Manuals: MLA, APA, CMS

The most widely used style manuals are those published by the Modern Language Association (MLA), the American Psychological Association (APA), and the University of Chicago Press (CMS). Other, more specialized style manuals are used in various fields.

- MLA style is used by writers in the fields of English language and literature, as well as by students of foreign languages and some humanities subjects. As writers in these fields can rely on sources from a wide range of time periods, the documentation style puts more emphasis on identifying specific editions of texts.

- APA style is favored by researchers in the fields of psychology and other social sciences. Publication date has a prominent place in the citation formats.

- CMS style is favored by researchers in art history, history, philosophy, religion, and other humanities subjects. It is also commonly used in business. A more "traditional" style, CMS style uses raised numbers (with footnotes or end notes) instead of parenthetical references within the text.

Elements Included in a Citation

Remember that the purpose of documentation is to identify others' contributions to your paper and to enable readers to find and evaluate for themselves those source materials. In-text citations identify sources in the text of your paper and direct the reader to the correct entries in your Works Cited (MLA style) list.

Generally speaking, the Works Cited list gives information for the sources you quote, summarize, or paraphrase in your paper. If your instructor asks you to include sources you consulted but did not use in the paper, call the list "Works Consulted."

Certain elements are common to all citation formats in all styles:

- Author or other creative individual or entity
- Title of the work
- Source of the work
- Publisher or distributor
- Relevant identifying numbers or letters
- Relevant dates

Constructing a Works Cited List in MLA Style

As an accompaniment to your English text, this guide explores MLA style. MLA lists are alphabetized by authors' last names. However, an individual item can also be alphabetized by article title (when there is no author), by editor (when, for example, you quote the editor in your paper), or by the sponsoring organization (when no author is given). Computerized programs can format and alphabetize a Works Cited list in a style that you choose using the data that you provide; however, these programs will *not* research the data for you. Understanding how documentation works can help you list and make use of sources more effectively.

The requirements of your topic may make some organizational choices more efficient than others. Whatever element you use to alphabetize an entry, remember to use the same element in the in-text citations. In the first example below, *An MLA In-Text Citation by Editor*, the focus of the paper is on what the editor has to say. As we can see from the Works Cited entry, the writer uses only the introduction to *Collected Poems*. In the second example, *An MLA In-Text Citation by Author*, the paper has several citations to *Collected Poems* in addition to the citation to the editor's introduction. In this example, the writer includes a single Works Cited entry for the book and specifies page numbers in each in-text reference.

An MLA In-Text Citation by Editor

```
    Bidart asserts that though Lowell was known as
a "confessional" writer, it was his "practice as
an artist," rather than simply his outspokenness, that
made Lowell one of the twentieth century's great poets
(Bidart vii).
```

Works Cited Entry

> Bidart, Frank. Introduction. *Collected Poems*.
>
> By Robert Lowell. Ed. Frank Bidart and David
>
> Gewanter. New York: Farrar, 2003. vii–xvi.

An MLA In-Text Citation by Author

> In his introduction to Robert Lowell's *Collected*
> *Poems*, Frank Bidart asserts that though Lowell was
> known as a "confessional" writer, it was his "practice
> as an artist," rather than simply his outspokenness,
> that made Lowell one of the twentieth century's great
> poets (vii). One memorable example can be found in
> "For the Union Dead" (376-78). In that poem Lowell's
> juxtaposition of the everyday commotion of life with
> St. Gaudens' depiction of a tragic historical event
> creates an almost palpable stillness for the reader.

Works Cited Entry

> Lowell, Robert. *Collected Poems*. Ed. Frank Bidart and
>
> David Gewanter. New York: Farrar, 2003.

MLA Style: Sample Formats

In the Works Cited list below, notice how in MLA style you spell out names in full, inverting only the first author's name. Elements are separated with a period. Observe the use of punctuation such as commas, colons, and angle brackets to separate and introduce material within elements. The Works Cited list below is organized by type of source (book, periodical, etc.) to illustrate the general differences in citation format. In an actual Works Cited list, all items are alphabetized by authors' last names in a single list.

Books

> Chernow, Ron. *Alexander Hamilton*. New York: Penguin, 2004.
>
> Conant, Jennet. *109 East Palace: Robert Oppenheimer and*
> *the Secret City of Los Alamos*. New York: Simon, 2005.

Conant. Jennet. *Tuxedo Park: A Wall Street Tycoon and the Secret Palace of Science That Changed the Course of World War II*. New York: Simon, 2002.

Maupassant, Guy de. "The Necklace." Trans. Marjorie Laurie. *An Introduction to Fiction*. Ed. X. J. Kennedy and Dana Gioia. 7th ed. New York: Longman, 1999. 160—66.

Woodward, Bob, and Carl Bernstein. *All the President's Men*. 1974. New York: Touchstone-Simon, 1994.

Periodicals

"Living on Borrowed Time." *Economist* 25 Feb.—3 Mar. 2006: 34—37.

"Restoring the Right to Vote." Editorial. *New York Times* 10 Jan. 2006, late ed., sec. A: 24.

Spinello, Richard A. "The End of Privacy." *America* 4 Jan. 1997: 9—13.

Williams, N. R., M. Davey, and K. Klock-Powell. "Rising from the Ashes: Stories of Recovery, Adaptation, and Resiliency in Burn Survivors." *Social Work Health Care* 36.4 (2003): 53—77.

Zobenica, Jon. "You Might As Well Live." Rev. of *A Long Way Down* by Nick Hornby. *Atlantic* July—Aug. 2005: 148.

Electronic Sources

Boehlert, Eric. "Artists to Napster: Drop Dead!" *Salon.com*. 24 Mar. 2000. Web. 17 Oct. 2004.

Human Rights Watch. *Libya: A Threat to Society? Arbitrary Detention of Women and Girls for "Social Rehabilitation."* Feb. 2006. Index No. E1802. Human Rights Watch. Web. 4 Mar. 2006.

Patronek, Gary J. "The Problem of Animal Hoarding." *Municipal Lawyer* May/June 2001: 6-9, 19. Hoarding of Animals Consortium, Center for Animals and

Public Policy, Cummings Animal Veterinary School,
Tufts University. Web. 12 Mar. 2006.
Reporters Without Borders. "Worldwide Press Freedom
Index 2005." *Reporters Without Borders*. 2005. Web.
28 Feb. 2006.

USING MATERIAL GATHERED FROM SOURCES: SUMMARY, PARAPHRASE, QUOTATION

You can integrate material into your paper in three ways: by summarizing, by paraphrasing, and by quoting. Each summary, paraphrase, or quotation must be used in a way that accurately conveys the meaning of the source; that is, no material should be taken out of context in a way that distorts the sense of the original.

Summary

A **summary** is a concise restatement in your own words of the source's main ideas. Summary is used to convey the general meaning of the ideas in a source without repeating the specific details or examples that appear in the original. A summary is always much shorter than the work it treats; a summary of an entire book might be just 50 to 100 words long. Some papers require particular types of summaries, such as reviews, plot summaries, annotated bibliography entries, and abstracts. Take care to give the essential information as clearly and succinctly as possible in your own words.

Write a summary when (1) the information is important enough to be included but not important enough to be treated at length; (2) the relevant material is too long to be quoted fully; or (3) you want to give the essence of the material without all the details.

Rules to Remember

1. Write a summary using your own words. If you "borrow" distinctive words or phrases from your source, you must use quotation marks within your summary to enclose that quoted material.
2. Indicate clearly where the summary begins and ends.
3. Use attribution and parenthetical reference to tell the reader where the material came from.

4. Make sure your summary is an accurate and objective restatement of the source's main ideas and that it preserves the source's tone or point of view.

5. See that the summary is clearly separated from your own ideas. One way to do this is to place the parenthetical reference immediately after the summary.

Paraphrase

A **paraphrase** is a restatement, using your own words and your own sentence structure, of specific ideas or information from a source. Paraphrase is useful when you want to capture certain ideas or details from a source but you do not need or want to quote the source's actual words. The chief purpose of a paraphrase is *to maintain your own writing style* throughout your paper. The most effective way to write a paraphrase is to read the original passage, then put the passage aside and compose your own restatement of the material in the passage. If you want to repeat particular words or phrases from the original, put them in quotation marks. A paraphrase can be about as long as the original passage.

Use a paraphrase when (1) you don't want to interrupt the flow of your writing with another person's writing; (2) you want to avoid using a long quotation or a string of quotations; or (3) you want to interpret or explain the material as you present it.

Rules to Remember

1. Use your own words and sentence structure; your paraphrase must not duplicate the source's words or phrases.

2. Use quotation marks within your paraphrase to indicate quoted material.

3. Make sure your readers know where the paraphrase begins and ends.

4. Verify that your paraphrase is an accurate and objective restatement of the source's specific ideas.

5. Conclude your paraphrase with a parenthetical reference indicating the source of the information.

Quotation

A **quotation** reproduces an actual part of a source, word for word. It can be used to support a statement or an idea, to provide an example, to advance an argument, or to add interest or color to a discussion. The length of a quotation can range from a word or phrase to several paragraphs. As a general rule, quote the fewest possible words that will get your point across to the reader.

Quoting many long passages from source material can make your paper seem choppy and may give the impression that you have no thoughts of your own.

Use quotations when (1) the original writing is especially powerful, descriptive, clear, or revealing; (2) the original contains language you are analyzing or commenting on; (3) the original provides authenticity or bolsters the credibility of your paper; or (4) the original material is difficult to summarize or paraphrase accurately.

Rules to Remember

1. Copy the material from your source to your paper exactly as it appears in the original. Do not alter the spelling, capitalization, or punctuation of the original. If a quotation contains an obvious error, you may insert [*sic*], the Latin for "so" or "thus," to indicate that the error appears in the original. Use regular type and brackets: "representatives from the 51 [sic] states plus the District of Columbia."

2. Enclose short quotations (four or fewer lines of text) in quotation marks; set off longer quotations as block quotations.

3. Provide clear attribution to your source so that your readers know the origin of the quotation.

4. Immediately follow each quotation with a parenthetical reference that gives the source information required.

CREATING IN-TEXT REFERENCES

Keep in mind that documentation has two parts: (1) a list of works used (the "Works Cited" list in MLA style) and (2) in-text references for all source material. The in-text references need to supply enough information to enable a reader to find the correct source in the Works Cited list. To properly cite a source in the text of your report, you generally need to give some or all of the following information for each use of the source:

- Name of the person or organization that authored the source
- Title of the source (when there is more than one source by the same author)
- Page, paragraph, or even line number. Some sources, such as Shakespeare's plays and the Bible, are customarily referred to by their own internal numbering system. And if more than one version of a work is used, the parenthetical reference must clearly show which version is being referenced in the Works Cited list.

The information on the previous page can appear as an attribution in your text ("According to Smith . . .") or in a parenthetical reference immediately following the summary, paraphrase, or quotation. The examples that follow are in MLA style.

Using an Introductory Attribution and a Parenthetical Reference

You can use the author's name, the publication, or a generalized reference to introduce source material. Remaining identifiers (title, page number) can go in the parenthetical reference, as shown in the first sentence of the example below. When a source, such as a Web site, does not have page numbers, it may be possible to put all the information into the in-text attribution, as in the second sentence of the example below.

A parenthetical reference should follow the source material as closely as possible, usually at the end of the sentence. This two-part format—attribution plus parenthetical reference—works well for quotations and is the best practice to follow for a paraphrase because it clearly separates the source material from the writer's own ideas.

MLA In-Text Citation

Recently *The Economist* noted that since 2004, "state tax revenues have come roaring back across the country" ("Living" 34). However, McNichol and Lav, writing for the Center on Budget and Policy Priorities, claim that recent gains are not sufficient to make up for the losses suffered.

Works Cited Entries

"Living on Borrowed Time." *Economist* 25 Feb–3 Mar. 2006: 34–37.

McNichol, Elizabeth C., and Iris J. Lav. "State Revenues and Services Remain below Pre-Recession Levels." *Center on Budget Policy Priorities*. 6 Dec. 2005. Web. 10 Mar. 2006.

Identifying Material by an Author of More Than One Work Used in Your Paper

When you refer to more than one work by a particular author, the attribution and the parenthetical reference combined must provide the title of the work as well as the author and the page number being cited.

> Describing the testing of the first atom bomb, Jennet
> Conant says, "The test had originally been scheduled for
> 4:00 A.M. on July 16, when most of the surrounding
> population would be sound asleep and there would be the
> least number of witnesses" (*109 East Palace* 304–05).

Placing All Identifying Information in the Parenthetical Reference

When using a quotation, you can often omit an introductory attribution; the quotation marks may be sufficient to set off the quotation from your own ideas. The page numbers in the in-text reference will guide the reader to the right source of the quotation.

> In its early days, America lacked many of the sophisticated
> financial mechanisms prevalent in other countries:
> "The creation of New York's first bank was a formative
> moment in the city's rise as a world financial center"
> (Chernow 199–200).

Placing All Identifying Information in the Attribution

In the following example, the writer combines paraphrase and quotation following an attribution that includes all necessary identifying information to locate this Web source on the Works Cited list.

> In its 2005 "Worldwide Press Freedom Index," Reporters
> Without Borders ranked the United States 44th among 167
> countries, a decrease of more than 20 places from the
> previous year, "mainly because of the imprisonment of
> *New York Times* reporter Judith Miller and legal moves
> undermining the privacy of journalistic sources."

Identifying Material That the Source Is Quoting

To use material that is quoted in your cited source, add *qtd. in*, for "quoted in," to the parenthetical reference. This example assumes that only one source by Conant is given in the Works Cited list.

> The weather was worrisome, but procrastination was even
> more problematic. General Groves was concerned that "every
> hour of delay would increase the possibility of someone's
> attempting to sabotage the tests" (qtd. in Conant 305).

USING CORRECT GRAMMAR AND PUNCTUATION TO BLEND QUOTATIONS INTO A PAPER

Quotations must blend seamlessly into your sentence or paragraph so that the result is neither awkward nor ungrammatical. Verb tenses, pronouns, and other parts of speech within the quotation must work grammatically with the rest of your writing, and punctuation must be handled properly.

Using a Full-Sentence Quotation of Fewer Than Four Lines

A quotation of one or more complete sentences can be enclosed in double quotation marks and introduced with a verb that takes a direct object, such as *says* or *writes*. Note that verbs in attributions are usually in the present tense and are followed by a comma. Omit the period at the end of a quoted sentence before the close-quotation marks (but keep a final question mark or an exclamation point). Then give the parenthetical reference, followed by the period.

> One commentator asks, "What accounts for the government's
> ineptitude in safeguarding our privacy rights?" (Spinello 9).

> "What accounts," Spinello asks, "for the government's
> ineptitude in safeguarding our privacy rights?" (9).

Introducing a Quotation with a Full Sentence

Use a colon after a full sentence that introduces a quotation.

> Spinello asks an important question: "What accounts for
> the government's ineptitude in safeguarding our privacy
> rights?" (9).

Introducing a Quotation with *That*

A single complete sentence can be introduced with a *that* construction. Do not put a comma after the word *that*.

```
Chernow suggests that "the creation of New York's first
bank was a formative moment in the city's rise as a world
financial center" (199–200).
```

Quoting Part of a Sentence

When you quote only part of a sentence, make sure the quoted material blends grammatically into your own sentence. The following examples are from a Web site and therefore, do not have page numbers attached to them.

```
McNichol and Lav assert that "an array of fiscal
gimmicks" helped state governments during that period.
```

```
McNichol and Lav assert that during that period, state
governments were helped by "an array of fiscal gimmicks."
```

Using a Quotation That Contains Another Quotation

To indicate a quotation within a quotation, replace the internal double quotation marks with single quotation marks.

```
Lowell was "famous as a 'confessional' writer, but he
scorned the term," according to Bidart (vii).
```

Adding Information to a Quotation

Any words added for clarity or any rewording for grammatical reasons should be placed within square brackets.

```
In 109 East Palace, Conant notes the timing of the first
atom bomb test: "The test had originally been scheduled
for 4:00 A.M. on July 16, [1945,] when most of the
surrounding population would be sound asleep" (304–05).
```

Omitting Words from the Middle of a Sentence

Indicate an omission from the middle of a sentence with an ellipsis mark (three spaced dots).

In *109 East Palace*, Conant says, "The test had originally been scheduled for 4:00 A.M. on July 16, when...there would be the least number of witnesses. But the weather was interfering with their plans, and there was talk of a postponement" (304–05).

Omitting Words at the End of a Sentence

When you omit words from the end of a sentence and another sentence follows inside your quotation, insert a period and then an ellipsis mark, with a space after the three dots.

In *109 East Palace*, Conant says, "The test had originally been scheduled for 4:00 A.M. on July 16.... But the weather was interfering with their plans, and there was talk of a postponement" (304–05).

When your omission at the end of a sentence also comes at the end of the quotation and a parenthetical reference follows, add the three dots with a space before the first one but no space after the third.

In *109 East Palace*, Conant says, "The test had originally been scheduled for 4:00 A.M. on July 16 ..." (304–05).

When your omission at the end of the quotation is not followed by a parenthetical reference, add a period and three dots, with no space after the third dot.

In its report, Human Rights Watch criticizes Libya for "arbitrarily detaining women and girls in 'social rehabilitation' facilities for suspected transgressions of moral codes...."

Omitting the End of One Sentence and the Beginning of the Next Sentence

When you omit words from the middle of one sentence to the middle of the next one, use an ellipsis mark but preserve any internal punctuation that makes the quotation work grammatically.

One expert provides a caution: "Although the stereotypical profile of a hoarder is an older, single female, living alone and known as the neighborhood 'cat

```
lady,' in reality . . . many can lead a double life with a
successful professional career . . ." (Patronek 6).
```

Omitting Information from the Beginning of a Quoted Sentence

(1) When you omit words at the beginning of a sentence you are quoting, you can integrate the quoted sentence into your text by using brackets to indicate a change in capitalization or, if your instructor permits, simply use proper capitalization without brackets.

```
One biographer notes that "the founding of the Bank of
New York cast him [Hamilton] in a more conciliatory role"
(Chernow 199).
```

Using a Quotation of More Than Four Lines

Use long quotations only when they are very important for the point you are making and they cannot be excerpted easily. Set off the quotation by indenting it one inch from the left margin. Begin the quotation on a new line, and double-space it throughout. Put the parenthetical reference *after* the period at the end of the quotation. Do not enclose a block quotation in quotation marks.

One international organization recently documented the repression of women's rights in Libya:

```
The government of Libya is arbitrarily detaining women
and girls in "social rehabilitation" facilities, . . .
locking them up indefinitely without due process.
Portrayed as "protective" homes for wayward women and
girls, . . . these facilities are de facto prisons . . .
[where] the government routinely violates women's and
girls' human rights, including those to due process,
liberty, freedom of movement, personal dignity, and
privacy. (Human Rights Watch)
```

IS IT PLAGIARISM? TEST YOURSELF ON IN-TEXT REFERENCES

Read the Original Source excerpt and then consider the examples that follow. Can you spot the plagiarism?

Original Source:

To begin with, language is a system of communication. I make this rather obvious point because to some people nowadays it isn't obvious: they see language as above all a means of "self-expression." Of course, language is one way that we express our personal feelings and thoughts—but so, if it comes to that, are dancing, cooking and making music. Language does much more: it enables us to convey to others what we think, feel and want. Language-as-communication is the prime means of organizing the cooperative activities that enable us to accomplish as groups things we could not possibly do as individuals. Some other species also engage in cooperative activities, but these are either quite simple (as among baboons and wolves) or exceedingly stereotyped (as among bees, ants and termites). Not surprisingly, the communicative systems used by these animals are also simple or stereotypes. Language, our uniquely flexible and intricate system of communication, makes possible our equally flexible and intricate ways of coping with the world around us: in a very real sense, it is what makes us human (Claiborne 8).

Works Cited Entry

Claiborne, Robert. *Our Marvelous Native Tongue: The Life and Times of the English Language.* New York: New York Times, 1983.

Plagiarism Example 1

One commentator makes a distinction between language used as **a means of self-expression** and **language-as-communication**. It is the latter that distinguishes human interaction from that of other species and allows humans to work cooperatively on complex tasks (8).

What's wrong?

The source's name is not given, and there are no quotation marks around words taken directly from the source (the words in **boldface** in the example).

Correction

One commentator makes a distinction between language used as "a means of self-expression" and "language-as-communication." It is the latter that distinguishes human interaction from that of other species and allows humans to work cooperatively on complex tasks (Claiborne 8).

Plagiarism Example 2

Claiborne notes that language "is the prime means of organizing the cooperative activities." Without language, we would, consequently, not have civilization.

What's wrong?
A parenthetical reference—with a page number—should immediately follow material being quoted, paraphrased, or summarized. You may omit a parenthetical reference only if the information you give in your attribution is sufficient to identify the source in your Works Cited list and no page number is needed.

Correction
Claiborne notes that language "is the prime means of organizing the cooperative activities" (8). Without language, we would, consequently, not have civilization.

Plagiarism Example 3

Robert Claiborne postulates that language makes it possible for human beings to work cooperatively with one another to achieve results that it might be difficult for a single person working alone to achieve.

What's wrong?
No page number reference follows the summary.

Correction
Robert Claiborne postulates that language makes it possible for human beings to work cooperatively with one another to achieve results that it might be difficult for a single person working alone to achieve (8).

Plagiarism Example 4

Other animals also **engage in cooperative activities**. However, these actions are not very complex. Rather they are either the very **simple** activities of, for example, **baboons and wolves** or the **stereotyped** activities of animals such as **bees, ants and termites** (Claiborne 8).

What's wrong?
The wording and the sentence structure follow the source too closely. A paraphrase should capture a specific idea from a source but must not duplicate the writer's phrases and words (the words in **boldface** in the example).

Correction
Other animals are known to work cooperatively. However, these actions are not very complex. Rather they are either the very "simple" activities of, for example,

"baboons and wolves" or the "stereotyped" activities of animals such as "bees, ants and termites" (Claiborne 8).

EVALUATING ELECTRONIC SOURCES

Because such a wealth of readily available information exists on the Internet, it can be difficult to separate helpful, reliable sources from questionable ones. Consequently, it's important to evaluate critically every source you consult. Ask these questions to help evaluate electronic sources:

- Is the material relevant to your topic?
- Is the source a respected one?
- Is the material accurate?
- Is the information current?
- Is the material from a primary source or a secondary source?

AVOIDING PLAGIARISM: NOTE-TAKING TIPS

The only effective approach to avoiding unintentional plagiarism is to keep in mind from the beginning of a writing project the necessity for documenting sources accurately and to follow a systematic method of note taking and writing.

- **Keep copies of your documentation information.** Writers often don't discover that they are missing documentation information until they are finalizing a paper and no longer have access to the original sources. *Tip*: Keep copies of the source material as reference. Photocopy the title and copyright pages of books you use and the pages with quotations you need. Send files of journal articles to your e-mail address or print out copies, making sure the journal title and the page numbers are evident. Highlight the relevant citation information in color. Keep these materials in a folder until you've completed your paper.

- **Quotation or paraphrase?** Writers consulting their notes are often unable to remember whether they recorded direct quotations or paraphrases. *Tip*: Assume that all the material in your notes is direct quotation unless you indicate otherwise. Double-check any paraphrases for quoted phrases and insert the necessary quotation marks. Later you can work on the paraphrase again if you know which portions are really quotations.

- **Create the Works Cited or References list *first*, before you start writing your paper.** It's easy to omit entries from a Works Cited list when, under pressure to finish, you only skim your paper looking for parenthetical references to document. *Tip*: Before you begin writing you paper, start your list as a **working bibliography**, a list of possible sources to which you add source entries as you discover them. As you finalize your list, you can delete the items you decided not to use.

LINDA STERN, PUBLISHING SCHOOL OF CONTINUING AND
PROFESSIONAL STUDIES, NEW YORK UNIVERSITY

INDEX

A

Academic essay. *See* Five-paragraph essay
Active reading, 22–23
Adjectives, 57–58
Adler, Jerry, "Vanity, Thy Name Is . . .",
    216–218
Adverbs, 58
Agreement, subject-verb, 156–157
"Andy Was Right" (Tyrangiel), 160–161
Annotation, 25
Anthology
    author's name, in MLA in-text
        citation, 282
    in MLA in-text citation, 282
    in MLA works cited style, 283
"Arranging a Marriage in India" (Nanda),
    132–141
Articles
    in electronic journal (in MLA works
        cited style), 286
    in electronic magazine (in MLA works
        cited style), 286
    in electronic reference database (in
        MLA works cited style), 286
    in electronic review (in MLA works
        cited style), 286
Atwood, Margaret, "Female Body, The,"
    254–257
Audience, 4
Authors (MLA in-text style)
    in anthology, 283
    corporate, 283

of entire work, 282
four or more, 280
named in text, 279
not named in text, 280
two or more works by same, 281
two or three, 280
unknown, 280
Authors (MLA works cited style), 282
    corporate, 283
    with editor, 282
    more than three authors or editors, 282
    one author, 282
    in translation, 283
    two or more works by same, 283
    two or three authors, 282
    unknown, 283
    works in anthology, 283

B

Base form, 101
Bible, in MLA works cited style,
    284–285
Black Boy (Wright), 126–130
Blake, William, "Tyger, The," 210–211
Body of essay, 11–12
Body of the paper, in MLA manuscript
    format, 279
Body paragraphs, 11–12
Books (MLA works cited style), 282–283
    electronic, 286
"Bracelet, A, an Odd Earring, Cracked
    Teacups" (Zadrynska), 35–37

Brainstorming, 4–5
"Brave Little Parrot, The" (Martin), 213–215
"Burgers for the Health Professional" (Santora), 238–241

C
Call of the Wild, The. *See* Nature
CD, in MLA works cited style, 285
Chronological organization, 15, 38
Citations. *See also* Sources
    example of cited essay, 273–275
    MLA in-text, 279–282
    MLA works cited, 282–287
Clarity, 16
Clustering, 8
Coherence, 14–16
Comma, 234–235
    beginning elements and, 234
    coordinating conjunctions and, 234
    dates, states, and, 234–235
    lists and, 234
    subordinating conjunctions and, 234
Commonly confused words, 148–150
Comprehension, exploratory writing for, 26
Conclusion of essay, 12–13
Conjunctions, 58
    coordinating, 234
    subordinating, 234
Consonant, doubling final, 207–208
Context clues, 23–24
Controversial issues, 237–277
    "Burgers for the Health Professional" (Santora), 238–241
    Declaration of Independence (Jefferson), 245–248
    "Female Body, The" (Atwood), 254–257
    "Have Today's Schools Failed Male Students?" (Dalton), 250–253
    "No Comprendo" (Mujica), 242–243
    "Reality Television: Issues and Controversies" (Facts on File), 266–268
    "Why One Peaceful Woman Carries a Pistol" (Hasselstrom), 258–264

Coordinating conjunctions, comma with, 234
Corporate author
    in MLA in-text citation, 280
    in MLA works cited style, 283
Credits, 9
Crispin, Jennifer, "No Place like Home," 51–53
Crucible, The (Miller), 17
Culture. *See also* Popular culture
    "Arranging a Marriage in India," 132–141
    Black Boy (Wright), 126–130
    "I'm Afraid to Look, Afraid to Turn Away" (Gonsales), 142–144
    "I Saw Anne Frank Die" (Menkel), 113–115
    "Pomegranates and English Education" (Lim), 117–124

D
Dalton, Patricia, "Have Today's Schools Failed Male Students?" (Dalton), 250–253
Database article, electronic in MLA works cited style, 286
Dates, commas with, 234–235
Declaration of Independence (Jefferson), 245–248
Direct quotation, 272
Discussion group posting, in MLA works cited style, 287
Diversity, cultural, 112–113
Documentation, MLA style, 278–287
Dorris, Michael, "Father's Day," 92–93
Drafting
    final draft, 16–19
    first draft, 9–10

E
e, silent final *e*, 207
Editor (MLA works cited style), 282
    author with, 283
    more than three authors or editors, 282
ei and *ie*, use of, 207

Electronic sources (MLA works cited style), 285–287
  book, 286
  graphic novels, 287
  online video clip, 287
  personal site, 285
  professional site, 285
E-mail, in MLA works cited style, 287
Ericsson, Stephanie, "Ways We Lie, The," 190–198
es, plural, 208
Essay
  body of, 12
  clarity in, 16
  coherence in, 14–15
  example of cited, 273–277
  five-paragraph, 10–13
  sample using reading strategies, 26–29
  unity in, 14
Ethnicity, 112–113
Evidence, 12
Exploratory writing, 26

F

Facts on File, "Reality Television: Issues and Controversies," 266–268
Family, 67–111
  "Father's Day" (Dorris), 92–93
  "Girl" (Kincaid), 86–87
  "Just a Normal Girl" (Kaufman), 68–74
  "My Mother Never Worked" (Smith-Yackel), 94–97
  "Turning Point, The" (Swanson), 89–91
  "Two Kinds" (Tan), 75–85
"Family Life" (Miller), 176–184
"Father's Day" (Dorris), 92–93
"Female Body, The" (Atwood), 254–257
Final consonant, doubling, 207–208
Final draft, 16–19
  student example, 17–19
Final *e*, silent, 207
Final *y*, 208
First draft, 9–10

Five-paragraph essay, 10–13
Frazier, Ian, "Trust Me. In These Parts, Hot Dogs Actually Repel Bears," 226–230
Freewriting, 5–6
French, Jeanie, "To Everything There Is a Season," 221–225
Frost, Robert, "Road Not Taken, The," 219–220
Future tenses, 104
  perfect, 104

G

"Girl" (Kincaid), 86–87
Goff, Karen Goldberg, "Social Networking Benefits Validated," 200–203
Gonsales, Denise, "I'm Afraid to Look, Afraid to Turn Away," 142–144
"Good Daughter, The" (Hwang), 42–45
Grammar. *See* Mechanics and grammar; specific issues

H

Hasselstrom, Linda M., "Why One Peaceful Woman Carries a Pistol" (Hasselstrom), 258–264
"Have Today's Schools Failed Male Students?" (Dalton), 250–253
Highlighting, 24
Hughes, Langston, "Salvation," 39–41
Humanities, MLA documentation style in, 278–287
Hwang, Caroline, "Good Daughter, The," 42–45

I

Identity, culture and, 112–157
ie and *ei*, use of, 207
"I'm Afraid to Look, Afraid to Turn Away" (Gonsales), 142–144
Interjections, 58
Interview, in MLA works cited style, 285

In-text citation (MLA style), 279–282
    author named in text, 279
    author not named in text, 280
    corporate author, 280
    entire work, 282
    four or more authors, 280
    novel, play, or poem, 281
    source quoted in another source, 281
    two or more works by same
        author, 281
    two or three authors, 280
    unknown author, 280
    work in an anthology, 282
Introductory paragraph, 10–11
Invention strategies, 3–9
    brainstorming as, 4–5
    clustering as, 8
    freewriting as, 5–6
    journalistic questions as, 8–9
    looping as, 6–7
    outlining as, 7–8
    starting to write, 3–4
    stream of consciousness as, 6
Introspection, 34–66
    "Bracelet, A, an Odd Earring, Cracked
        Teacups" (Zadrynska), 35–37
    "Good Daughter, The" (Hwang),
        42–45
    "No Place like Home" (Crispin),
        51–53
    "Salvation" (Hughes), 39–41
    "What's in a Name?" (Work), 46–50
Irregular verbs, 105–107
    list of, 105–107
"I Saw Anne Frank Die" (Menkel),
    113–115
Issues, controversial, 237–277

J
Jefferson, Thomas, Declaration of
    Independence, 245–248
Journal article (MLA works cited style), 284
    electronic, 286
Journalistic questions, 8–9
"Just a Normal Girl" (Kaufman), 68–74

K
Kaufman, Leslie, "Just a Normal Girl,"
    68–74
Kincaid, Jamaica, "Girl," 86–87

L
Letter to the editor, in MLA works cited
    style, 285
Lifestyle. *See* Nature
Lim, Shirley Geok-lin, "Pomegranates
    and English Education," 117–124
Lists, commas with, 234
Looping, 6–7

M
Magazine article (MLA works cited
    style), 284
    electronic, 286
Manuscript format. *See* MLA
    manuscript format
Martin, Rafe, "Brave Little Parrot, The,"
    213–215
Mechanics and grammar
    comma, 234–235
    commonly confused words,
        148–150
    correction symbols for errors, 30
    parts of speech, 57–58
    semicolon, 235
    spelling, 207–208
    subject–verb agreement, 156–157
    verbs, 101–102
Mechanics and style, using and
    acknowledging sources, 272–277
Menkel, Irma Sonnenberg, "I Saw Anne
    Frank Die," 113–115
Miller, Arthur, *Crucible, The,* 17
Miller, Marie Winn, "Family Life,"
    176–184
MLA documentation style, 278–287
    in-text citation, 279–282
    manuscript format, 278–279
    works cited, 276–277, 282–287
*MLA Handbook for Writers of Research
    Papers,* 278

MLA manuscript format. *See also* MLA
    documentation style
    body of the paper in, 279
    list of sources in, 279
    page layout in, 278–279
*MLA Style Manual and Guide to Scholarly
    Publishing*, 278
Modern Language Association
    of America. *See* MLA
    documentation style
Mujica, Barbara, "No Comprendo"
    (Mujica), 242–243
"M Word," The: Why It Matters to Me"
    (Sullivan), 163–165
"My Mother Never Worked" (Smith-
    Yackel), 94–97

N
Nanda, Serena, "Arranging a Marriage in
    India," 132–141
Narration, 38
Nature, 210–236
    "Brave Little Parrot, The" (Martin),
        211–213
    "Road Not Taken, The" (Frost),
        219–220
    "To Everything There Is a Season"
        (French), 221–225
    "Trust Me. In These Parts, Hot Dogs
        Actually Repel Bears" (Frazier),
        226–230
    "Tyger, The" (Blake), 210–211
    "Vanity, Thy Name Is . . ." (Adler),
        216–218
Netburn, Deborah, "Young, Carefree and
    Hooked on Sunlamps," 170–174
Newspaper article, in MLA works cited
    style, 284
"No Comprendo" (Mujica),
    242–243
"No Place like Home" (Crispin),
    51–53
Noun, 57
Novel, title
    (in MLA style), 279

O
Ogunnaike, Lola, " 'Yours Truly,' The
    E-Variations," 166–169
Organization
    space, 15–16
    time (chronological), 15, 38
Outdoors. *See* Nature
Outlining, 7–8

P
Page layout, in MLA manuscript format,
    278–279
Paragraph, body, 12
Paraphrase, 272
Parts of speech, 57–58
Past participle, 101
Past tenses, 101
    perfect, 104
    simple, 104
Perfect tenses, 101
    future, 104
    past, 104
    present, 103–104
Periodicals, in MLA works cited
    style, 284
Personal e-mail, in MLA works cited
    style, 287
Personal interview, in MLA works cited
    style, 285
Personal Web site, in MLA works cited
    style, 285
Phrases, transitional, 14–15
Plagiarism, 9, 20, 272
Play, title in MLA style, 281
Plural *es*, 208
Poem
    electronic in MLA works cited style, 286
    title in MLA style, 281–282
Pollitt, Katha, "Why Boys Don't Play
    with Dolls," 186–189
"Pomegranates and English Education"
    (Lim), 117–124
Popular culture, 158–208. *See also*
    Culture
    "Family Life" (Miller), 176–184

"M Word," The: Why It Matters to Me" (Sullivan), 163–165

"Ways We Lie, The" (Ericsson), 190–198

"Why Boys Don't Play with Dolls" (Pollitt), 186–189

"Young, Carefree and Hooked on Sunlamps" (Netburn), 170–174

" 'Yours Truly,' The E-Variations" (Ogunnaike), 166–169

Prepositions, 58
list of common, 64
multiword, 64

Present continuous tense, 102

Present perfect tense, 102, 103–104

Present tense, 101
simple, 101, 103

Primary sources, using and acknowledging, 272

Professional Web site, in MLA works cited style, 285

Progressive tenses, 101

Pronoun, 57

Purpose, of writing assignment, **4**

Q

Questioning, journalistic, 8–9

Quotation, direct, 272

R

Reading to write, 21–33
active, 22–23
college reading strategies, 24–29
as interactive process, 22
to understand, 23
vocabulary expansion through reading, 23–24

"Reality Television: Issues and Controversies," 266–268

Record, in MLA works cited style, 285

Reference database article (electronic), in MLA works cited style, 286

Regular verbs, 101, 105

Religion, culture and, 112

Review, electronic (in MLA works cited style), 286

Revision, 3, 13–14

"Road Not Taken, The" (Frost), 219–220

S

"Salvation" (Hughes), 39–41

Santora, Marc, "Burgers for the Health Professional," 238–241

Secondary sources, using and acknowledging, 272

Semicolon
commas and, 234–235
using, 235

Silent final *e,* 207

Simple tenses
future, 104
past, 104
present, 101, 103

Smith-Yackel, Bonnie, "My Mother Never Worked," 94–97

"Social Networking Benefits Validated" (Goff), 200–203

Source list, in MLA manuscript format, 279

Sources. *See also* MLA documentation style
crediting, 9
direct quotation of, 273
paraphrasing of, 272
quoted in another source, 281
summary of, 272–273
using and acknowledging, 272–277

Space organization, **15**

Spelling, 207–208
doubling final consonant, 207–208
final *y,* 208
silent final *e,* 207
use of *ei* and *ie,* 207

States, commas with, 234–235

Storytelling, narration and, 38

Stream of consciousness writing, **6**

Student essay
example of cited essay, 273–277
final draft, 16–19

Student writing sample, title and
    introductory paragraph, 11
Subject–verb agreement, 156–157
Subordinating conjunctions, comma
    with, 234
Sullivan, Andrew, "M Word," The: Why
    It Matters to Me," 163–165
Summary, 12, **25–26,** 272–273
    as reading strategy, 25–26
Swanson, Craig, "Turning Point, The,"
    89–91

T

Tan, Amy, "Two Kinds," 75–85
Tape, in MLA works cited style, 285
Telephone interview, in MLA works cited
    style, 285
Tenses, 101
Thesis, evidence supporting, 10–11
Thesis statement, 10
Time organization, **15**
Title, 10
    of novel, play, or poem (MLA in-text
        citation style), 281
"To Everything There Is a Season,"
    (French), 221–225
Transitional words and phrases, **15,** 25
Translation, in MLA works cited
    style, 283
"Trust Me. In These Parts, Hot Dogs
    Actually Repel Bears" (Frazier),
    226–230
"Turning Point, The" (Swanson),
    89–91
"Two Kinds" (Tan), 75–85
"Tyger, The" (Blake), 210–211
Tyrangiel, Josh, "Andy Was Right,"
    160–161

U

Underlining, 24
Understanding, reading for, 23
Unity, 14

V

"Vanity, Thy Name Is . . ." (Adler),
    216–218
Verbs, 57, 101–102
    irregular, 105–107
    regular, 105
    subject–verb agreement and,
        156–157
Verb tenses, 101
    future perfect, 104
    past perfect, 104
    present perfect, 103–104
    simple future, 104
    simple past, 104
    uses in English, 104–105
Vocabulary, expanding, 23–24

W

"Ways We Lie, The" (Ericsson),
    190–198
Web sites (MLA works cited style)
    personal, 285
    professional, 285
"What's in a Name?" (Work), 46–50
"Why Boys Don't Play with Dolls"
    (Pollitt), 186–189
"Why One Peaceful Woman Carries a
    Pistol" (Hasselstrom), 258–264
Words
    commonly confused, 148–150
    transitional, 14–15
Work, Deborah, "What's in a Name?,"
    46–50
Works cited (MLA style), 282–287
    Bible, 284–285
    books, 282–284
    electronic sources, 285–287
    in example of cited essay, 276–277
    letter to the editor, 285
    periodicals, 284
    personal or telephone interview, 285
    record, tape, or CD, 285
Wright, Richard, *Black Boy,* 126–130

Writing
    correction symbols for mechanics and
      grammar, 30
    elements of good writing, 14–16
Writing process, 3–20
    core elements of, 3
    first draft, 9–10
    five-paragraph essay, 10–13
    invention strategies for, 4–9
    revision, 13–14
Writing technique, narration and, 38

Y

y, final, 208
"Young, Carefree and Hooked on
    Sunlamps" (Netburn), 170–174
" 'Yours Truly,' The E-Variations"
    (Ogunnaike), 166–169

Z

Zadrynska, Ewa, "Bracelet, A, an
    Odd Earring, Cracked Teacups,"
    35–37